Swipe LEFT

THE SAVVY WOMAN'S GUIDE TO DECODING MEN'S DATING PROFILES

- THE GOOD, THE BAD, THE CRINGEWORTHY -

NANCY LEE GULBRANDSEN

© 2025 Nansealee Enterprises LLC

All rights reserved. No part of this publication may be reproduced, distributed, or transmitted in any form or by any means, including photocopying, recording, or other electronic or mechanical methods, without the prior written permission of the publisher, except in the case of brief quotations embodied in critical reviews and specific other noncommercial uses permitted by copyright law.

First Edition ISBN: 979-8-218-55379-1
Published by Nansealee Enterprises LLC
For permissions requests, contact: Nansealee Enterprises LLC
www.nancyleegulbrandsen.com

DISCLAIMER

This is a work of fiction. All characters, dating profiles, conversations, and incidents portrayed in this book are products of the author's imagination. Any resemblance to actual persons, living or dead, or actual dating profiles is purely coincidental.

The content of this book includes generalizations, stereotypes, and satirical observations about dating profiles and behavioral patterns, intended for entertainment and educational purposes only. These descriptions and characterizations are not intended to represent or define any specific individual, group, or demographic.

The examples, stories, and interpretations presented are for illustrative purposes only and do not represent specific individuals or their online dating profiles. The author and publisher assume no responsibility for any similarities readers may perceive between the fictional content and real people or profiles, or for any claims of defamation, libel, or personal identification with the content.

The author and publisher assume no responsibility for:

- Any similarities readers may perceive between the fictional content and real people or profiles
- Personal interpretations of the content
- Actions taken based on the information provided
- Any emotional or psychological reactions to the content
- Any claims of defamation, libel, or personal identification with the fictional content

By reading this book, you acknowledge that the content is fictional, subjective, and for entertainment purposes only.

Dedication

To my Mother,

Whose love knew no bounds and whose wisdom lights my path even now.

You taught me the value of self-worth and the courage to remain strong, independent, and confident. You showed me how to seek what I deserve and instilled in me an unwavering resolve never to settle.

Your voice still whispers in my heart, guiding me through life's seasons. Your influence lives on in every word of this book.

Your legacy of love, strength, encouragement, and humor continues to shape my path.

Thank you for being my first and most outstanding teacher in the art of living and loving.

I feel your presence in every laugh, every choice, and every page.

This book is for you, Mom.

The Dating Disaster Directory

WHY THIS BOOK EXISTS	1
SWIPE LEFT POEM	4
READY, SET, SWIPE LEFT	14
CHAPTER 1: The Digital Dating Disasters	18
CHAPTER 2: The Communication Catastrophes	35
CHAPTER 3: The Attachment Arena	49
CHAPTER 4: The Love Language Labyrinth	67
CHAPTER 5: The Personality Extremes	88
CHAPTER 6: The Financial Follies	100
CHAPTER 7: The Lifestyle Extremists	114
CHAPTER 8: The Obsession Overloads	128
CHAPTER 9: The Quirky Quotient	145
CHAPTER 10: The Commitment Enthusiasts	159
CHAPTER 11: The Commitment Conundrums	170
CHAPTER 12: The Perpetual Peter Pans	183
CHAPTER 13: The Overly Attached	194
CHAPTER 14: The Midlife Mayhem	208
CHAPTER 15: The Red Flag Parade	226
CHAPTER 16: The Toxic Masculinity Troupe	270
CHAPTER 17: The Green Flag Gallery	318
CHAPTER 18: The Swipe Smart Survival Guide	351
CHAPTER 19: Resources - The Savvy Swiper's Safety Net	361
THE ROAD AHEAD	412
SWIPING RIGHT ON GRATITUDE	415

Why This Book Exists

It all started with a poem, because when life gives you dating lemons, you make literary lemonade. And honey, the dating apps were serving up lemons by the truckload.

I'm a walker. Not the zombie kind, though, after enough dating app disasters, the comparison feels accurate. Whether it's a leisurely stroll with my dog or a brisk 5-miler, walking works for me. It helps me clear my head, organize my thoughts, and achieve that peaceful state of mind that usually only comes after blocking a bad match. Additionally, it allows me to appreciate the natural beauty of Central Florida.

Three years ago, after one of my invigorating and often inspiring morning walks, I began scribbling my thoughts, which just happened to rhyme. I giggled as the words effortlessly flowed, which I can only compare to a full garden hose finally relieved of a kink. It began with a few starry-eyed stanzas about finding love online, followed by the crushing realization that the sea of infinite possibilities is mainly stocked with bottom feeders.

"Wow!" I thought as I wrote. "This is fun and feels kinda therapeutic." With snarky wit and blunt-force honesty, my silly little poem grew, and then she (yep, it's a she) continued to grow, like a collection of dating app horror stories. I affectionately and aptly named her "Swipe Left" because that's precisely what I wish I'd done from the very beginning.

I began sharing "Swipe Left" with family and close friends. They loved her, mainly because they were right there with me during what was, at times, an emotional rollercoaster ride. They had a proverbial front-row seat to it all, so they got it. When I shared her story with women who had been (and some still are) on dating apps, they didn't just get it; they lived it. They laughed, they cried, they shared their own tales of dating app woe. It turned out that we were all starring in different episodes of the same reality show, "Project Red Flag." These women generously and hilariously shared their stories of men who, at first, appeared to be Prince Charming, only to discover they were more like Prince Alarming.

I was strongly encouraged to share my poem "Swipe Left" with women, but wasn't quite sure how to go about doing so. So she sat quietly on my desk while I contemplated. I had written two children's books and was preoccupied with their editing, illustration, and formatting process. Yet, "Swipe Left" kept nudging me (more persistently than a desperate ex). It took a while, but on a beautiful spring morning while walking, naturally, the idea of turning "Swipe Left" into a book occurred to me. Nineteen chapters later, here she is. Phew!

Let's be clear: Swipe Left isn't meant to be mean-spirited or hurtful. It's a satirical, enlightening, and occasionally painful look at online dating profiles from my perspective. So don't get your panties in a wad, ladies (and gents). Just sit back and enjoy reading about guys like Ghosting Gary (who disappeared faster than your last match), Halitosis Hal (whose breath could clear a stadium), and Flatulent Floyd (no explanation needed). Although embellished for fun, men like them do exist, as do, unfortunately, men like Philandering Phil, Bitter Brett, and Toxic Tom.

In writing "Swipe Left," I had to break down the various personalities (or archetypes) of men on dating apps into distinct chapters. Whether I read a guy's profile and swiped left (self-preservation at its finest), blocked him (often the block button is the best match), or swiped right then proceeded to message, speak with, meet, or date them, each one belonged in a category befitting their personality and behavior, or lack thereof.

It was also important to include chapters on attachment styles and love languages. If we understand our attachment style(s) and love language(s), we'll better understand the importance of recognizing and learning about others. Sometimes, the red flags come from inside the house.

I also wanted to include a guide for women that summarizes and encourages them to recognize behavior, so that they "Know When to Hold 'Em, Know When to Fold 'Em, and Know When to Run" (spoiler alert: there's a lot more running than holding). Thus, the Dating Traffic Light Roadmap, your GPS through the dating danger zones, was born.

What started as a personal catharsis has evolved into a shared experience, a communal laugh, and hopefully, a helpful guide. Through writing this book, I've realized that while our individual dating stories are unique, the emotions, frustrations, and occasional triumphs are universal, like bad fish pics and gym selfies, but with better lighting.

By sharing these experiences, we create a supportive community of women who can manage the challenging landscape of online dating together, armed with knowledge, humor, and the comforting thought that we're not alone in this crusade through the digital dating world.

Throughout this adventure, I've learned that laughter isn't just the best medicine; it's also the best defense mechanism against questionable dating profiles. Finding humor in these experiences doesn't just protect our hearts; it helps us spot the red flags before they turn into relationship horror stories.

"Swipe Left" is my way of turning potential heartache into hearty laughter, dating disasters into delicious karma, and hopefully helping you do the same.

Consider this book your dating app survival guide. It is a place where wisdom meets wit and where every cringeworthy experience becomes a stepping stone to better choices, or at least better stories.

Swipe Left

Tales from the Trenches of Online Dating

Ain't love grand with a swipe of my hand
This dating app shows great potential
Men all showcasing a variety of traits
Women find most essential

So many men! The options seem endless
They appear handsome, witty, successful, and bright
I swipe right on a few; they swipe right back
One even calls me that night!

We chat, all goes well
And he asks for a date
Lo and behold
He shows up late

Older and heavier
Still thinks he's a catch
I chuckle to myself
This ain't no match

The next date, same thing
Two hours of boasting
Good Lord, this one was convinced
He's utterly engrossing!

He's gross, alright
So it's back to the App
Should've stayed home
And taken a nap!

So I swiped some more
It became rather funny
I'm beginning to think
I'm just wasting money

A plethora of men's photos
Holding dead fish, reptiles, birds, and deer
Always gives me the creeps. Why, you ask?
Because now they're hunting here!

Once beautiful living creatures
On land and in the sea
Can't help but wonder
If that's what he'll do to me

Surely there's a gent
Who has it all together
Possesses character and integrity
And is seeking his forever

He'll make me laugh
After a challenging day
Patiently listen to whatever
I feel the desire to say

He'll put on a chick flick
And massage my sore feet
Then disappear into the kitchen
To make us a treat

He won't roll his eyes or ignore me
Rip loud stinky farts, burp or snore
Why is it that so many men these days
Possess the manners of a boar?

I embraced online dating without trepidation
Excited to meet a good man
I'm slim and attractive, have a keen sense of humor
And look pretty good with a tan

Thought finding love
Would be a breeze
Not fraught with concerns
Of mug shots and STDs

To quote a famous songwriter
A tortured poet, she claims to be
Who proudly declares aloud
"All's fair in love and poetry"

Is this poetic justice, you ask?
That's a topic I'll gladly debate
My experiences tell a story
To which many women can certainly relate

Some men made me giggle
A couple even made me cry
All of them made it easy
To walk away and say goodbye

I should write a book
But this poem shall suffice
Enjoy as I recount
As I paid quite the price

So let me recall
A few of the guys
Who turned out to be
An utter waste of my time

The fiscally irresponsible drunk
Drank vodka like water
And spent his evenings in a funk

Claimed he was my prince
With his martini glass full of grog
Turns out that he was really
Nothing more than a frog

A midnight call from jail
With a desperate plea for bail
"What happened this time?" I reply
"Was drunk, lost my cool, punched a guy."

He smoked too much weed
Said it calmed his anxiety
Put my life in his hands?
I'd surely need psychiatry!

He was seeking a drinking buddy
Disguised as a wife
I'd be nothing more than his enabler
24/7 for life!

The freak who liked feet
Oh, and the one who looked pregnant
Can't forget the chap
Who was repulsively arrogant

"Let's drink some beers."
Said the dude from Boston.
"No thanks,
Going to FaceTime my son in Austin."

A very sweet guy with a twinkle in his eye
Possessed the energy of a youth
One crucial thing was missing
Which happened to be his front tooth

My heart went out
To a really nice guy
Shallow me
Couldn't get past his lazy eye

The love bomber extraordinaire
Was anything but lazy
The ultimate charming chameleon
To earn my affection
He provided constant attention
And claimed all his exes were crazy

He vilified me, too
That's precisely what narcissists do
That relationship?
An award-winning script for Scorsese

To be more explicit, a song comes to mind
The lyrics to which I don't tire
To give you an idea of what dating him was like
Listen to Olivia Rodrigo's "Vampire"

I pity the women before me
And those, after, if they only knew
They're dating the devil incarnate
An evil man through and through

Broken and damaged
Bitter, angry, and sad
They blame their exes, her attorney
Their Mom and Dad

Some men I met were clingy
While others quite aloof
One dude had the audacity
To expect me to provide his roof!

His next big deal will make him rich
He'll retire and live at the beach
I doubt that will ever happen
Yet, he's convinced success is within reach

Dreamers and schemers
And scammers galore
Will host you, then ghost you
Their only goal is to score

I'm confident there are men
Who will say
Many women online
Are exactly the same way

We claim we are genuine
And seeking our honey
When our agenda is all about
Chasing the money

Some are convinced we're all too needy
A mess in a dress or worse
But wealthy older gents sure seem willing
To trade their purse for a young nurse

Look, I'm not perfect
Far from it, in fact
I bite my nails and worry
At times, tend to overreact

I must have space and freedom
And quality time with my sons
For if you're controlling or jealous
I'm surely going to run!

A girl's night out is no reason to doubt
My interest in you or intentions
You must understand we're just dating
I'm not one of your possessions

I choose my friends wisely
I'm generous, honest, and sincere
But if you lie to or betray me
I'll surely disappear

Self-confident and outgoing
With a four-year college degree
Not seeking a man
To complete or rescue me

Independent and strong
And have an opinion
Been told I'm quite funny
In most situations

Many interests I have
The list is quite long
Love white sandy beaches, island rum
A steel drum song

Billy Joel, The Eagles, and Pink
To me, there's nothing better!
I've Sailed Across the Sun with Train
While singing Drops of Jupiter

Music fills my soul
Transports me to a beautiful place
Countless concerts have provided
Vivid memories I'll never erase

Sometimes I ask Alexa
For my favorite list to play
And dance around my living room
To Robbie Dupree's "Steal Away"

Children's books, I love to write
A creative outlet I employ
The looks on the kids' darling faces as they read them
Fills my heart with tremendous joy

But where's the trusted friend and confidant
Who is always happy to see me?
We'll spend our days together
And rarely disagree

We'll cuddle on the sofa
Binge-watch the latest show
Feeling utterly content
As I sip a nice Bordeaux

Then one evening, it occurred to me
He's been here all along
Through thick and thin, he's remained
Affectionate, loyal, and strong

His temperament is even
He allows me to relax
This wonderful creature I lovingly speak of
Is my precious little dog, Max!

So, rather than date clowns just to have a man in my life
I spend time with my family and friends
For these are the people who love me
And will be here till the end

At this stage of my life
I'm very content
Watching the drama unfold
On the Golden Bachelorette

But make no mistake
I'd love nothing more
If Kevin Costner, himself
Showed up at my door

Martha Stewart and Drew Barrymore
Have given it a try
Mariah Carey and Sharon Stone
Joined the online search for a guy

Picture them swiping left and right
Then, meeting for a drink, did they dare?
If so, you can be sure
They have some stories to share!

Burn that Haystack
Says Jennie Young, very loud and clear
Or you'll never find your needle
So you'd best listen up, dear

Follow Jennie's strategy
To keep Mr. Wrong out of sight
Block all those pathetic profiles
To discover your Mr. Right

Men who put forth minimal effort
Should not be given a chance
Move on with your goal, remain steadfast
In seeking true love and romance

Raise that bar, girl
Communicate clearly, be direct, and furthermore
You shouldn't go fishing for a good man
With inferior bait on your lure

Comedian Chris Munch's Steven Steven's
Is the ultimate cringeworthy type
Loves "Mother", offers blessings
And implores you to swipe right

Donning a gold necklace
A snappy turtleneck, how divine!
He offers long-stemmed roses
And boxed chocolates that say "Be Mine"

The apps are full of men like him
As well as toxic jerks
I've met more than my fair share
From creeps to guys with quirks

For those of you still searching
On Bumble, Match, or Tinder
The man of your dreams may be there
But here's something to consider

After meeting a variety of men
Like Robert, David, and Tim
You may come to realize, as I did
The pickens are mighty slim

A friend found her husband's profile on Tinder
How do you suppose she knew?
That wasn't a difficult thing to discover
Because she had a profile there, too!

So pack your sense of humor
It'll come in mighty handy
As you begin a journey, encountering men
Like Charlie, Trent, and Randy

That's how people meet these days
It's become a fact of life
So, be sure to do your research to discover
If he's bankrupt, been arrested, or has a wife!

Some words of wisdom I'd like to share
This I guarantee
That people aren't always who
They portray themselves to be

When it comes to matters of the heart
Love is blind and often deaf
So, consider family and friends' opinions
Towards Edward, Johnny, or Jeff

They'll tell it like it is
Good or bad or indifferent
Take those blinders off, girl
Before you make a lifelong commitment

One final thought before I wrap
Here is my epilogue
Save your money, time, and energy
Swipe Left and adopt a cat or a dog!

"Swipe Left: Tales from the Trenches of Online Dating" poem
© 2025 Nancy Lee Gulbrandsen
Published by Nansealee Enterprises LLC
All Rights Reserved

Ready, Set, Swipe Left!

Welcome to Swipe Left, my survival guide from the trenches of online dating, complete with field notes on a veritable parade of archetypes you're bound to encounter (if you haven't already).

In an age where love is just a swipe away (or so they say), dating apps have become the modern-day Cupid, minus the archery skills and plus a lot more shirtless bathroom selfies. As of 2025, there are over 1,500 dating apps and websites available globally, with an estimated 360 million people worldwide swiping, liking, and desperately trying to decipher whether "entrepreneur" means "successful business owner" or "sells questionable supplements from their parents' basement."

While these apps promise to help us find everything from our soulmate to our next regrettable decision, they've also turned dating into a veritable circus of characters that would make even the most seasoned ringmaster throw up their hands in despair. According to recent studies, 55% of online daters report feeling more frustrated than hopeful about their experience (I bet that number is much higher). If you're part of that frustrated majority, congratulations! You're about to find your tribe.

This book is a tribute to every woman who has ever stared at her phone, wondering if she's stumbled into an alternative universe where every man is either a gym enthusiast, a world obsessed with bathroom mirror selfies, or suspiciously fond of fish photography.

I'm here to shine a spotlight on the archetypes that roam the digital dating savanna, from the Narcissistic Cyclone to the Perpetual Peter Pan, with a healthy dose of humor and a dash of "oh honey, no."

But it's not all fun and games (unlike Sugar Daddy Sean's profile might suggest). Online dating can present significant challenges and potential dangers. That's why, amidst the laughter, I've included resources for various issues mentioned in the book. Because while I'm here to poke fun at Mugshot Mick, I also want you to stay safe, sane, and swipe-savvy.

This book is the result of extensive research, including:

- My voyage through the wild world of online dating (where the only thing more abundant than red flags was my determination to document them)

- Countless hours analyzing dating app behavior patterns (someone had to do it, and my therapist suggested a hobby)

- A deep dive into relationship psychology (think less "formal study," more "3 AM rabbit holes into attachment theory while wondering why Gary ghosted")

- Interviews with fellow dating app survivors (with friends and online group chats fueled by wine and war stories)

- A genuinely concerning amount of time spent scrolling through profiles (my thumb may never recover)

- More dating self-help books than I'd like to admit (my Kindle history looks like a therapist's bookshelf having an identity crisis)

16

Chapter 1
THE DIGITAL DATING DISASTERS

Let's Set the Scene

Welcome to The Digital Dating Disasters, where we examine the fascinating species of Homo sapiens that have evolved (or devolved) in the age of swipes, likes, and digital dopamine hits. This chapter is dedicated to those individuals whose personalities have been shaped, warped, or completely consumed by the digital world.

In this pixelated parade, you'll encounter men who seem to have forgotten that life exists beyond a screen. Meet Catfish Calvin, whose online persona is more fiction than fact, Catch-of-the-Day Carl, who thinks dead fish are the ultimate thirst trap. There's Picture-Perfect Perry, who never reads beyond the photos, and Grammatically Grating Greg, waging war on the English language one typo at a time.

These archetypes represent the extremes of digital-age dating, where the lines between online and offline personas blur, and where the curated image often overshadows the real person. They're in this chapter because they've let technology overtake their personalities, social skills, or sense of reality to a degree that makes meaningful connections challenging.

But fear not, intrepid dater! This chapter will equip you with the tools to navigate this new and challenging world. Remember, behind every profile is a person; the trick is finding the ones who remember that, too.

So charge up your phone, update your apps, and get ready to swipe through the digital dating jungle. Just don't forget to look up from your screen once in a while, your next great date might be right in front of you, in that crazy place we call "real life."

The Digital Deceiver

Catfish Calvin

Too good to be true: Calvin's photos showcase a chiseled jawline, six-pack abs, and a full head of luscious hair, all courtesy of FaceApp and Photoshop. His bio claims he's a 32-year-old entrepreneur/pilot/philanthropist who splits his time between his penthouse in New York and his villa in the Virgin Islands. In reality, Calvin is a balding, 45-year-old IT support technician living in his mom's basement in New Jersey.

Catfish Calvin's profile is a masterpiece of digital deception:

About Me: "Adventure-seeking entrepreneur with a passion for high-altitude philanthropy. When I'm not piloting my jet to exotic locales, I'm changing lives one charity gala at a time. Looking for a co-pilot in love and life. Swipe right if you're ready for a first-class voyage to happily ever after!"

Calvin's hobbies include crafting elaborate backstories, googling "rich people hobbies," and staging "luxury vacation" selfies in front of his neighbor's swimming pool. His idea of travel is using Google Earth to "visit" exotic locations, and his philanthropic efforts mostly involve donating his leftover pizza to the neighborhood stray cats.

Calvin's profile is a minefield of suspicious signals. His photos look suspiciously like they're ripped straight from a men's fashion magazine, and he oddly claims to be "verified" on a dating app that doesn't even have a verification system. His Instagram feed consists entirely of stock photos of luxury cars and tropical beaches. Despite his seemingly endless collection of professional-looking pictures, he's mysteriously "camera-shy" when it comes to video calls.

Communicating with Calvin is like playing a real-life version of "Catch Me If You Can," minus the Leonardo DiCaprio charm and a hefty dose of mom's basement musk. The chances of meeting Calvin in person are about as likely as finding a unicorn in your backyard. Typically, he'll ghost faster than you can say "video call verification" if you push for a real-life encounter.

The Mythical First Date (on the off chance it ever happens): If by some miracle Calvin agrees to meet in person (and you haven't caught on to his game), prepare for a shock. Instead of the chiseled Adonis from his profile, you'll be greeted by a balding, middle-aged man with a dad bod that screams, "I debug computers, and have never seen the inside of a gym." He'll likely show up in a wrinkled polo shirt that's seen better days, possibly with a mustard stain from his lunchtime Hot Pocket.

Love Language: Quality time spent with his alternate identities

Attachment Style: Securely attached to his Photoshop subscription and collection of stolen profile pics

The Last Word:

Calvin: Hey there, Discount DiCaprio! I see you're still playing "Fake It Till You Make It." Here's a revolutionary idea: try being yourself for once. You might find that honesty is more attractive than your imaginary jet. But what do I know? I'm just someone who can tell the difference between the Virgin Islands and a New Jersey pool. Oh, and by the way, your mom called; she wants her credit card and Photoshop subscription back.

Ladies: Real men don't need Photoshop to show their best angles. Your time is too valuable to waste on someone else's digital fantasy; you deserve authenticity, not artfully filtered fiction. Besides, if he's lying about his looks, imagine what else he's decorating with deception! When a man's photos look like they belong in GQ but his messages belong in spam, it's time to swipe left faster than Calvin can come up with another excuse to avoid video calls! Your time, truth detector, and dating expectations will thank you.

The Piscatorial Poser

Catch-of-the-Day Carl

Observe Carl, the human embodiment of a Bass Pro Shops catalog. This walking, talking fish tale has turned aquatic conquests into a dating strategy and considers "plenty of fish in the sea" a personal challenge rather than a metaphor.

Carl's dating profile follows the puzzling male dating app tradition that assumes women are powerless to resist the allure of a man clutching a lifeless fish, a strategy that continues to baffle female dating app users worldwide.

About Me: "Reel catch seeking a partner to sea my true potential. Looking for someone who appreciates a man who can provide (as long as you like fish... a lot). My ideal match? A gal who thinks 'impressive length' refers to my latest catch and finds the aroma of fish bait irresistible. Swipe right to join my school of admirers!"

Photos showcase Carl in his natural habitat: squinting into the sun while awkwardly holding a fish, grinning next to a massive cooler (contents: obvious), and a "candid" shot of him locked in an intense staring contest with a mounted bass. His attempt at a sexy pic? A shirtless selfie on a boat, with more fishing rods than abs visible.

First Date: A date with Carl is like being trapped in an endless loop of "The Old Man and the Sea." He'll suggest meeting at a seafood restaurant (where he'll critique the freshness), arrive smelling faintly of worm dirt and boat fuel, and spend the evening regaling you with epic tales of "the one that got away." Be prepared for detailed descriptions of fish anatomy, impromptu knot-tying demonstrations, and at least one attempt to plan your next date at 4 AM on a foggy lake.

Love Language: Sharing his prized lures, secret fishing spot, and letting you hold his favorite rod

Attachment Style: Securely attached to his fishing pole and the belief that dead fish are an aphrodisiac

P.S. Carl's idea of Netflix and chill involves a marathon of "River Monsters" followed by a spirited debate about the best bait for catfish.

P.P.S. If you make it to a second date, expect an invitation to watch him get his latest catch stuffed at the taxidermist because nothing says romance like formaldehyde and glass eyes!

The Last Word:

Carl: Oh, Carl. Sweet, scaly Carl. Let's have a heart-to-heart, buddy. Women are about as impressed by your dead fish photos as they would be by a collection of toenail clippings. Your Tinder isn't a seafood market, and that carp isn't Cupid. Unless you're trying to date a mermaid (spoiler: they're not on Bumble), consider showcasing some interests that don't involve hooking unsuspecting sea creatures through the mouth. The goal is to reel in a partner, not make them feel like they've been catfished. So please, for the love of all things holy and scaled, put down the trout. Your future matches (and the fish population) will thank you!

Ladies: Swipe Left and throw this one back faster than Carl can say 'you should've seen the one that got away!' Your sense of smell, weekend sleep schedule, and fish-free photo gallery will thank you.

The Photo Skimmer

Picture-Perfect Perry

Behold Perry, whose attention span is inversely proportional to a woman's neckline. He's never met a profile he's read, but he's an expert in judging photo angles. His ideal match is 80% legs, 20% flattering filter, and 0% substance.

Perry's profile is a museum of shirtless selfies where words go to die, each image more carefully filtered than his dating standards.

About Me: "Hey, beautiful! I'm all about the visual. They say a picture's worth a thousand words, so why bother with all that reading? Looking for a hottie who catches my eye. If you've got it, flaunt it! Swipe right if you want a guy who appreciates the finer things in life, like your profile pic."

First Interaction with Perry: Prepare for a Masterclass in Shallow Conversation. He will:

- Compliment your looks while completely ignoring your listed interests
- Ask questions that are answered in your profile
- Send you a gym selfie without prompting

- Suggest meeting up based solely on your physical appearance.

- Act confused when you bring up any information from your written profile.

Perry's hobbies include rapid-fire swiping, sliding into DMs with "hey", and being genuinely surprised when his matches have personalities.

First Date: A carefully selected craft beer bar with strategic mirror placement and low lighting, perfect for selfies, a self-guided tour of his mirror selfie collection at the gym, followed by him asking what you do for a living (which is clearly stated in your bio)

Love Language: Visual validation and unsolicited gym selfies

Attachment Style: Superficially attached to profile pics and deeply committed to his zoom function

Interacting with Perry is like trying to have a deep conversation with a billboard: flashy, one-dimensional, and ultimately disappointing.

P.S. Pierce's idea of "getting to know you" is zooming in on your beach vacation photos.

The Last Word:

Perry: The shallow end of the pool called, they're missing their lifeguard. Pro tip: Women are three-dimensional beings with thoughts and personalities, not just profile pictures you can scroll through like an Instagram feed. Try reading a bio sometime; it's the text below the photos.

Ladies: A picture may be worth a thousand words, but his vocabulary stops at "hey, beautiful." Unless you want a relationship that's as deep as a profile thumbnail, swipe left faster than Perry skims through photos. Your intellectual curiosity, conversational needs, and un-objectified self-worth will thank you.

The Spell Check Skeptic

Grammatically Grating Greg

Presenting Greg, the human embodiment of a typo-riddled text message. This walking, talking autocorrect nightmare has turned butchering the English language into an extreme sport, and considers proper grammar as optional as turn signals in a BMW.

Greg's dating profile reads like a high school English teacher's worst nightmare:

About Me: "Your gonna love me! Im a grate guy who's looking four his sole mate. I like long walks on the beech, good food (accept pineapple on pizza, thats just wrong), and intelligent conversashun. If your ready too meat your prince charming, swipe write!"

Photos showcase Greg in his natural habitat: posing next to signs with obvious spelling errors (giving a thumbs up), caught mid-text with a look of intense concentration, and a "candid" shot of him appearing genuinely confused with Grammarly's corrections.

First Date: A date with Greg is like playing a real-time game of "Guess What I Meant to Say." He'll suggest meeting at "Star Bucks" (because apparently, it's owned by a celebrity deer), and spend the evening mangling idioms with the confidence of a motivational speaker. Be prepared for texts that require a decoder ring, misplaced apostrophes galore, and at least one heated debate about why "could of" is totally valid English. Pack your patience, a pocket dictionary, and maybe a red pen for those moments when you can't resist the urge to correct.

Attachment Style: Securely attached to his spelling errors but perpetually detached from the English language's attempt to love him back

Love Language: Expressing affection through creatively misspelled terms of endearment

Note: Prolonged exposure to Greg's writing may result in a nervous tic, an irresistible urge to correct restaurant menus, and the nagging feeling that somewhere, a dictionary is crying.

P.S. Greg's idea of proofreading is giving his message a quick glance and thinking, "Eh, they'll figure it out."

P.P.S. If you somehow agree to a second date, expect a follow-up text that reads, "Can't weight too sea you again! Your the most beautiful women I ever scene!"

The Last Word

Greg: Your grasp of grammar is as shaky as your understanding of 'your' versus 'you're.' Maybe it's time to let spellcheck be your wingman instead of your nemesis.

Ladies: When a man's red flags include turning the English language into a crime scene and treating autocorrect like a sworn enemy, save yourself (and your sanity). Unless you want your future children learning that "definitely" has an 'a' in it and "loose" means to misplace something, swipe left faster than you can say "their/there/they're." English teachers everywhere will thank you!

Chapter 1
THE TAKEAWAY

And there you have it, the wild west of Dating Apps, where profile pics are more filtered than a fancy coffee shop's water, and the line between "putting your best foot forward" and "complete fiction" is thinner than Greg's grasp of grammar!

Let's get real. Dating apps promise us a buffet of potential soulmates but often deliver a digital version of those "expectations vs. reality" food memes instead. The characters in this chapter aren't just swiping right; they're swiping reality right out the window.

Red Flags With Extra Notification Alerts:

- Their photos require more disclaimers than a pharmaceutical commercial.

- They treat dating apps like Pokémon GO, where you 'gotta catch 'em all,' but with less walking and more ghosting.

- Their communication skills make autocorrect throw up its digital hands in surrender.

- They're more committed to their swiping routine than any actual relationship.

- They judge profiles faster than a New Yorker judges tourists wearing "I ♥ NY" shirts.

- Their idea of a meaningful connection is a stable WiFi signal.

- They're allergic to transitioning from charming texts to actual face-to-face conversation.

Behind every profile is a real person, well, except for Calvin, who's crafting tales of his 'private jet adventures' while waiting for his bus pass to recharge. The digital dating world might be a circus, but you don't have to be the clown. Trust your gut when someone's profile seems fishy (looking at you, Carl), their grammar makes your eyes bleed, or they seem more interested in your filtered photos than your actual personality.

Your time is valuable, your standards are valid, and your dating app experience should be more than an endless scroll through red flags. So, put down that phone occasionally and look up, because sometimes the best connections happen when you're not staring at a screen.

Chapter 2

THE COMMUNICATION CATASTROPHES

Let's Set the Scene

Welcome to The Communication Catastrophes, where conversation is an extreme sport and clarity is as rare as a timely text from Later Luke! In this chapter, we're diving into the murky waters of men who've turned basic human interaction into an Olympic event of misunderstanding.

Introducing our cast of conversational conundrums: Flirtatious Flynn, who thinks every exchange should come with a wink, and 20-Questions Quentin, who turns every coffee date into a Senate hearing. There's Friend-Zone Fred, masterfully avoiding romantic signals while sending mixed ones of his own, and Later Luke, whose response time makes snail mail look speedy. Whether they're flirting inappropriately, interrogating intensely, or responding three weeks late, these communication catastrophes have turned social interaction into a masterclass in confusion.

While everyone has their own communication style, these men have turned theirs into indecipherable codes. They're living proof that sometimes, the most attractive quality is the ability to express yourself clearly, or at least respond within the same calendar year.

So grab your decoder rings and universal translators as we maneuver through this labyrinth of linguistic landmines. Keep in mind, in the world of dating, sometimes the most profound thing you can say is "goodbye."

Now, let's examine these communication quagmires and see if we can find a method to the madness!

The Smooth Operator

Flirtatious Flynn

Prepare yourself for Flynn, the human embodiment of a pick-up line generator with legs. This walking, talking charm offensive has turned flirtation into an extreme sport, considering subtlety a foreign concept.

Flynn's dating profile reads like a romance novel written by a horny teenager:

About Me: "Professional heartbreaker seeking someone to finally tame this wild stallion. Looking for a partner who appreciates a man who can make even a grocery list sound seductive. My ideal match? Someone who thinks 'Are you a parking ticket? Because you've got FINE written all over you' is the height of wit. Swipe right if you're ready for a relationship that's more sizzle than steak, but oh, what a sizzle!"

Photos showcase Flynn in his natural habitat: winking at the camera in various locations, and a "candid" shot of him pretending to be surprised while flexing. His attempt at a serious pic? A smoldering gaze into the camera that's one step away from a Zoolander "Blue Steel."

First Date: A date with Flynn is like being trapped in a B-grade rom-com. He'll suggest meeting at a place where he's on a first-name basis with all the staff (and openly flirts with them), arrive with a rose clenched between his teeth, and spend the evening peppering every sentence with innuendos and exaggerated eyebrow waggles. Be prepared for cheesy one-liners, impromptu attempts at hand-kissing, and at least one instance of him trying to recreate the spaghetti scene from Lady and the Tramp.

Love Language: Showering you with compliments and gifting you with personalized pick-up lines

Attachment Style: Indiscriminately attached to anything with a pulse

The Last Word

Flynn: Hey Romeo, the 1970s called, they want their pick-up lines back. Your endless flirtation isn't charm, it's a museum piece that belongs next to disco balls and polyester suits. While you're busy practicing your eyebrow waggle in the mirror, real men have evolved past treating women like a game of "who can drop the cheesiest line." Try having a conversation that doesn't sound like it came from a fossilized dating manual. Real chemistry happens when you drop the act and join us here in 2025.

Ladies: No amount of smooth talk can compensate for being emotionally trapped in an era when men thought "hey baby" was a conversation starter. This walking time capsule of outdated charm might seem amusing at first, but don't let his retro routine fool you; there's a reason this style of flirting went out with phone books and fax machines. Unless you want your entire relationship to feel like a rejected script from "Love Boat," swipe left on this vintage variety show host faster than he can say "What's your sign?" Your dating dignity, conversation standards, and eye roll muscles will thank you.

The Interrogator

20-Questions Quentin

Check out Quentin, a walking, talking FAQ session who has turned conversation into a one-way interrogation and considers dialogue a series of rapid-fire questions with no room for natural flow.

Quentin's dating profile is the human embodiment of a survey monkey questionnaire.

About Me: "Curious mind seeking someone who enjoys in-depth conversations (meaning: answering my endless questions). Looking for a partner who appreciates thorough discussions (translation: being interviewed like it's a job application). Let's really get to know each other (but mostly you, through my detailed questionnaire)!"

Photos showcase Quentin in his natural habitat: looking intensely interested in various settings, notebook always at the ready, and "candid" shots of him mid-question with raised eyebrows. His attempt at a casual pic? A contemplative pose with his famous list of first-date questions visible in the background.

A date with Quentin is like being on the receiving end of a verbal tennis ball machine, except there's no chance to return serve. He'll suggest meeting for coffee (an optimal questioning environment), arrive with his mental checklist ready, and spend the evening firing questions at a machine-gun pace. Be prepared for zero natural conversation flow, constant interruptions with follow-up questions, and at least one moment where you realize you haven't completed a full sentence in 30 minutes.

First Date: Any quiet venue where he can hear your answers clearly while simultaneously planning his following seven questions.

Love Language: Asking rapid-fire questions and completely ignoring your answers

Attachment Style: Interrogatively attached, treating first dates like FBI investigations

The Last Word

Quentin: Conversation is a two-way street, not a police interrogation. If you spent half as much time listening as you do compiling your next question, you might learn something. But hey, if you're looking for a career change, I hear the FBI is hiring.

Ladies: When a man treats every date like he's auditioning for Law & Order and you feel like you should have brought your lawyer, swipe left faster than he can say "But wait, I have a follow-up question!" Your vocal cords, personal boundaries, and mental stamina will thank you.

The Unattainable Adonis

Friend-Zone Fred

Next up is Fred, the human equivalent of a "Do Not Enter" sign in the realm of romance. This charming, oblivious Adonis has mastered the art of unintentional rejection, leaving a trail of lovestruck friends in his perfectly platonic wake.

Fred's dating profile is a masterclass in mixed signals:

About Me: "Looking for my soulmate... to watch rom-coms with platonically! Just a regular guy who loves his dog, hitting the gym, and being oblivious to romantic advances. I'm told I'm a great listener, excellent shopping companion, and the perfect 'guy friend' to make your crush jealous. Warning: May accidentally friend-zone you before the first date. Swipe right if you're cool with keeping things strictly platonic!"

His photos are a gallery of missed opportunities: Fred giving a side hug to a visibly swooning woman, Fred as the "man of honor" at his best friend's wedding, Fred obliviously flexing at the beach while surrounded by admiring gazes, volunteer work with puppies, and inexplicably artistic shots of him reading philosophy books in coffee shops.

With Fred, you'll find yourself in a rom-com where you're the lead, but he thinks he's the quirky sidekick. He'll compliment your outfit, then ask for fashion advice for his date with someone else. He'll share intimate details about his life, then high-five you for being such a great "bro." He'll charm your parents, make your friends swoon, and then spend the entire evening talking about how you're "such a good friend" and asking for advice about other women.

First Date: A cozy night in, watching "When Harry Met Sally" while Fred explains why men and women can totally just be friends, missing the irony entirely.

Love Language: Quality friend time, punctuated by oblivious flirting and accidental heartbreak

Attachment Style: Deeply attached to the concept of friendship, utterly detached from romantic reality, and permanently bonded to his role as everyone's favorite "totally platonic" guy pal

P.S. If you match with Fred, be prepared to join his ever-growing collection of "best friends." Your romantic advances will be met with confused laughter and playful shoulder punches.

P.P.S. Fred's idea of "making a move" is asking you to be his wingwoman at the bar. He's always happy to set you up with his friends or be your plus-one at weddings, blissfully unaware that you only have eyes for him.

The Last Word:

Fred: Your communication blindness isn't cute, it's a defense mechanism in designer jeans. Try seeing the signals instead of collecting 'friends' like Pokémon. Sometimes the best friend you could be is the one who's honest about what's really happening.

Ladies: When a man's emotional intelligence has more blind spots than a highway's worth of side mirrors, save yourself the frustration. No amount of meaningful glances can penetrate romantic cataracts. Unless you want your romantic overtures to be met with high-fives and "buddy" talks, swipe left on this walking friend zone faster than he can say 'You're like a sister to me!' Your emotional clarity and romantic dignity will thank you.

The
Delayed Responder

Later Luke

Meet Luke, the human embodiment of Internet Explorer's loading screen. This walking, talking time lag has turned response delays into a talent and considers "eventually" an acceptable timeframe for communication.

Luke's profile is a time capsule of unmet expectations, where messages go to age like fine wine:

About Me: "Relaxed communicator seeking someone who appreciates that time is relative (very relative in my case). Great at maintaining suspense through strategic response delays. If you enjoy wondering whether I'm alive or just composing the perfect reply to your 'hey' from last week, we'll get along great... eventually."

Photos showcase Luke in his natural habitat: staring contemplatively at unanswered messages, mid-yawn while typing a response to last month's text, and "candid" shots of him with his phone showing 847 unread notifications. His attempt at being prompt? Responding to a "Good morning" text before midnight.

In Luke's world, every message exists in a temporal void. He doesn't just take his time; he bends it, turning simple exchanges into exercises in patience that would impress a Buddhist monk. His idea of rapid response? Anything within the same calendar month.

First Date: A spontaneous midnight picnic that he starts planning at 11:55 PM, featuring whatever he can scrounge from his nearly empty fridge

Love Language: Leaving messages on "read," responding to time-sensitive questions after they're irrelevant, and the ability to make people question the concept of time itself

Attachment Style: Securely attached to procrastination, treating deadlines like friendly suggestions and punctuality like a foreign concept

The Last Word:

Luke: Communication isn't wine; it doesn't get better with age. Your delayed responses aren't 'laid-back,' they are conversation killers. Try existing in the same temporal plane as your messages.

Ladies: When a man's response time is longer than a presidential term, and his idea of "be right back" means next season, swipe left faster than he can type "k" (estimated completion time: next week). Your texting etiquette and concept of time will thank you.

Chapter 2

THE TAKEAWAY

So, what have we learned from Communication Catastrophes? That the art of conversation goes to die here! These men aren't just missing the mark in their communication; they're in an entirely different zip code from where the mark is located.

When it comes to connection, the medium really is the message. And the message from these guys ranges from "I only speak in pick-up lines" to "I'll respond to your text sometime before the next solar eclipse."

Red Flags With Sound Effects:

- Their idea of conversation is either an interrogation, a monologue, or a disappearing act.

- They use words as weapons, shields, or occasionally, complete afterthoughts.

- They're fluent in everything except emotional availability and appropriate timing.

- They've mastered the art of saying nothing while talking constantly (or saying nothing by not talking at all)

- Their response time could be measured with carbon dating rather than minutes.

- They've turned "mixed signals" into an Olympic sport, complete with medals for the most confusing message.

- Their emotional intelligence has the processing power of a 1990s calculator watch.

Communication isn't just about words; it's about timing, balance, and emotional attunement. From Flynn's flirtation overload to Quentin's question barrage, Luke's eternal delays to Fred's friendship façade, these men demonstrate that how we communicate is often more revealing than what we say.

Good communication shouldn't feel like solving a puzzle, surviving an interview, waiting for Godot, or friend-zoning yourself into oblivion. It should flow, connect, and build bridges rather than walls.

Your time deserves responses, your questions deserve conversations (not interrogations), your romantic interest deserves clarity, and your messages deserve timely replies. Don't lower your standards for someone who treats communication like an optional feature rather than the foundation of connection.

The right person won't make you decode their messages like you're working for the CIA. They'll be clear, present, and engaged because they'll want to communicate with you.

Chapter 3

THE ATTACHMENT ARENA

Let's Set the Scene

Welcome to The Attachment Arena, where dating isn't just a game; it's a full-contact emotional sport with no referee. In this chapter, we delve into the world of attachment styles, where your childhood experiences become your adult dating playbook, whether you wanted them to or not.

Think of attachment styles as your emotional operating system; they're running in the background of every relationship, determining how you connect, conflict, and comfort each other. Some of us have the premium version with regular updates, while others are still running on Windows 95 with occasional crashes.

In our attachment lineup, you'll discover:

The Secure Sweetheart (Balanced Ben): The rare unicorn who approaches relationships with the confidence of someone who received emotional validation as a child. Mind-blowing!

The Anxious Adherent (Clingy Clint): The Olympic gold medalist in text message frequency who treats "seen" notifications like personal rejections.

The Fearful Flip-Flopper (Distant Dylan): The emotional equivalent of that person who keeps one foot out the door at parties, simultaneously afraid you'll leave and terrified you'll stay.

The Dismissively Distanced (Detached Daniel): The emotional equivalent of a cactus, self-sufficient, prickly when touched, and somehow thriving in conditions that would kill most relationships.

Understanding these attachment styles isn't just about labeling the men you date; it's about recognizing the patterns that drive behavior (yours included). Because let's face it: when two different attachment styles collide, it's less "romantic comedy" and more "psychological thriller" with occasional heartwarming moments.

So adjust your emotional armor, grab your field guide to the human heart, and let's traverse this fascinating arena where past meets present, and "it's not you, it's me" takes on a whole new meaning.

Caution: Side effects of reading this chapter may include sudden self-awareness, a desire to call your therapist, and the ability to psychoanalyze your date before the appetizers arrive.

The Secure Sweetheart

Balanced Ben

Ben embodies a warm cup of tea on a rainy day, comforting, reliable, and surprisingly refreshing. His emotional baggage fits neatly in the overhead compartment, and he's not afraid to talk about his feelings without turning every conversation into a therapy session.

Ben's profile is an oasis of emotional stability in the dating desert, where security feels like a superpower and drama is something that happens to other people.

About Me: "Emotionally available guy seeking a partner for a drama-free connection. I'm like a sturdy oak tree, rooted, reliable, but not clingy (unless you're into tree hugging). Looking for someone to share life's adventures without the emotional rollercoaster. Warning: May cause feelings of stability and genuine happiness."

First Date: Prepare for a shockingly normal and pleasant experience. Ben will:

- Arrive on time, looking like his profile pictures (gasp!)
- Ask about your interests and listen to your answers
- Share about himself without dominating the conversation

- Respect your boundaries and not push for more than you're comfortable with
- End the night with clear communication about his interest and future plans.

Green Flags: (because you deserve them):

- Has a healthy relationship with his ex(s)
- Maintains close friendships without neglecting romantic relationships
- Can handle conflict without ghosting or blowing up
- Supports your goals and independence
- Is comfortable with both intimacy and autonomy

Ben's hobbies include maintaining healthy boundaries, communicating clearly, and making his partner feel secure without suffocating.

Dating Ben is like finding a unicorn that's also a magical financial advisor, but with a solid retirement plan. If you find yourself falling for Ben, don't panic! That fluttering in your chest might be the foreign feeling of emotional security.

P.S. Ben's idea of keeping the spark alive is surprising you with your favorite takeout when you've had a long day.

P.P.S. He once argued with a friend and resolved it through open communication. The shock was felt nationwide.

The Last Word:

Ben: In a dating landscape full of storms, you're the calm harbor we didn't know we needed. Continue to be that rare combination of emotional intelligence and genuine warmth; you're proof that good men aren't just mythical creatures in dating advice columns. Your green flags are giving the red ones a run for their money!

Ladies: Hold onto your emotional support animals because Ben is here to revolutionize your dating world! These unicorns might be rare, but they're worth every moment of the search. After all, sometimes the best love stories begin with solid foundations rather than red flags. When you find a man whose emotional baggage fits in a carry-on instead of requiring a cargo ship, whose communication is more transparent than your therapist's, and whose green flags are greener in person, swipe right faster than Ben can say "I understand your perspective". Your future happiness and emotional well-being will thank you.

The Anxious Adherent

Clingy Clint

Clint mirrors a pop-up notification, always there, often when you least expect it. His love language is "constant contact," and his idea of personal space involves texting instead of calling.

Clint's profile is a study in separation anxiety masquerading as devotion, where every word promises the romantic equivalent of being slowly suffocated by a love-scented pillow.

About Me: "Devoted guy seeking constant reassurance... I mean, romance! I'm like a smartphone; I'm always on and always connected, and I panic when left alone. Looking for someone to share every waking moment with. And sleeping moments. And all moments in between. Did I mention I'm available 24/7?"

First Date: Prepare for an experience that's equal parts flattering and overwhelming. Clint will:

- Arrive 30 minutes early, having already texted you 12 times to confirm
- Shower you with compliments and hang on your every word

- Share his entire life story, hopes, dreams, and deepest fears before the appetizers arrive

- Suggest a second date halfway through the first

- End the night with a 12-part text message about what a great time he had

Red Flags: (or as Clint calls them, "signs of devotion"):

- His longest relationship was three weeks because that's when his phone died.

- Considers "You up?" a romantic greeting at any hour.

- Has already added you to his family group chat.

- Gets visibly anxious when you take more than 5 minutes to reply to a text.

- His idea of a surprise gift is a tracking device... for safety, of course!

Clint's hobbies include overthinking text response times, planning your wedding after the first date, and turning "seen" notifications into reasons for existential crises.

Dating Clint is like adopting an overly enthusiastic puppy, cute at first, but you'll soon be longing for some alone time. If you find yourself falling for Clint, prepare for a relationship that's one part romance, two parts emotional support hotline.

P.S. Clint's idea of giving you space is waiting in your driveway instead of your living room.

P.P.S. He once called in sick to work because his date didn't end a text with the usual number of exclamation points.

The Last Word:

Clint: Clint, buddy, your attachment style is more suffocating than a wetsuit three sizes too small. Here's a revolutionary idea: try giving people room to breathe. You might find that absence really does make the heart grow fonder – or at least less likely to file a restraining order. A watched pot never boils, and a constantly watched date never calls back.

Ladies: If you're considering swiping right on Clint, prepare for a relationship that's more crowded than a rush-hour subway – and about as comfortable. Sure, constant attention might seem flattering at first, but trust me, you'll soon be longing for the sweet silence of a dead phone battery. If your ideal date involves zero personal space and a side of codependency, Clint's your guy. Otherwise, swipe left faster than Clint can type "Where are you?" Your relationship boundaries, personal space, and phone battery will thank you.

The Fearful Flip-Flopper

Distant Dylan

Dylan is the human personification of an emotional seesaw. He desperately wants a connection one moment and flees in terror the next. His heart yearns for closeness, while his fear simultaneously pushes it away.

Dylan's profile is a contradiction wrapped in ambivalence and tied with the ribbon of "I want you, but I'm terrified of you":

About Me: "Seeking connection... but also space? I'm like a moth to a flame, drawn to relationships but scared of getting burned. Looking for someone patient enough to handle my hot-and-cold patterns. Fair warning: I might text you 12 times in a day and then disappear the next. It's not you, it's my crippling fear of both rejection AND intimacy."

First Date: Prepare for an emotional rollercoaster of mixed signals. Dylan will:

- Appear genuinely interested and share surprising personal details
- Suddenly pull back when feeling too connected, as if catching himself being vulnerable

- Show flashes of deep connection followed by obvious discomfort
- Make plans for a second date with authentic enthusiasm
- Become overwhelmed with anxiety afterward and nearly cancel before forcing himself to show up

Red Flags: (or as Dylan calls them, "self-protection mechanisms"):

- Has a relationship history full of intense beginnings and abrupt endings.
- Idealizes partners from afar but finds reasons to create distance when they get close.
- Gets equally panicked by the thought of abandonment AND the thought of commitment.
- Sends mixed signals because he genuinely feels mixed emotions.
- Craves emotional intimacy but becomes overwhelmed when he experiences it.

Dylan's hobbies include overthinking texts before sending them, yearning for relationships he sabotages, and fighting his competing fears of being both too close and too distant. He's simultaneously afraid of being alone and afraid of being trapped.

Dating Dylan is like riding a relationship pendulum, swinging between moments of surprising connection and frustrating withdrawal. If you find yourself falling for Dylan, prepare for a relationship where "it's complicated" isn't just a status, it's a permanent state of being.

P.S. Dylan's idea of emotional progress is admitting he has feelings, only to disappear for three days to recover from the vulnerability.

The Last Word

Dylan: Your fear of both closeness AND distance has you trapped in a relationship purgatory of your own making. The mixed signals you send aren't mysterious; they're exhausting. Consider that healing means facing your fears of both abandonment and engulfment, not just toggling between them endlessly.

Ladies: When a man pulls you close only to push you away, then misses you once you're gone, save yourself from emotional whiplash. If you enjoy relationships with more plot twists than a telenovela, he's your guy. You deserve consistent care, not just passionate comebacks after unexplained absences. Swipe left faster than Dylan can say "I miss you" after ghosting you for a week. Your emotional stability, relationship predictability, and unconfused heart will thank you.

The Dismissively Distanced

Detached Daniel

Daniel has all the qualities of an emotional fortress with impenetrable walls. This walking, talking island of self-sufficiency has turned independence into an extreme sport and considers emotional vulnerability a weakness to be avoided at all costs.

Daniel's profile is a masterclass in subtle dismissiveness, where every word creates more distance than it bridges:

About Me: "Self-sufficient individual seeking... well, not much actually. I value my space and independence above all else. Seeking someone who understands that silence doesn't need to be filled and that weekends apart are healthy. Not interested in excessive talking, texting, or 'processing feelings.' Drama-free means emotion-free in my book. Ideal match: Someone with their own life who won't constantly need validation or attention."

First Date: Prepare for an exercise in emotional distancing. Daniel will:

- Arrive precisely on time and suggest a venue with enough background noise to prevent deep conversation

- Maintain polite but surface-level chat, smoothly deflecting any personal questions

- Share impressive accomplishments while revealing nothing about his actual feelings

- Keep a careful physical distance and check his phone regularly

- End the evening with a firm handshake and vague mention of "doing this again sometime"

Red Flags: (or as Daniel calls them, "signs of healthy independence"):

- Dismisses past relationships as "no big deal" with a shrug.

- Considers emotional needs "clingy" and regards vulnerability as weakness.

- Has mastered the art of changing subjects when conversations get personal.

- Responds to your expressed feelings with logical solutions rather than empathy.

- His idea of opening up is telling you his career goals.

Daniel's hobbies include solo activities, dismissing the importance of connection, and maintaining an emotional distance that would make the Grand Canyon feel intimate by comparison. He prides himself on never "needing" anyone and views self-sufficiency as the ultimate virtue.

Dating Daniel is like trying to embrace a cactus; the more you reach out, the more you'll get pushed away. If you find yourself falling for Daniel, prepare for a relationship where you're always kept at arm's length and your emotional needs are consistently dismissed as "dramatic" or "too much."

P.S. Daniel's idea of commitment is adding you to his calendar once every two weeks.

The Final Word:

Daniel: Your dismissive attitude isn't independence; it's a shield against vulnerability that creates real connections. While self-sufficiency has its merits, your emotional fortress isn't protecting you; it's imprisoning you. Consider that true strength lies in the courage to connect, not in the ability to distance.

Ladies: When a man dismisses emotions like they're spam emails and treats intimacy like an allergic reaction, save yourself the emotional frostbite. If you enjoy having your feelings invalidated and your needs dismissed as "clingy," he's the guy for you. You deserve a partner who sees your emotions as valuable, not inconvenient. So swipe left faster than Devin can say "I need my space." Your emotional well-being, undiminished needs, and un-dismissed feelings will thank you.

Chapter 3

THE TAKEAWAY

After touring this relationship coliseum, you've now met the full roster of attachment-style gladiators you might encounter in the dating world! From Balanced Ben's refreshing emotional stability to Clingy Clint's text message marathons, Distant Dylan's hot-and-cold routine, and Detached Daniel's emotional fortress, men's attachment styles explain why some dates feel like peaceful picnics while others resemble psychological obstacle courses.

We've decoded these masculine attachment mysteries throughout this chapter, revealing why some men are comfortable with both intimacy and independence, while others treat vulnerability like kryptonite or cling to you like you're their emotional oxygen tank. These patterns aren't just quirky personality traits; they're deeply ingrained relationship blueprints that determine how he'll respond when things get serious, stressful, or suspiciously quiet on the text front.

Red Flags With Attachment Labels:

Secure Attachment (Balanced Ben):

- Communicates like a grown-up (shocking, we know).
- Handles both togetherness and alone time without a meltdown.
- Manages conflicts without declaring emotional bankruptcy.
- Offers support without suffocation.
- Sets boundaries without building walls.

Anxious Attachment (Clingy Clint):

- Treats text response time like a medical emergency.
- Interprets "I need space" as "I'm planning your replacement".
- Needs more reassurance than a toddler at their first sleepover.
- Overanalyzes your tone, text, emoji choice, and probably your breathing pattern.
- Jumps into relationships with the speed and caution of a caffeinated lemming.

Fearful-Avoidant Attachment (Distant Dylan):

- Approaches and retreats with the predictability of a malfunctioning robot.
- Wants intimacy but runs from it as if it were on fire.
- Sends more mixed signals than a broken traffic light.
- Creates emotional whiplash with hot/cold behavior.
- Simultaneously fears both abandonment AND closeness.

Dismissive-Avoidant Attachment (Detached Daniel):

- Treats emotional needs as inconvenient allergies.
- Maintains independence with the fervor of a cat who's been picked up against its will.
- Dismisses feelings faster than spam email.
- Views vulnerability as a character flaw rather than a human connection.
- Considers self-sufficiency a religion and dependency a sin.

Understanding these attachment styles isn't just about judging his emotional baggage; it's about deciding if you want to help carry it! Whether you're swiping on a Balanced Ben or decoding Detached Daniel's latest disappearing act, recognizing these patterns can save you months of confusion and countless emergency calls to your girlfriends. The silver lining? These attachment styles aren't emotional prison sentences; with self-awareness, therapy, and perhaps a minor miracle, even the most commitment-phobic men can develop more secure patterns.

His attachment style explains why he sends 47 consecutive texts or ghosts for a week after you mention meeting your parents, but it doesn't give him a free pass for treating your heart like an emotional yo-yo. And while we've focused on men's attachment styles in this chapter, I hope you've also spotted yourself in these descriptions, because understanding your attachment style is just as crucial as identifying his! Whether he's securely supporting, anxiously pursuing, fearfully flip-flopping, or dismissively distancing (and whether you're doing the same), the question isn't just about recognizing these patterns; it's about deciding whether to stick around for the reruns or change the channel entirely!

Chapter 4

THE LOVE LANGUAGE LABYRINTH

Let's Set the Scene

Welcome, intrepid explorers of the heart, to The Love Language Labyrinth, a maze so complex it makes solving a Rubik's cube blindfolded look like a game of tic-tac-toe! Here, we'll make our way through the twisting corridors of affection, where one wrong turn can lead you from "be mine" to "be gone" faster than you can say "it's not you, it's me."

Our voyage takes us through five distinct districts, each with its unique dialect of devotion:

1. **Words of Affirmation:** Where compliments flow like wine, and silence is more deadly than a thousand insults. Here, "you look nice" is small talk, and sonnets are casual greetings.

2. **Quality Time:** The realm where watching paint dry together is considered a hot date. Phones are forbidden, and eye contact is an Olympic sport.

3. **Physical Touch:** Enter at your own risk, the land where personal space goes to die. Hugs are handshakes, and handshakes are practically third base.

4. **Acts of Service:** Welcome to the kingdom of "I love you, now let me do your taxes." Where changing oil is foreplay and folding laundry is pillow talk.

5. **Receiving Gifts:** Behold the province where "it's the thought that counts" is heresy. Here, love is measured in price tags, and gift receipts are love letters.

But hold onto your heart-shaped hats, folks! While we're poking fun at these love languages, let's not forget they're as crucial to relationships as caffeine is to Monday mornings. These languages, when spoken fluently and reciprocated, can transform a good relationship into a great one. However, like that friend who won't stop quoting their favorite movie, some folks take their preferred love language to extremes. Balance is key – a harmonious relationship is more like a well-mixed cocktail than a shot of pure tequila. It shouldn't feel like a full-time job as a personal gift shopper or a professional compliment dispenser.

So grab your map (and maybe your wallet, just in case), and let's embark on this treacherous trek through the topsy-turvy terrain of romantic dialects. Who knows? By the end, you might be fluent in the language of love or at least able to pilot the choppy waters of dating without capsizing your emotional boat.

In the Love Language Labyrinth, every turn is an adventure, every dead end a lesson, and every successful navigation a victory. May the odds be ever in your favor, and may your love tank always be full!

The Compliment Collector

Validation Vince

Vince could pass for a peacock with a praise kink. His self-esteem is more delicate than a soufflé, and his ego requires more maintenance than a vintage sports car.

Vince's profile is a masterclass in ego maintenance disguised as a dating bio, where every word begs for praise.

About Me: "Seeking a sweet-talker who can make my ego purr like a well-fed kitten. If your compliments flow like wine and your praise is as abundant as cat videos on the internet, we might be a match made in flattery heaven. Warning: May develop an allergic reaction to constructive criticism."

First Date: Prepare for an exercise in verbal gymnastics. Vince will:

- Arrive looking expectantly at you, waiting for praise on his outfit choice.

- Drop not-so-subtle hints about his accomplishments, pausing for your applause.

- Deflate visibly if you go more than 5 minutes without complimenting him.

- Offer you backhanded compliments, hoping you'll counter with better ones.

- End the night by asking you to rate his date performance on a scale of "amazing" to "life-changing".

Red Flags (or as Vince calls them, "praise deficiency symptoms"):

- Gets moody when not the center of attention.

- Turns every conversation back to his achievements.

- Struggles to genuinely compliment others.

- Has a framed collection of participation trophies from adulthood.

Vince's hobbies include fishing for compliments, basking in adoration, and practicing his "oh, stop it, you" face in the mirror (while secretly hoping you won't stop). He believes in a world where participation trophies are given out for breathing and "you tried" is the highest form of praise.

Dating Vince is like being a one-person PR team for the world's neediest client. If you find yourself falling for Vince, make sure your compliment thesaurus is up to date and your praise tank is always full!

The Last Word:

Vince: Your self-worth shouldn't need more validation than an expired parking meter. Perhaps if you spent less time fishing for compliments and more time developing actual self-esteem, you'd realize that confidence is sexier than constant neediness.

Ladies: Unless you're looking for a full-time position as an unpaid personal cheerleader for a man whose ego is more fragile than a soap bubble, treats compliments like oxygen, and self-esteem has more needs than a newborn, swipe left faster than he can say "Tell me I'm handsome." Your patience and praise tank will thank you.

The Timeshare Enthusiast

Togetherness Tony

Tony resembles a needy golden retriever with separation anxiety. His ideal day involves 24 uninterrupted hours of togetherness, and his nightmare is a partner with hobbies that don't include him.

Tony's profile is a clingy cuddle manifesto disguised as a dating bio, where personal space is treated as an optional luxury rather than a basic human need:

About Me: "ISO a partner who thinks 'quality time' is the only time that matters. If you can put your phone down longer than it takes to order takeout, we might have a shot. Seeking someone who believes eye contact is the ultimate extreme sport. Warning: May experience separation anxiety when you go to the bathroom."

First Date: Prepare for an intense one-on-one experience that would make a Siamese twin uncomfortable. Tony will:

- Arrive early and text you his exact location every 30 seconds until you get there.
- Maintain eye contact so intensely you'll wonder if he's trying to hypnotize you.

- Suggest activities that maximize talking time, like a silent movie or a mime show.

- Look hurt if you check your phone, even if it's to tell your family you're still alive.

- End the night by suggesting a weekend getaway for your second date... tomorrow.

Red Flags (or as Tony calls them, "togetherness deficiency indicators"):

- Gets anxious when you mention having separate hobbies.

- Considers "I need some space" fighting words.

- Has never heard of the concept of "absence makes the heart grow fonder."

- His ideal vacation is being stranded on a desert island... with you, of course.

Tony's pastimes include staring lovingly into his date's eyes, planning couple activities, and panic-texting "where are you?" if his partner takes too long grocery shopping. He believes multitasking is a dirty word and divided attention is grounds for relationship counseling.

Dating Tony is like joining a two-person cult whose central doctrine is "thou shalt not part, even for bathroom breaks." If you find yourself falling for Tony, make sure your schedule is clear for the rest of your life!

The Last Word:

Tony: Hey, Koala Bear, quality time doesn't mean ALL the time, and "joined at the hip" isn't a relationship goal, it's a medical condition. Being someone's everything isn't romantic; it's exhausting. Try developing a personality that exists beyond your partner's presence. Your bathroom mirror might be a good place to start that independent course.

Ladies: When a man's clinginess rivals that of a barnacle and his idea of personal space is measured in millimeters, swipe left faster than Tony can say, "Where are you going?" Your healthy sense of independence, combined with the tracking device he installed on your phone, will thank you.

The Affection Aficionado

Touchy-Feely Ted

Ted functions as a sticky note, always looking to attach himself to someone. His personal bubble is microscopic, and his ideal date involves more physical contact than Black Friday at the Outlet Mall.

Ted's profile is a tactile tsunami where consent is treated as a suggestion and every interaction is viewed as an opportunity for skin-to-skin contact.

About Me: "Searching for a human octopus who believes personal space is overrated. If your love language is more tactile than a Braille dictionary, we'll get along just fine. Caution: May cause spontaneous cuddling in public places."

First Date: Prepare for a hands-on experience that would make an octopus blush. Ted will:

- Greet you with a hug that lasts longer than most people's relationships.

- Find any excuse to initiate contact (You've got an eyelash! No, let me get it...).

- Suggest activities that involve touching, like a massage class or full-contact origami.

- Look hurt if you don't hold his hand while he's chewing.
- End the night with a goodbye hug that turns into an impromptu slow dance... in the parking lot.

Red Flags (or as Ted calls them, "affection deficiency symptoms"):

- Considers "I need some space" a personal insult.
- Has been banned from multiple petting zoos for being "too handsy" with the animals.
- Thinks "no touching" signs are merely suggestions.
- His idea of respecting boundaries is leaving a millimeter of space between you.

Ted's hobbies include inventing new ways to hug, finding excuses for incidental touches, and planning dates to crowded places so he has a reason to stand extremely close. He believes handshakes are for cowards and a pat on the back is practically foreplay.

Dating Ted is like signing up to be a professional hugger in a world where everyone has a cold. If you find yourself falling for Ted, make sure you're ready for a relationship that's more hands-on than a surgeon's career!

The Last Word:

Ted: Hey there, Tentacles Ted! Your understanding of personal space is about as developed as a toddler's concept of sharing. Here's a revolutionary idea: meaningful connection doesn't require constant physical contact, and consent is sexier than surprise snuggles. Try developing a personality that doesn't rely on breaking the touch barrier every 3.5 seconds.

Ladies: When a man's emotional intelligence is smaller than his personal space bubble and he treats 'no touching' signs like they're written in invisible ink, swipe left faster than he can say, 'Come here, you need a hug!' Your public dignity, personal boundaries, and elbow room will thank you.

The Task Asker

Do-It-For-Me Drew

Drew doubles as a to-do list, always full of tasks for others to complete. His love tank fills up faster than his laundry basket, and his idea of romance is coming home to find all his chores magically done.

Drew's profile is an unpaid internship disguised as a dating opportunity, where love is measured in completed tasks and romance comes with a clipboard and checklist:

About Me: "ISO a partner fluent in the language of 'doing stuff for me.' If your idea of romance is surprising me with a spotless kitchen or a reorganized closet, I'm already swooning. Seeking someone who shows love through actions, not words. Because who needs poetry when you can pick up my dry cleaning?"

First Date: Prepare for a bizarrely task-oriented romantic experience. Drew will:

- Casually mention his dog needs a bath.

- Drop hints about his chaotic pantry and how great it would be if someone organized it.

- Suggest "fun" future activities like deep cleaning his apartment or meal prepping for his work week.

- Look disappointed if you don't offer to pick up the check and his dry cleaning.

- End the night by wondering aloud if you're free to wait for his handyman while he's at work next week.

Red Flags (or as Drew calls them, "service deficiency indicators"):

- Gets visibly anxious when you don't offer to do things for him.

- Considers "Let's just hang out" as fighting words.

- Has never heard of the concept "It's the thought that counts."

- His idea of reciprocating is letting you bask in the glory of a job well done.

Drew's hobbies include creating to-do lists, dreaming up new organizational systems for others to implement, and perfecting his "you shouldn't have" face. He believes "I love you" is best expressed through a well-stocked fridge and an empty hamper.

Dating Drew is like being a very under-appreciated personal assistant who pays for the privilege. If you find yourself falling for Drew, make sure your servant's heart is strong and your boundaries are stronger!

The Last Word:

Drew: Hey there, Delegation Dave! Your love language isn't "acts of service", it's "acts of servitude." A relationship shouldn't come with a job description, and romance isn't measured by the number of completed chores. Try picking up something other than your phone to ask for favors, like maybe your own dry cleaning.

Ladies: When a man's idea of romance is treating you like his personal TaskRabbit and his dating profile reads more like a job posting on Indeed, Swipe left faster than he can say "while you're up..." Your to-do list, work-life balance, and self-respect will thank you.

The Gift Gatherer

Present-Pursuing Pat

Pat is a human mood ring whose color changes based on present proximity. This walking, talking gift receipt has never met a wrapped package it didn't like or a gift-giving occasion it could pass up.

Pat's profile is the dating equivalent of leaving a Christmas list on the refrigerator year-round:

About Me: "Thoughtful romantic who speaks fluent Gift. My love language isn't just receiving presents, it's interpreting them like a relationship archaeologist. That keychain? Evidence you were listening last Tuesday. That coffee mug? Proof that our souls are connected. Looking for someone who knows that sometimes, the right carefully chosen token can say more than words, though words written on gift tags count double!"

The three most romantic words in Pat's world aren't "I love you" but "I got you something." While he's perfectly capable of connecting through conversation, his pupils visibly dilate at the crinkle of wrapping paper. It's not about price tags (though his hints about that watch have become less subtle than a neon sign); it's about the concrete evidence that he occupies space in your mental real estate.

First Date: An enjoyable evening where Pat arrives with a surprisingly thoughtful small gift, perhaps a book you mentioned, or a coffee mug featuring your profession's inside joke. Watch how he casually drops that his birthday is only seven months away while maintaining direct eye contact. The smallest reciprocal gesture will make his face light up like Times Square on New Year's Eve.

Love Language: Receiving gifts, with the enthusiasm of a kid on Christmas morning and the memory of an elephant. He remembers every gift he's ever received and can rank them by thoughtfulness, presentation, and whether they made his friends jealous.

Attachment Style: Materially motivated but emotionally genuine. His bedside drawer isn't filled with love letters; it's a carefully cataloged museum of relationship artifacts, each with its own mental display card.

Pat isn't just a one-way gift vacuum; he gives as good as he gets, often remembering details you mentioned while half-asleep three weeks ago. His gifting accuracy is so precise it's slightly unsettling, like he's been taking notes while you browse online (spoiler alert: he has).

The challenge with Pat isn't materialism, it's that during emotional turbulence, he'll show up with a perfectly wrapped peace offering instead of perfectly chosen words. Who needs apologies when there's Amazon Prime?

The Last Word:

Pat: Your gift radar is impressive, but relationships need more sustenance than what fits in gift bags. Try unwrapping your actual feelings sometimes; they're the only present that appreciates over time.

Ladies: If you enjoy the language of thoughtful tokens and a partner who notices what makes you smile, Pat might be refreshingly attentive. Just ensure your connection extends beyond the material. If the gifts feel like emotional shorthand rather than enhancement, consider whether you're building a relationship or just an elaborate gift exchange program. Your emotional fulfillment, disposable income, and the storage space in your closet will thank you.

Chapter 4

THE TAKEAWAY

Having traversed the twists and turns of The Love Language Labyrinth, we've discovered what happens when good intentions get lost in translation and relationship GPS systems mysteriously malfunction! These men aren't just speaking different love languages, they're shouting them through megaphones while wearing noise-canceling headphones.

Understanding love languages should enhance connection, not hijack it. Yet our characters have turned balanced preferences into obsessive demands, creating relationship obstacle courses where their partners must navigate increasingly complex expressions of love.

Red Flags In Multiple Languages:

Words of Affirmation (Validation Vince):

- Treats compliments like oxygen, can't survive without hourly doses.
- Has turned fishing for compliments into an Olympic sport.
- Interprets any criticism as a declaration of war.
- Needs more validation than a parking ticket machine.
- Believes silence equals hatred, regardless of context.

Quality Time (Togetherness Tony):

- Has never met a boundary he wouldn't cheerfully trample in the name of "togetherness."

- Monitors your attention like a security guard with separation anxiety.

- Considers "alone time" a personal insult rather than a human need.

- Treats your schedule as an offensive obstacle to his master plan.

- Believes "quality time" means "all time, all places, no exceptions".

Physical Touch (Touchy-Feely Ted):

- Approaches personal space like it's an optional concept.

- Treats PDA as mandatory regardless of setting or comfort.

- Believes "I'm a physical touch person" exempts him from consent conversations.

- Interprets a lack of constant contact as emotional abandonment.

- Has never met a hug he couldn't turn into a full-body experience.

Acts of Service (Do-It-For-Me Drew):

- Confuses "partner" with "personal assistant".

- Has mysteriously forgotten how to perform basic tasks since meeting you.

- Measures love by your willingness to be his unpaid housekeeper.

- Interprets self-sufficiency as a sign that you don't care.

- Has elevated learned helplessness to a craft.

Receiving Gifts (Present-Pursuing Pat):

- Measures emotional connection through tangible tokens and wrapped surprises.
- Interprets gifts with the intensity of an archaeologist examining ancient artifacts.
- Has memory storage exclusively dedicated to cataloging every gift ever received.
- Reads more meaning into a simple present than a literature professor analyzing symbolism.
- Defaults to gift-giving as a form of emotional shorthand when actual conversations become complicated.

Healthy love languages enhance connection rather than demand it. They're preferences, not prescriptions; desires, not demands. The right partner won't just speak their love language at maximum volume; they'll learn to become multilingual, appreciating your dialect while teaching you theirs.

When someone's love language becomes their love obsession, they're not seeking connection but imposing demands. You deserve a relationship where love is expressed in many languages, all spoken with respect, balance, and the understanding that true love is a conversation, not a monologue.

Chapter 5

THE PERSONALITY EXTREMES

Let's Set the Scene

Welcome to The Personality Extremes, where we dive into the deep end of the human psyche pool, no lifeguard on duty! In this chapter, we're exploring a veritable smorgasbord of personality quirks, each dialed up to eleven. It's like a psychiatric ward met a comedy club, and they decided to start a dating app together.

Say hello to our cast of characters: Arrogant Arnold, whose ego needs its own zip code, and Boring Bob, who could make a fireworks display feel like watching paint dry. Let's not forget Sarcastic Sean, who is ironically attached to his defense mechanisms and collection of cutting remarks.

These archetypes represent the colorful extremes of human personality, the spice of life that sometimes feels more like a mouthful of wasabi. They're in this chapter because they've taken one aspect of their personality and run with it... straight off a cliff.

While these extreme personalities can be entertaining in small doses, they often pose significant challenges in building balanced and healthy relationships. They remind us that there's a fine line between being uniquely yourself and being, well, too much.

So get ready. We're about to take a roller coaster ride through the highs, lows, and loop-de-loops of human personality. In the world of dating, sometimes the most attractive quality is a little thing we like to call... balance.

Now, let's see if we can find some method to this madness, or at least have a good laugh trying!

The Ego Extraordinaire

Arrogant Arnold

Let me present Arnold, the man who doesn't just think he's God's gift to women, he's convinced he's God's gift to the entire universe. His ego is so massive it has its own gravitational pull, and his self-esteem is higher than his outrageously gelled hair.

Arnold's dating profile reads like a megalomaniac's manifesto.

About Me: "Looking for someone who appreciates excellence in human form, my form, specifically. Must be comfortable with being the second most attractive person in the room at all times (though let's be honest, it's not even close). If you can't handle me at my best, you don't deserve me at my... still best."

His profile pics are a gallery of selfies taken at angles designed to make him look down on you, literally and figuratively.

This walking, talking superlative considers himself the winner of every competition, including ones that don't exist. He doesn't just enter a room; he graces it with his presence. His conversations are less dialogue and more one-man show, with you as the captive audience. Arnold's definition of a balanced conversation: He talks, you nod admiringly.

Dating Arnold is like being a supporting character in the blockbuster movie of his life. He doesn't ask questions; he makes statements about your life that you're expected to confirm. His idea of compromise is letting you agree with him.

First Date: A meal at one of his favorite spots, where the walls are adorned with mirrors, followed by a riveting slideshow of his selfies, culminating in a two-hour TED talk about his path to greatness, with audience participation limited to applause

Love Language: Monologuing about his achievements while you gaze at him adoringly, with bonus points if you take notes and ask for his autograph

Attachment Style: Securely attached to every reflective surface that shows his face

Arnold's favorite topic? Arnold, of course. His second favorite topic? How everyone else doesn't measure up to Arnold. He's not just confident; he's confidently incorrect about almost everything. But don't try to correct him; in Arnold's world, facts are just opinions that haven't had the privilege of being validated by him yet.

P.S. If you match with Arnold, be prepared for dates that feel like an endless acceptance speech for an award he gave himself. In Arnold's world, the sun doesn't just revolve around him; it asks for his permission to rise each morning.

The Last Word:

Arnold: Hey there, Emperor of Ego! I hate to break it to you, but the world doesn't revolve around you – it just feels that way because you're spinning so fast in your own self-importance. Here's a revolutionary idea: try listening to someone else for a change. You might learn something, like humility, for instance.

Ladies: Don't let his inflated ego deflate your self-worth! You deserve someone genuinely interested in you, not just in hearing their own voice. If you encounter an Arnold in the wild, swipe left faster than he can say 'I'm the best thing that will ever happen to you!" Your personal achievements, attention span, and eardrums will thank you.

The Tedium Titan

Boring Bob

Have you ever encountered Bob? He's the human equivalent of watching grass grow in slow motion. This walking, talking sedative doesn't just embrace routine; he's elevated monotony to a practice that would make even beige paint yawn.

Bob's dating profile is a masterpiece of mediocrity:

About Me: "Seeking a partner for life's great adventure (as long as it's scheduled between 6:05 PM and 8:30 PM. Interests include watching paint dry, collecting lint, and alphabetizing my spice rack. Looking for someone who appreciates the thrill of a well-organized sock drawer."

His photos are a gallery of bland: Bob staring blankly at his oatmeal, Bob meticulously folding laundry, Bob's extensive collection of beige sweater vests.

In Bob's world, every day is Groundhog Day, minus the excitement. He doesn't just like routine; he worships at the altar of the mundane, turning even the most potentially exciting activities into exercises in tedium. His idea of spontaneity? Eating dessert before dinner, once a year, after careful consideration.

First Date: A riveting evening of watching infomercials, followed by a thrilling discussion about the optimal way to sort recycling. If you're lucky, he might spice things up with a detailed account of his latest trip to the post office.

Love Language: Punctuality, discussing the weather in excruciating detail, and the ability to appreciate the subtle differences between eggshell and ecru

Attachment Style: Steadfastly attached to his routine of watching paint dry

P.S. If you match with Bob, be prepared for dates that feel like you're starring in a very slow, very dull version of "Groundhog Day." In Bob's universe, "Netflix and chill" means watching documentaries about the history of cardboard while he provides a running commentary on the benefits of his new filing system. Just don't be surprised if you find yourself envying the excitement of your grandmother's bridge club.

The Last Word:

Bob: Hey there, Captain Mundane! Even elevators have more ups and downs than your personality, and watching paint dry called, it wants its excitement back. Your daily routine has less variation than a stop sign, and your conversation topics have all the spice of unflavored oatmeal at room temperature.

Ladies: Thinking of swiping right on Bob? You're in for the most predictable ride of your life! If you've ever wondered what it's like to date a human screensaver, Bob's your guy. However, if your idea of romance doesn't include timing how long it takes a stoplight to change or categorizing paperclips by size and color, swipe left faster than Bob can say, "Did you know there are 37 different types of manila folders?" Your zest for life, conversation topics, and will to live will thank you.

The Verbal Viper

Sarcastic Sean

Get ready to swipe left on Sean, the human embodiment of an eye-roll wrapped in a defense mechanism. This walking, talking snark machine has turned "I'm fluent in sarcasm" into code for "I'm just mean but I'll call it wit."

About Me: "Professional cynic seeking someone with skin thicker than my walls. Looking for a partner who thinks 'brutally honest' is a compliment and 'just being sarcastic' is a valid excuse for emotional damage. If you can't handle me at my snarkiest, you don't deserve me at my... well, I'm pretty much always like this."

Photos showcase Sean in his natural habitat: smirking at inspirational quotes, posing mockingly next to "Live, Laugh, Love" signs, and taking "ironic" selfies that convey a sense of humor as a means to avoid genuine connection. His attempt at sincerity? A raised eyebrow and "This is my caring face. Really."

First Date: Save your time for someone who doesn't treat emotional damage like a competitive sport. The only date Sean deserves is with his therapist.

Love Language: Backhanded compliments, creating inside jokes at others' expense, and making sure everyone knows he's the funniest guy in the room

Attachment Style: Ironically attached to his defense mechanisms and collection of cutting remarks that keep genuine connection safely at bay

In Sean's world, every interaction is a verbal gladiator arena. He doesn't just converse; he performs, turning casual chats into opportunities to demonstrate his superiority through carefully crafted burns. His favorite phrase? "Can't you take a joke?" is the battle cry of those who use humor as a weapon rather than joy.

The Last Word:

Sean: Your 'wit' isn't a personality trait, it's a shield made of sharp edges and defensive humor. Try developing actual personality traits that don't require making others feel small. Spoiler alert: being mean isn't a substitute for being interesting."

Ladies: When a man's profile proudly proclaims he's "fluent in sarcasm," translate that as "I'll insult you and call it humor." Unless you want your self-esteem to be the punchline of a very unfunny joke, swipe left faster than Sean can say "I was just kidding!" and then BLOCK this walking defense mechanism. No amount of "wit" is worth the emotional paper cuts. Your self-esteem, pride, and women everywhere will thank you.

Chapter 5

THE TAKEAWAY

Having survived our expedition through The Personality Extremes, we've witnessed firsthand how dating can become an extreme sport without safety equipment! These men don't just display quirks; they showcase personality traits amplified to nuclear levels.

Our field research has confirmed what many suspected: from mind-numbing boredom to ego inflation that would make hot air balloons jealous, these exaggerated traits explain why some dates feel less like getting to know someone and more like surviving a personality tsunami.

Red Flags With Volume Controls:

- Their personality settings are permanently stuck on maximum, with no dimmer switch in sight.

- They've turned single traits into entire personalities, like one-note songs on an endless loop.

- They approach self-awareness like vampires approach mirrors; they avoid it entirely.

- Their emotional range runs from A to A½, with no stops at any other letters.

- They've mistaken "being yourself" for "being your most extreme self at all times."

- Their personality quirks aren't seasoning, they're the entire meal, drink, and dessert.

- They've never met a middle ground they couldn't avoid with Olympic-level skill.

Personality certainly matters in dating, but issues of proportion matter even more. From Bob's boredom marathon to Arnold's ego explosion to Sean's sarcasm tsunami, these men demonstrate that how we express ourselves is just as important as what we're expressing.

A healthy personality shouldn't feel like enduring a one-man show, surviving an ego assault, or defending against verbal paper cuts. It should be balanced, adaptable, and considerate of others in the room.

Your attention deserves engagement, your achievements deserve recognition, and your feelings deserve respect. Don't lower your standards for someone whose personality trait has mutated into their entire identity.

The right person won't make you feel like an audience member in their personality show. They'll bring their unique qualities to the table without forcing you to drown in them, because they'll want to know your personality too.

Chapter 6

THE FINANCIAL FOLLIES

Let's Set the Scene

Welcome to The Financial Follies, where wallets are always empty but excuses are abundant! In this chapter, we're diving into the shallow end of the money pool with men who've turned financial responsibility into a game of hot potato.

Allow me to introduce Divorced-Dad Dirk, whose wallet is stretched thinner than the ice he's skating on with creditors. Dutch-Treat Doug, on the other hand, calculates everything shared down to the last penny. We've got Pyramid Pete, turning every date into a multi-level marketing pitch, and Bitcoin Bill, who's more committed to his crypto wallet than any human relationship.

These fiscal fumblers have turned dating into an economic obstacle course, leaving a trail of split checks, investment schemes, and awkward silences when the bill arrives. They're the guys who make you wonder: Is he also calculating how much complimentary bread I ate?

While financial compatibility is essential, these men have taken it to the extreme by pinching pennies until they scream or gambling their life savings on the next big crypto surge. They're living proof that sometimes, the most attractive quality is the ability to handle money with maturity and grace.

So, grab your calculator and your sense of financial fairness as we face the perilous path of monetary mismanagement. In the world of dating, sometimes the richest experiences come from those who understand the actual value of things and people.

Now, let's count the ways these cash-conscious Casanovas can make your romantic account run dry!

The Penny-Pinching Papa

Divorced-Dad Dirk

Say hello to Dirk, the poster child for "champagne taste on a tap water budget." This divorced dad is stretching his dollars so thin, you could read a newspaper through his wallet. Dirk's financial situation is tighter than his high school jeans, between alimony, child support, and his kids' endless supply of growth spurts.

Dirk's profile is a financial tightrope act where his wit is inversely proportional to his bank balance:

About Me: "Financially savvy single dad (translation: I can make a Costco sample tray last three meals) seeking someone who appreciates the finer things in life, like buy-one-get-one-free deals and early bird specials. Expert in creative date planning (park benches are nature's fine dining). My credit score and bank account are playing limbo, how low can they go?"

In Dirk's world, every dollar has a job, a backup job, and a side hustle. He doesn't just budget; he performs financial gymnastics, turning bill-paying into an extreme sport. His idea of splurging? Using name-brand ketchup packets (borrowed from McDonald's) for his home-cooked pasta.

First Date: Dirk's dates are a masterclass in low-cost entertainment. Romantic walks in the park? Free. Window shopping? Doesn't cost a dime. Pretending the playground is an amusement park? Priceless. He's turned bargain hunting into an extreme sport, and every date is the Olympics.

Love Language: Sharing half-off happy hour appetizers, collecting grocery store points together, and the ability to find romance in comparing coupon expiration dates

Attachment Style: Permanently attached to his Excel spreadsheet of shared expenses

This modern-day Robin Hood robs from his meager savings to give to his ex-wife, kids, and the occasional lucky lady who doesn't mind splitting a kids' meal at McDonald's. Dirk's credit cards are maxed out faster than his ex-wife's patience. His wallet is a graveyard of declined plastic, and his credit score is so low it needs a ladder to reach rock bottom. He's on a first-name basis with every debt collector in the tri-state area, and his financial strategy is best described as "robbing Peter to pay MasterCard." But hey, at least he's got enough points for a free flight... to Bankruptcy Town.

Despite his financial gymnastics, Dirk's determined to find love, or at least someone willing to pick up the check occasionally. He's proof that you can't put a price on love, mainly because he can't afford to.

Swipe right if you enjoy creative budgeting, don't mind being paid in compliments instead of actual currency, and think love is all you need (because it's all he can afford).

P.S. If you match with Dirk, be prepared for dates that are high on imagination and low on expenditure. When Dirk says he wants to "invest in your future together," he means it literally – he needs an investor!

The Last Word

Dirk: Your dedication to your kids is admirable, but maybe it's time for a dating timeout. Love might not cost a thing, but dating sure does. Try focusing on financial recovery before attempting romantic discovery. Your future self (and your credit score) will thank you.

Ladies: When a man's financial obligations have obligations of their own, and his idea of fine dining involves drive-thru coupons, consider that sometimes the kindest swipe is to the left. Not because he's a bad guy, but because good guys sometimes need time to get their lives (and finances) in order before adding romance to the mix.

The Stingy Splitter

Dutch-Treat Doug

Enter Doug, the human embodiment of a calculator with trust issues. This walking, talking spreadsheet has turned bill-splitting into an extreme sport.

Doug's profile is a financial red flag waving from behind a fortress of separate checks and coupons:

About Me: "Fiscally meticulous bachelor seeking equally economical partner who understands that love doesn't pay the bills (which we'll be splitting down to the penny). Looking for someone who appreciates that romance is best served with separate checks. Warning: Must be willing to Venmo before leaving the table."

Photos showcase Doug in his penny-pinching habitat: comparing prices on identical water bottles, clutching his beloved coupon organizer, and "casual" shots of him looking triumphant over a 2-for-1 happy hour deal. His attempt at a romantic pic? A selfie with his prized possession: a Casio calculator watch from 1987.

First Date: A venue with a BOGO offer, followed by detailed negotiations over who should leave the tip

Love Language: Immediate Venmo requests, sharing Groupons, and the ability to calculate your portion of the bill in nanoseconds

Attachment Style: Mathematically attached to his calculator and the belief that love can be itemized. His strongest emotional bonds are with discount codes and his monthly budget spreadsheet.

In Doug's world, every date is an accounting exercise and every meal a mathematical equation. He doesn't just split bills; he performs financial forensics, turning dinner into a spreadsheet-worthy event. His idea of romance? Letting you keep the extra penny when the bill is odd.

The Last Word

Doug: Your relationship with money is tighter than your grip on that calculator. Try investing in generosity instead of spreadsheets. The only thing you're successfully splitting is your chance at a genuine connection.

Ladies: When a man's idea of romance includes itemized receipts and his Venmo requests arrive before the meal is digested, swipe left faster than he can say "separate checks, please". Your financial freedom, fiscal dignity, and restaurant servers everywhere will thank you.

The MLM Guru

Pyramid Pete

Next up is Pete, the human embodiment of a motivational poster gone rogue. This walking, talking sales pitch has turned the art of alienating friends and family into a lucrative "business opportunity."

Pete's dating profile is a masterclass in thinly-veiled recruitment:

About Me: "Entrepreneur extraordinaire seeking a partner in life and business (but mostly business). Looking for someone who appreciates the finer things in life, like financial freedom and the sweet smell of essential oils. Swipe right to join my team... I mean, my heart! #BossBabe #RelationshipGoals #ButReallyItsAboutTheDownline"

Photos showcase Pete in his natural habitat: posing next to a rented sports car, hosting a "party" where everyone looks uncomfortable, and a suspiciously professional shot of him on stage with a headset, captioned "Living the dream!"

First Date: A date with Pete is like sitting through a timeshare presentation, but with more emoji use. He'll arrive precisely on time (because time is money, hun!), insist on meeting at a coffee shop (where he'll try to recruit the barista), and spend the evening explaining how you too can be your own boss by selling leggings/shakes/questionable supplements. Be prepared for constant compliments that segue into how much better your life could be if you just signed up under him.

Love Language: Giving you the "opportunity of a lifetime" and showering you with sample products that definitely aren't expired

Attachment Style: Hierarchically attached to his downline and the belief that it's not a pyramid, it's an "opportunity triangle"

P.S. Pete's idea of Netflix and chill involves watching motivational speakers on YouTube and chilling... with his vision board.

P.P.S. If things get serious, be ready for a proposal... to sign up as his downline. Because nothing says "I love you" like a binding contract and a garage full of unsold inventory.

The Last Word

Pete: Your relationship pyramid scheme has left you with nothing but a garage full of dreams and a contacts list of people who won't answer your calls. It's time to sell yourself on reality.

Ladies: Unless you want your love life to become an endless sales pitch (and your garage to become a legging museum), swipe left. The only thing that'll grow faster than his 'business' is your debt.

The Crypto Bro

Bitcoin Bill

Here comes Bill, the human embodiment of a cryptocurrency crash. This walking, talking blockchain has invested his entire personality in digital currency and considers "To the moon!" appropriate pillow talk.

Bill's profile is a digital currency prospectus disguised as a dating bio, equal parts techno-evangelism and financial fantasy.

About Me: "Future crypto billionaire (currently living in mom's basement) seeking a partner to Hold On for Dear Life (HODL) through the dips. Must appreciate a man who's all in on digital currencies and doesn't mind that I sold my car for more speculative crypto investments. Warning: May need to reschedule dates based on market fluctuations."

Photos showcase Bill in his digital habitat, posing with his cryptocurrency mining computers (which double as space heaters), pointing at indecipherable charts, and candid shots of him pretending to use Bitcoin ATMs. His attempt at a professional pic? A selfie wearing a suit with a laser-eyes filter captioned "Future of Finance."

In Bill' 's world, every moment is an opportunity to shill crypto. He doesn't just talk; he preaches, turning casual coffee dates into unsolicited financial seminars. His idea of romance? Showing you his expensive digital art collection (NFTs) while explaining why traditional banking is a government conspiracy.

First Date: Watching crypto prices fluctuate while he explains why this latest 90% drop is bullish news

Love Language: Sharing his favorite digital coins, explaining blockchain technology to strangers, and the ability to understand what HODL means (he has it tattooed on his arm)

Attachment Style: Cryptically attached to his digital wallet and the conviction that "diamond hands" (never selling despite losses) is a personality trait

The Last Word

Bill: Your personality is more volatile than your crypto portfolio, and that's saying something. Try investing in some real-world social skills instead of another meme coin. The only thing you're HODLing is delusion.

Ladies: When a man's financial strategy is based on internet memes, run faster than his portfolio loses value. Unless you want your relationship to feel like a never-ending crypto convention, swipe left on this walking market crash. No amount of potential future gains is worth dating a human Bitcoin bubble. Your fiscal responsibility, financial advisor, and retirement plan will thank you.

Chapter 6

THE TAKEAWAY

After examining the balance sheets of Financial Follies, we've seen firsthand how wallets speak louder than words and red flags come with price tags attached! These men haven't just demonstrated financial challenges - they've revealed how money matters can transform into relationship minefields that would make accountants weep.

Our audit of these fiscal fiascos confirms what savvy daters suspect: while money might not buy happiness, financial compatibility certainly helps sustain it. From penny-pinchers to crypto evangelists, these characters have illustrated how money behaviors reveal more profound truths about values, responsibility, and potential for partnership.

Red Flags With Dollar Signs:

- Their relationship with money is more dysfunctional than their last three breakups combined.

- They've mistaken "financial partnership" for either "your wallet is my wallet" or "my wallet stays locked in a safe you can't access."

- Their financial literacy stops at either "spend it all" or "hoard it like a dragon."

- They treat joint expenses like advanced calculus - unnecessarily complicated and designed to make one person cry.

- Their financial planning consists entirely of either "someone else will handle it" or "I've invested our future in digital cat pictures."

- They've turned money discussions into emotional hostage situations.

- Their financial red flags are so bright they're visible from space.

Financial compatibility isn't about matching bank accounts – it's about matching values, honesty, and partnership approaches. These men demonstrate that how someone handles money often reveals how they'll handle you: with respect, transparency, and balance... or not.

Whether it's Dirk's post-divorce penny-pinching, Doug's Dutch treat dictatorship, Pete's pyramid scheming, or Bill's crypto crusade, these financial follies aren't just annoying quirks – they're relationship deal-breakers masquerading as money habits.

You deserve a partner who approaches finances with maturity, transparency, and a reasonable level of flexibility. Someone who understands that money is a tool for building a life together, not a weapon, a secret, or their entire personality.

Money talks in relationships – and sometimes what it's saying is "Run!"

Chapter 7

THE LIFESTYLE EXTREMISTS

Let's Set the Scene

Welcome to The Lifestyle Extremists, where moderation is a four-letter word and every hobby is a full-blown identity crisis! In this chapter, we dive into the deep end of dedication with men who have turned their lifestyles into religions and their passions into pathologies.

Step into a world where Buckshot Brock tries to woo you with his fresh kill, Bible Thumper Bobby quotes scripture in his pickup lines, Kama Sutra Kyle's yoga poses are pure innuendo, and Stoner Steve's idea of "higher consciousness" comes in a very different package.

These men have taken "passion" to pathological levels, from evangelical dating to tantric timing, from venison valentines to perpetual highs. They're living proof that sometimes, the most attractive thing you can be is... well, balanced.

So grab your Bible (Bobby insists), your Tantric manual (Kyle recommends), your hunting gear (Brock demands), your rolling papers (Steve supplies), and let's venture into the world of men who don't just have interests, they have obsessions with tax-exempt status!

The Primal Pursuer

Buckshot Brock

Feast your eyes on Brock, the man who thinks courting is best done with a crossbow. This walking, talking Bass Pro Shops catalog doesn't just enjoy the outdoors; he's convinced that the path to a woman's heart is paved with animal carcasses and camo print.

Brock's dating profile is a veritable trophy room of machismo:

About Me: "Looking for a filly to join my herd. Must love the smell of gunpowder in the morning and the taste of freshly caught venison. Seeking a woman who understands that camouflage is a neutral and taxidermy is just interior decorating for real men. If you think 'field dressing' is a fashion term, we're not compatible. City slickers swipe left!"

His photos are a gallery of conquered beasts: Brock proudly displaying various dead animals, Brock in a tree stand at dawn, Brock's truck with more antlers attached than a reindeer convention.

First Date: A "romantic" dinner at Wild Game Grill, where Brock will spend the entire meal critiquing the amateur preparation of meats he's "harvested better himself.

Don't be alarmed when he pulls out his phone to show the waitstaff pictures of his latest kill while explaining why zebra should be served medium-rare, not medium.

Love Language: Sharing jerky, comparing rifle scopes, and the ability to appreciate the nuances between deer and elk droppings

Attachment Style: Securely attached to his hunting rifle and emotionally bonded to his collection of mounted trophies, while maintaining the stealth to avoid any real human connection

In Brock's world, every conversation is a chance to showcase his primal prowess. His retirement plan involves stockpiling ammunition and building a cabin "off the grid" where he can live out his days scaring hikers. "Netflix and chill" means watching hunting documentaries while he cleans his extensive gun collection. Just don't be surprised if your goodnight kiss tastes suspiciously like venison jerky.

P.S. If you match with Brock, be prepared for dates that feel like you're auditioning for a very niche survival reality show.

The Last Word

Brock: Hey there, Rambo of Romance! Your outdoor skills are impressive, but not every woman dreams of being a Camo Cinderella. Try hunting for some social skills instead of big game. You might find that the most exotic prey is a meaningful connection.

Ladies: If you're considering joining Brock's wilderness expedition, prepare for a relationship where "romantic getaway" means a weekend in a damp tent. Unless your idea of Prince Charming is a man who can skin a deer faster than he can text back, swipe left quicker than a startled pheasant. Your manicure (and your sense of smell) will thank you.

The Zealot

Bible-Thumper Bobby

Presenting Bobby, the man whose dating radius is determined by how far he can drive and still make it back for evening service. This devoted dater has turned "getting to know you" into a spiritual vetting process and considers his dating profile an extension of his testimony.

Bobby's dating profile reads like a religious tract mixed with a marriage application:

About Me: "God-fearing gentleman seeking God-fearing lady for a relationship that puts the 'holy' in holy matrimony. (1 Corinthians 7:9, 'But if they cannot control themselves, they should marry, for it is better to marry than to burn with passion'). Looking for someone whose idea of a perfect Sunday is two church services followed by a potluck dinner and an evening of prayer. Must love Christian acoustic guitar worship songs and understand that my pastor gets the first vote on our compatibility."

Bobby's photos are a carefully curated spiritual resume: solemnly pointing at Bible verses, raising one hand in worship while taking the selfie with the other, posing with elderly church ladies who "would love to see him find a Godly woman," and a selfie at a Christian rock concert, eyes modestly averted because pride is a sin.

First Date: He'll suggest meeting at a local Christian bookstore or coffee shop. Be prepared for prayer before, during, and after your coffee, plus a detailed questionnaire about your relationship with the Lord that makes the SATs look like a BuzzFeed quiz, and whether you'd be willing to homeschool your future 5-8 children. Next stop is a surprise drop-in on his Bible study group, who have "coincidentally" gathered to meet his "friend."

Love Language: Daily scripture texts at 5:30 AM, sharing his favorite sermons, and praying for your "spiritual growth" in areas he's identified as concerning

Attachment Style: Equally yoked to his church community, who collectively have more input on his dating life than he does

In Bobby's world, every conversation is a chance to gauge your spiritual temperature. He doesn't just ask about your day; he asks how your "walk with the Lord" is going this week.

P.S. Bobby's idea of getting physical is a side-hug with witnesses present and possibly a chaste forehead kiss after Sunday services.

The Last Word

Bobby: Faith is beautiful, but turning dating into a theological exam isn't. Remember, Jesus's first miracle was at a wedding, not a sermon - perhaps there's a lesson there about balance.

Ladies: When a man's dating profile features more scripture references than personal details and he considers ordering a glass of Pinot Noir with dinner to be walking dangerously close to the edge, swipe left faster than Jonah fled from Nineveh. Your Sunday mornings, relationship autonomy, and spiritual journey will thank you!

The Sensual Savant

Kama Sutra Kyle

Behold, Kyle, the self-proclaimed PhD in Prurient Studies. This walking encyclopedia of erotica doesn't just have game; he's got an entire Olympic event of romantic rituals. Kyle's dating profile reads like the index of an adult bookstore, carefully skirting the line of app guidelines while leaving no doubt about his area of expertise.

About Me: "Expert in alternative healing, energy alignment, and making every conversation uncomfortably intimate. My spirit animal is a pretzel with commitment issues. Looking for someone who appreciates the finer art of sensual living and doesn't mind that my bedroom looks like a meditation center had a wild night with a massage parlor."

Kyle's profile pics are a masterclass in suggestive posing. There he is, sensually eating a banana. Here's Kyle doing yoga in improbably tight shorts. Oh look, it's Kyle winking at the camera while suggestively polishing a suspiciously shaped vase.

In Kyle's world, every interaction is an opportunity for innuendo. He doesn't just text; he sexts. A simple "How are you?" is answered with a dissertation on the erogenous zones. His idea of small talk is discussing the finer points of Tantric breathing techniques.

First Date: Planning a date with Kyle requires stretching exercises and possibly a safe word. He doesn't just want to meet for coffee; he wants to delve into the sensual art of coffee bean selection, followed by a hands-on latte foam art session that somehow takes a risqué turn.

Love Language: Teaching ancient bedroom arts through inappropriate metaphors and turning every activity into an audition for Cirque du Soleil's adults-only show

Attachment Style: Flexibly attached to his collection of sensual arts manuals while maintaining the limberness to dodge any real emotional connection

Kyle's idea of romance isn't just wine and roses; it's a full-on sensory experience complete with mood lighting, carefully curated playlist, and more scented oils than an aromatherapy convention. He doesn't just want to hold your hand; he wants to introduce your hand to pleasures it never knew existed.

Swipe right if you enjoy feeling like you're dating a contortionist with a thesaurus, don't mind stretching before every date, and think "flexibility" should be listed as a love language.

P.S. In Kyle's universe, "Netflix and chill" is a euphemism for a night of acrobatic adventures that would make a yoga instructor blush!

The Last Word

Kyle: Hey Kyle, while your expertise is... impressive, not every conversation needs to be a lesson in linguistics and limberness. Sometimes, 'How's your day?' can mean 'How's your day?', without any contortions required. Try dialing it back from 'Kama Sutra' to 'Karma Subtle' occasionally. Your dates (and their unsuspecting yoga instructors) will thank you!"

Ladies: Unless you're looking for a date that requires a liability waiver, three years of yoga training, and a dictionary of Sanskrit terminology, swipe left faster than Kyle can say "tantric alignment." Your chiropractor will thank you!

The Perpetual Pothead

Stoner Steve

Observe Steve, the human embodiment of a lava lamp. This walking, talking chill pill has turned relaxation into an extreme sport and considers stress a foreign concept.

Steve's dating profile reads like a dispensary menu crossed with a philosophy textbook:

About Me: "Laid-back dude seeking a partner for deep conversations and snack adventures. Looking for someone who appreciates the greener side of life and finds profound meaning in late-night infomercials. My ideal match? Someone who thinks 'wake and bake' is the most important meal of the day. Swipe right if you're ready to explore the cosmos from the comfort of my couch!"

Photos showcase Steve in his natural habitat: gazing pensively at house plants, caught mid-laugh at something off-camera, and a "candid" shot of him intensely focused on a lava lamp. His attempt at a formal pic? A selfie with his prized glass "art collection."

First Date: A date with Steve is like a passage through time, if time were to move really, really slowly. He'll suggest meeting at a 24-hour diner, arrive in a cloud of incense, and spend the evening pondering life's great mysteries.

Be prepared for philosophical debates about the sentience of snack foods, impromptu meditation sessions, and at least one attempt to order pizza to a park.

Love Language: Sharing his gummies and gifting you with homemade tie-dye creations

Attachment Style: Hazily attached to his bong collection while maintaining the most relaxed relationship with reality ever documented

Dating Steve comes with the promise of never having to worry about high-stress situations or any situations that require being fully alert. Pack your sense of humor, your comfiest clothes, and maybe some eye drops, you know, for the wind or whatever.

P.S. Steve's idea of getting ready for a big night out is changing his sweatpants.

P.P.S. If you make it to a second date, expect an invitation to his weekly drum circle. Because in Steve's world, the only thing better than good vibes is... more good vibes!

P.P.P.S. Steve's spirit animal is a sloth crossed with a golden retriever, slow-moving but eternally optimistic about snacks.

The Last Word

Steve: Dude, your life isn't The Big Lebowski, and "high functioning" doesn't just mean functioning while high. While your laid-back approach has its charms, relationships require you to occasionally remember what day it is and distinguish between deep thoughts and "deep, man." Perhaps try being fully present in the moment instead of just being present-ish.

Ladies: Unless you're cool with dates that start at 4:20, conversations that never quite conclude, and a partner whose most ambitious life goal is finding the perfect ratio of Cool Ranch to Nacho Cheese, swipe left faster than Steve can say "Wait... what was I saying?" Your short-term memory and future ambitions will thank you.

Chapter 7

THE TAKEAWAY

So you've just toured the Lifestyle Extremist amusement park, where the rides are intense, the exits are hard to find, and the souvenirs leave lasting mental scars. These men aren't just enthusiastic about their chosen lifestyles; they're one-note symphonies playing at maximum volume while ignoring all requests to turn it down.

Here's the unfiltered truth with a side of Jersey Girl realness: There's a Grand Canyon-sized difference between having passions and being possessed by them. When a guy's entire personality is wrapped around his Bible, bong, bow and arrow, or bedroom acrobatics manual, you're not dating a man; you're dating his obsession while he rides shotgun.

Red Flags With Extra Flair:

- His lifestyle choice isn't just a preference; it's his moral high ground, and honey, he's looking down at you from it.

- Conversations somehow always circle back to his obsession faster than your aunt circles back to her gallbladder surgery story.

- He judges anyone who doesn't share his lifestyle with the intensity of a fashion critic at Walmart.

- His friend circle consists exclusively of clones who validate his extreme choices.

- Your relationship milestones will always take a backseat to his lifestyle milestones.

- His bank account is emptier than a Times Square subway car at 3 AM, thanks to his lifestyle expenses.

- He's more rigid than a frozen flagpole in January when it comes to accommodating non-lifestyle activities.

Passion is sexy, obsession is exhausting. A healthy relationship needs room for two full personalities, not one personality and a lifestyle support system. When you're constantly playing second fiddle to his beliefs, practices, or peculiar pastimes, it's not a duet; it's a solo performance with you as the unpaid audience.

Trust your gut, protect your boundaries, and never apologize for wanting a multi-dimensional relationship. There's nothing wrong with swiping left on someone whose life's mission is to convert you, hunt with you, hotbox with you, or turn you into their personal Kama Sutra study buddy.

Take this to heart: If his first love isn't you, you'll always be number two.

Chapter 8

THE OBSESSION OVERLOADS

Let's Set the Scene

Welcome to The Obsession Overloads, where passion meets persistence, and hobbies become lifestyles! In this chapter, we're diving headfirst into the deep end of dedication, where moderation is a foreign concept and "too much" is just the beginning.

Prepare to discover a cast of characters who've never heard the phrase "everything in moderation. Introducing Gym-Rat Jake, whose biceps have biceps and whose personality is as sculpted as his abs. There's Football-Fanatic Freddy, who's more committed to his team than most people are to their marriages, and Par-for-the-Course Parker, who thinks eighteen holes is a personality trait. Don't forget Tattoo Tate, turning his body into a walking art gallery, while Tin-Foil Hat Tim searches for conspiracy theories in his breakfast cereal.

These obsession overloads represent the fine line between passion and fixation. From the weight room to the golf course, from the tattoo parlor to the panic room, these guys have taken their interests and cranked them up to eleven. They remind us that while having interests is excellent, there's a point where a hobby becomes hubris.

While their dedication can be admirable, it often presents unique challenges in the dating world. After all, it's hard to build a relationship when your partner's first love is CrossFit, their football team, their putting average, their next ink session, or their latest conspiracy theory.

So, get comfy, as we embark on a trek through the wild world of obsessions. You'll laugh, you'll cry, you'll wonder how someone can talk about protein shakes, draft picks, golf handicaps, tattoo aftercare, and government conspiracies for three hours straight. In the realm of dating, sometimes the most attractive quality is having a personality that extends beyond a single interest.

The Fitness Fiend

Gym-Rat Jake

Feast your eyes on Jake, the man who treats his body like a temple and the gym like his second home (or first, depending on his workout schedule). This walking, talking protein shake doesn't just work out; he's on a lifelong crusade to achieve physical perfection, one grunt and selfie at a time.

Jake's dating profile is a shrine to the Church of Iron:

About Me: "Looking for a spotter in life and love. Must love the smell of sweat, the sound of clanging weights, and the sight of veins popping out like a road map. Leg day is every day, rest days are for the weak!"

Photos showcase Jake in his natural habitat: flexing in gym mirrors, posing with weights heavier than most small cars, and struggling to fit through doorways in shirts two sizes too small. His attempt at a casual pic? A "candid" shot of him bench-pressing a palm tree at the beach.

First Date: A date with Jake is like a high-intensity interval training session for your patience. He'll suggest meeting at a smoothie bar (but only if they have the proper protein-to-carb ratio), arrive in gym clothes because he "just finished a quick 3-hour workout", and spend the evening flexing subconsciously and checking his reflection in every shiny surface. Be prepared for long monologues about the superiority of free weights over machines, impromptu nutrition lessons, and at least one attempt to turn your coffee date into a squat challenge.

Love Language: Complimenting muscle definition, spotting during workouts, and the ability to differentiate between his 17 different protein shakes

Attachment Style: Securely attached to his gym membership, protein shaker, and mirror reflections

Dating Jake comes with the guarantee that you'll always have a gym buddy... whether you want one or not! Pack your workout gear, a thesaurus of compliments for his muscles, and maybe some earplugs for when he inevitably grunts.

The Last Word

Jake: Hey there, Hercules! Your dedication to fitness is impressive, but there's more to life than bicep curls. Try flexing your personality muscles for a change. You might find that emotional depth is just as attractive as a six-pack. But what do I know? I'm just someone who thinks the brain is the most important muscle to exercise.

Ladies: If you're considering swiping right on Jake, prepare for a relationship where "gym" is a four-letter word for "love." Unless you dream of dating a sentient protein shake or fancy being a distant second to his gym membership, swipe left faster than Jake can say "one more rep." Your social life (and your nostrils) will thank you!

The Gridiron Groupie

Football-Fanatic Freddy

Here comes Freddy, the man who's turned sports spectating into a full-contact sport. This walking, talking ESPN highlight reel doesn't just watch games; he lives them, turning every sports season into a rollercoaster of emotions that would put soap operas to shame.

Freddy's dating profile is a sports bar on your screen:

About Me: "Seeking MVP for my heart team. Must love the thrill of victory and be able to console me in the agony of defeat. Warning: I may be emotionally unavailable during playoffs."

His photos are a fan's fantasy: Fred in face paint at stadiums, Fred buried under team merchandise, Freddy's shrine-like man cave that would make professional athletes jealous.

In Freddy's world, every conversation is a potential sports debate, and every life event is scheduled around game days. He doesn't just talk; he commentates, turning casual chats into sports analytics worthy of a pre-game show. His idea of a perfect date? Watching the game, of course (yes, whatever game is on, and there's always a game on).

Freddy's year is divided into two seasons: football season and waiting for football season. His mood swings correlate directly with his team's performance, and he's been known to call in sick to work after a particularly devastating loss. Freddy's idea of couples therapy is co-managing a fantasy league, and he measures relationship milestones by Super Bowls rather than anniversaries.

First Date: A romantic evening at his favorite sports bar where you'll compete for his attention with six TV screens, learn more about his favorite team than his actual life, and watch him emotionally collapse when his team fumbles

Love Language: Fantasy stats and draft picks, treating relationships like his backup quarterback option

Attachment Style: More emotionally invested in his team than any human relationship

P.S. If you match with Freddy, be prepared for dates that feel like you're trapped in a very enthusiastic sports bar. In Freddy's universe, "Netflix and chill" means rewatching classic games while he provides a detailed play-by-play commentary of every move.

The Last Word

Freddy: Hey, Armchair Quarterback! Your passion for the game is impressive, but life isn't just a series of downs and time-outs. Try investing some of that energy into your personal playoffs. You might find that relationships need more than just a good fantasy draft to succeed. But what do I know? I'm just someone who thinks "touchdown" shouldn't be the highest form of emotion in your life.

Ladies: If you're considering joining Fred's fan club, prepare for a relationship where you'll always be competing with 22 men on a field. Unless you can recite stats like a human Wikipedia or you're cool with being a football widow 5 months a year, swipe left faster than a referee can throw a flag. Your Sundays (and your sanity) will thank you.

The Fairway Fundamentalist

Par-for-the-Course Parker

Next up is Parker, the man who believes life is just one big game of golf, and he's always aiming for a hole in one. This walking, talking pro shop doesn't just love golf; he's turned it into a lifestyle, a religion, and possibly a diagnosable obsession.

Parker's dating profile is a virtual country club brochure:

About Me: "Seeking a caddy... I mean partner... for life's 18 holes. Must love early mornings, plaid pants, and the sweet sound of a driver connecting with a ball. Handicap: 7. Emotional availability: Par for the course."

In Parker's world, every conversation is an opportunity to talk about golf. He doesn't just chat; he provides a play-by-play commentary of his latest round, complete with sound effects and impromptu swing demonstrations. His idea of flirting? Comparing your eyes to perfectly manicured putting greens.

Parker's condo is a shrine to the sport. He doesn't just have golf clubs; he's got more shafts than a skyscraper and enough balls to sink a small island. His decor theme? "Augusta National meets bachelor pad," with more golf trophies than furniture and a living room carpet that suspiciously resembles a putting green.

First Date: Hope you enjoy the great outdoors and the gentle whack of club meeting ball, because you're in for 18 holes of pure golfing bliss. He doesn't just plan activities; he schedules tee times. Expect to spend your evening at the driving range, where Parker will critique your form and mansplain the intricacies of choosing the right club.

Love Language: Golf metaphors and unsolicited swing advice. He doesn't want a girlfriend; he wants a playing partner who can appreciate a good sand save and doesn't mind being referred to as his "favorite birdie."

Attachment Style: Securely attached to his nine iron while maintaining a long-distance relationship with reality and treating emotional intimacy like a water hazard to be avoided

Swipe right if you enjoy feeling like you're dating the lovechild of Tiger Woods and a golf cart, don't mind spending every weekend chasing a little white ball across manicured lawns, and think that "dressing up" means donning your finest polo shirt and cleats.

P.S. If you match with Parker, be prepared for dates that feel like you're trapped in a never-ending country club commercial. In Parker's universe, "Netflix and chill" means watching golf tournament reruns while he practices his putting on a portable green in the living room. Forewarned is forearmed!

The Last Word

Parker: Hey there, Tiger Woulds-be! Your dedication to golf is impressive, but life's not just about getting it in the hole. Try swinging for some personal growth instead of that little white ball. You may find that relationships require more than a good handicap to succeed.

Ladies: If you're considering teeing off with Parker, prepare for a relationship where you'll always come second... to a stick and a ball. Unless your idea of romance is spending every waking moment on the links or you fancy being a golf widow before you're even married, swipe left faster than Parker can shout "Fore!" Your weekends (and your wardrobe) will thank you.

The Walking Canvas

Tattoo Tate

Take a good look at Tate, the man who never met a blank patch of skin he didn't want to ink. Tate's not just wearing his heart on his sleeve; he's got it tattooed there, along with his ex's name (poorly covered up), a dragon, and something that might be a dolphin or a very confused shark.

Tate's dating profile is a masterpiece of body art exhibition:

About Me: "Living proof that you can't judge a book by its cover – but you can definitely judge me by mine, because I've got my entire life story inked on my body. Each tattoo tells a tale (especially the one I got in Vegas that I still can't explain). Professional canvas seeking someone who appreciates fine art and doesn't mind dating a man who's spent more on ink than his car. Warning: May spontaneously remove shirt to show you my newest masterpiece."

His photos look like a flip book of "Name That Tattoo." Is that a butterfly on his neck, or did he fall asleep on an ink-soaked Rorschach test? Only Tate knows for sure (and sometimes, not even him).

Tate's idea of opening up emotionally is showing you the Chinese symbol on his bicep that he swears means "strength" (spoiler alert: it actually translates to "soup"). He doesn't just wear his emotions on his sleeve; he's got them permanently etched across his entire epidermis.

In Tate's world, commitment isn't scary, unless you count the lifelong commitment to that tribal armband he got in the '90s. He's not afraid of needles, but he might be terrified of ever holding a job that doesn't involve a guitar or a motorcycle.

First Date: This human coloring book treats first dates like a show-and-tell for grown-ups. "Want to see my tattoos?" isn't just a pickup line; it's his entire personality. Hope you're ready for a detailed tour of every inked inch, complete with a backstory longer than War and Peace for each design.

Love Language: Skin-deep affection, expressing emotions through permanent body art, and the ability to appreciate the subtle nuances between "tribal" and "Celtic" designs, prefers to say "I love you" with a tattoo gun rather than words, and believes the most valid form of commitment is having your partner's face inked on your body (preferably somewhere visible)

Attachment Style: Permanently attached to his ink addiction and the belief that there's always room for one more

Swipe right if you enjoy dating a man who's more illustrated than your favorite children's book, don't mind playing "guess that faded ink blob" on every date, and think that the ultimate show of affection is getting your name tattooed on his body (right next to the "Mom" heart, of course).

The Last Word

Tate: Hey, Michelangelo of the Epidermis! Your commitment to body art is impressive, but some canvases are best left blank. Try investing in some inner depth to match your outer illustrations. You might find that personality isn't something you can ink on.

Ladies: When a man's body resembles a kindergartener gone wild with permanent markers and his idea of commitment is getting your name tattooed next to his ex's (poorly covered) one, run faster than he can say, "This Chinese symbol means 'destiny'" (it doesn't). Unless you want your future children asking why Daddy has a misspelled philosophy quote wrapped around his neck, swipe left on this human art gallery. Some masterpieces are best admired from a distance.

The Conspiracy Theorist

Tin-Foil Hat Tim

Connect the dots to Tim, the man who never met a conspiracy theory he didn't like. This walking, talking WikiLeaks doesn't just question authority; he's convinced that everything from the moon landing to his neighbor's cat is part of an elaborate global conspiracy.

Tim's dating profile is a rabbit hole of cryptic warnings and coded messages.

About Me: "Seeking a fellow truth-seeker. Must be open-minded about flat earth, lizard people, and the real reason for daylight saving time. WAKE UP, SHEEPLE!" His photos are a collage of "evidence": Tim pointing at "chemtrails," Tim with his homemade Faraday cage, Tim wearing his finest tin foil hat.

In Tim's world, every conversation is an opportunity to uncover the "truth." He doesn't just talk; he unravels vast conspiracies, turning even a simple "How's the weather?" into a 30-minute lecture on government weather control programs.

First Date: A carefully vetted meeting in a "secure location" (the corner booth at Denny's) where he'll scan for surveillance devices, explain why the menu is actually a coded government message, and whisper his theories about why they really discontinued the Grand Slam

Love Language: Sharing "classified" information, gift-wrapping in tin foil, and the ability to spot "hidden messages" in everyday objects

Attachment Style: Securely attached to his conspiracy theories while maintaining deep suspicion of any emotional connection (because feelings might be a government plot)

P.S. If you match with Tim, be prepared for dates that feel like you're trapped in a Dan Brown novel. In Tim's universe, "Netflix and chill" means binge-watching documentaries about Bigfoot while he checks the room for hidden cameras.

The Last Word

Tim: Hey there, Conspiracy Connoisseur! Your dedication to "uncovering the truth" is impressive, but sometimes a cigar is just a cigar. Try applying your investigative skills to self-reflection. You might find that the biggest cover-up is how much you're hiding from reality. But what do I know? I'm just a satirical dating profile writer... or am I?

Ladies: If you're considering joining Tim's truth-seeking crusade, prepare for a relationship where "date night" means decoding grocery receipts for hidden messages. Unless you find paranoia sexy or you've always wanted to live off the grid, swipe left faster than Tim can say "false flag operation."

Chapter 8

THE TAKEAWAY

Having cataloged the specimens in Obsession Overloads, we've witnessed firsthand how hobbies aren't just pastimes; they're all-consuming lifestyle cults. These men haven't just found interests; they've discovered religions, complete with daily worship rituals and a fervor for evangelism.

Being passionate about something can be healthy. Having passions that devour your entire personality like a black hole consumes light? Not so much. From fitness fixations to fairway fanaticism, these characters illustrate how enthusiasms can evolve from attractive interests into relationship-consuming obsessions.

Red Flags With Obsession Alarms:

- Their personality has been entirely replaced by their singular focus, like a body-snatcher scenario, but with hobbies.

- They measure your compatibility solely by your willingness to become their obsession's supporting character.

- Their calendar has room for their passion, more of their passion, and absolutely nothing else.

- They've turned casual interests into competitive sports where they're always the self-appointed champions.

- Their financial priorities read: 1) obsession, 2) obsession accessories, 3) basic survival.

- They can't hold a conversation that doesn't circle back to their fixation faster than a boomerang.

- Their identity is so fused with their interest that questioning one feels like attacking the other.

Passions should enhance life, not consume it. When someone's entire existence revolves around gym schedules, football statistics, golf handicaps, tattoo appointments, or conspiracy theories, they're not just enthusiasts – they're one-dimensional characters in their own single-plot story.

True compatibility doesn't require identical interests, but it does require balanced attention. You deserve someone who brings their passions to the relationship without expecting the relationship to revolve around them. Someone who can put down the weights, turn off the game, step off the green, pause the tattoo session, or remove the tin foil hat long enough to genuinely engage with the world around them, too.

Life is a buffet of experiences, not a single-item menu. Choose someone who samples widely rather than someone who's convinced the only dish worth eating is the one they're obsessed with.

Chapter 9

THE QUIRKY QUOTIENT

Let's Set the Scene

Welcome to The Quirky Quotient, where normal is just a setting on a washing machine and eccentricity is the new black! In this chapter, we delve into the delightfully bizarre world of men who have turned their peculiarities into personality traits and their oddities into effective dating strategies.

Witness Puppy Love Paul, who'd rather spend his life with four legs than two, Flatulent Floyd, whose idea of breaking the ice is breaking wind, Lazy Eye Larry, whose wandering eye makes eye contact a guessing game, and Good-'Ol-Boy Gordon, bringing his backwoods charm to city life.

These quirky quixotes have turned the dating world into their personal circus, leaving a trail of raised eyebrows, nervous laughter, and memorable (for better or worse) first dates in their wake. They're the guys who make you wonder: Is it possible to be too unique? (Spoiler alert: yes, and it might involve inappropriate bodily functions and dates with his best friend, Rover.)

While everyone has their quirks, these men have turned theirs into full-fledged personas. They're living proof that sometimes, the most attractive quality is the courage to be unabashedly yourself, even if that self comes with sound effects, an entourage of canines, a geographic identity crisis, or optical navigation challenges.

So grab your sense of humor and your open mind as we traverse the carnival of curiosities that is The Quirky Quotient. In the world of dating, sometimes the strangest fruit is the sweetest, or at least makes for the best stories at brunch.

Now, let's uncover this menagerie of misfits and see if we can find the fine line between endearingly quirky and alarmingly eccentric! Because one woman's adorable oddity is another woman's reason to fake an emergency phone call and flee the restaurant.

The Dog Dad

Puppy-Love Paul

Leading the pack, here's Paul, the human embodiment of a dog treat dispenser. This walking, talking fire hydrant has turned canine companionship into an extreme sport, and considers "who's a good boy?" a term of endearment for all species.

Paul's dating profile reads like a pet adoption flyer:

About Me: "Package deal seeking a co-petter for life's adventures. Looking for someone who appreciates a man who's loyal, playful, and occasionally sheds. My ideal match? Someone who thinks 'three's company' means me, you, and my four-legged chaperone. Swipe right if you're ready to join our pack!"

Photos showcase Paul in his natural habitat: buried under a pile of puppies at the local shelter, mid-frisbee toss at the dog park, and a "candid" shot of him sharing an ice cream cone with Max. His attempt at a solo pic? A selfie where Max's nose takes up 90% of the frame.

First Date: A date with Paul is like a dog-themed amusement park. He'll suggest meeting at a pet-friendly café, arrive with Max in tow (sporting a "Wing-Dog" bandana), and spend the evening alternating between charming conversation and impromptu games of fetch. Be prepared for lengthy discussions about the merits of various chew toys, impromptu puppy playdates, and at least one attempt to sneak Max into a "no pets allowed" establishment.

Love Language: Belly rubs and sharing his premium doggy daycare membership

Attachment Style: More securely attached to his dog than any human could hope to be

P.S. Paul's idea of Netflix and chill involves a marathon of dog movies and cuddling... with Max in the middle.

P.P.S. If things get serious, expect a proposal that comes with a "Package Deal?" tag attached to Max's collar. Because in Paul's world, the only thing better than puppy love is finding a human who loves puppies just as much!

The Last Word

Paul: Your heart is as big as Max's puppy eyes, and your loyalty is definitely best in show! While Max might be your first love, there's room in that big heart for a two-legged companion too.

Ladies: Dating Paul comes with the promise of unconditional love... from at least one member of the household. Pack your lint roller, some treats (for Max, of course), and maybe some obedience training tips, for Paul, not the dog!

The Human Whoopee Cushion

Flatulent Floyd

Brace yourself for Floyd, the man whose body is a one-man wind symphony. This walking, talking gas factory doesn't just break wind; he conducts it, turning every date into an olfactory adventure that would make a skunk blush.

Floyd's dating profile is a masterpiece of misdirection:

About Me: "Looking for someone who appreciates natural music. Enjoy long walks (downwind), candlelit dinners (with scented candles), and have a great sense of humor (you'll need it). Warning: I'm a bit of an air bender."

Floyd's photos are carefully curated to hide his extraordinary talent: Floyd in wide-open spaces, Floyd near aromatic food trucks, Floyd's extensive collection of scented candles and air fresheners.

In Floyd's world, every meal is a ticking time bomb and every quiet moment a potential symphony. He doesn't just eat; he fuels up, treating his body like a biogas plant with an overambitious production schedule. Floyd's grocery cart contains the equivalent of high-octane fuel: cabbage, beans, broccoli, and dairy. Floyd gives new meaning to the term natural gas.

First Date: Anything with background noise to muffle his internal orchestra

Love Language: Sharing gas-relief remedies, finding well-ventilated date spots, and the ability to laugh (and breathe) through any situation

Attachment Style: Gastronomically attached to his belief that bodily functions are high comedy

P.S. If you match with Floyd, be prepared for dates that feel like you're starring in a very smelly episode of "Silent But Deadly." In Floyd's universe, "Netflix and chill" means watching documentaries about the digestive system while he provides live sound effects. Just don't be surprised if your romantic evening is frequently interrupted by his sudden need to "check the perimeter."

P.P.S. If you're brave enough to go on a road trip with Floyd, it's best to pack a gas mask, roll down all windows, and pray for tailwinds. His car doesn't need a fuel gauge; it has a Scoville scale. Long rides with Floyd turn "Are we there yet?" from a question of impatience to a desperate plea for survival. On the bright side, you'll never need to worry about falling asleep at the wheel – staying conscious becomes an act of self-preservation!

> ### The Last Word
>
> **Floyd:** Well, at least you're not full of hot air... oh wait. While your particular talent might clear a room, your honesty about it is refreshingly breezy. Keep floating on, you gassy guardian of gut-level truth.
>
> **Ladies:** If you're looking for a man who can clear a room faster than a fire alarm and turn every date into an aromatic adventure, Floyd's your guy. Love may be in the air, but with Floyd, so is everything else.

The Wandering Eye

Lazy-Eye Larry

Keep an eye on Larry, a guy whose view of the world is as unique as his vision. This optimistic soul has turned an ocular quirk into a superpower, enabling him to see the best in every situation.

Larry's dating profile reads like a heartwarming pep talk:

About Me: "Seeking someone who appreciates a man with a different point of view, literally and figuratively! I might not always meet your gaze directly, but I promise my attention is fully on you. Looking for a partner who values substance over surface and finds confidence more attractive than perfection. Swipe right if you're ready for a guy who sees the world (and you) in his special way!"

Larry's superpower? He's an expert at making people feel truly seen, even if his gaze doesn't always land where expected. His genuine interest in others and self-deprecating humor about his condition often win people over.

What Larry lacks in ocular coordination, he makes up for in heart. His unique perspective has gifted him with an uncanny ability to spot the beauty in life's imperfections. While one eye might wander, his attention never does; he's mastered the art of making people feel truly seen, even if he's technically looking slightly to their left.

First Date: A date with Larry is an exercise in understanding and patience. He'll suggest meeting somewhere quiet where it's easier to focus on conversation. He might sometimes seem to be looking elsewhere, but his warmth and attentiveness prove his eyes don't always tell the whole story.

Love Language: Making heart-to-heart connections while maintaining eye-to-somewhere-else contact, and seeing the beauty in life's imperfect angles

Attachment Style: Simultaneously attached to looking at you and the person next to you

Larry's unique perspective often leads to insightful observations and a refreshing outlook on life. In a world of superficial swipes, Larry offers a chance to connect with someone who truly looks beyond the surface.

P.S. Larry's favorite joke? "I may not have a good aim, but I've got my sights set on finding true love!"

The Last Word

Larry: Keep seeing the world your way, Larry! While one eye might be exploring the scenery, your heart's got perfect 20/20 vision when it comes to what really matters. You're proof that the best views don't always come from ideal alignment.

Ladies: When a man can turn life's quirks into superpowers and make you feel truly seen (even when he's technically looking at the plant behind you), you might want to give him a second look. After all, the sweetest connections often come from unexpected angles!

The Backwoods Beau

Good-'Ol-Boy Gordon

Y'all say howdy to Gordon, the self-proclaimed guardian of "the good 'ol days," who thinks modern dating is more complicated than the instructions on his microwave dinner. This country-fried Casanova is here to bring Southern charm to the dating scene, whether you want it or not, bless your heart.

Gordon's dating profile is a masterpiece of down-home clichés:

About Me: "Just a good 'ol boy lookin' for his Daisy Duke. Must love huntin', fishin', and muddin'. City slickers need not apply. The South will rise again... in my heart!"

His profile pics are a Gallery of Grit: Gordon with his truck, Gordon with his gun, and Gordon with what might be a possum (it's hard to tell under all that mud).

In Gordon's world, chivalry isn't dead; it's just been preserved in Mason jars alongside his mama's pickles. He doesn't just open doors; he builds them from scratch, using wood he chopped himself. His idea of a perfect date? Tailgating at a NASCAR race, followed by a romantic dinner at the nearest Waffle House.

Conversation with Gordon is like playing redneck Mad Libs. He doesn't just talk; he drawls, each word dripping with more syrup than a stack of flapjacks. His vocabulary is a unique blend of country idioms and questionable political opinions, sprinkled liberally with "y'all" and "ain't."

Gordon's idea of oral fixation isn't what most dating apps had in mind. His love for chewing tobacco is so strong, you'd think Skoal was sponsoring his dating life. He doesn't just have a tin of snuff; he's got a whole apocalypse bunker stocked with the stuff. His kisses don't taste like mint or strawberries, they're more 'eau de tobacco plant.' Don't worry about finding a spittoon on your dates; Gordon's truck has more makeshift spit receptacles than cup holders.

He claims it's part of his rugged charm, but let's be honest, nothing says 'Southern gentleman' quite like a well-placed tobacco stain. When Gordon says he wants to 'dip' with you, he's not talking about dancing or skinny-dipping!"

First Date: Hope you enjoy the great outdoors, because you're in for a wild ride. He doesn't just pick you up; he arrives in a monster truck that's more mud than vehicle, expecting you to hoist yourself up without smudging your Sunday best. Don't worry about dinner reservations, he's already packed a cooler full of beer and beef jerky.

Love Language: It isn't words of affirmation or physical touch; it's acts of providing, preferably involving something he shot, skinned, and barbecued himself. He doesn't want a partner; he wants a co-pilot for his John Deere and a fellow enthusiast for states' rights.

Attachment Style: Firmly attached to his Confederate flag collection and "it's heritage, not hate" manifesto

Swipe right if you enjoy feeling like you've time-traveled to 1952, don't mind debating the merits of Confederate statues over moonshine, and think that "librul" is just another word for "city folk."

P.S. If you match with Gordon, be prepared for dates that feel like you're starring in a country music video meets "Duck Dynasty" spin-off. And, in Gordon's universe, "Netflix and chill" means watching reruns of "The Dukes of Hazzard" while sitting at least six inches apart... until marriage.

The Last Word

Gordon: Bless your heart, sugar, keep that Southern charm flowing like sweet tea on a Sunday afternoon. You're as genuine as your mama's biscuit recipe!

Ladies: Y'all might find this good 'ol boy as comfortable as your favorite pair of worn-in cowboy boots, or as puzzling as a vegetarian at a BBQ. Either way, Gordon comes with more authenticity than a Mason jar full of moonshine, take him or leave him, but he is what he is!

Chapter 9

THE TAKEAWAY

After our unusual excursion through The Quirky Quotient, we've discovered that dating profiles sometimes come with asterisks and first impressions often include footnotes. These men haven't just embraced their uniqueness; they've turned it into their entire brand, complete with warning labels that practically flash in neon.

Our field guide to these eccentric specimens has made one thing clear: there's charming quirky (collecting vintage typewriters) and then there's alarming quirky (collecting toenail clippings). From flatulence fanatics to backwoods behaviors, these characters demonstrate how the line between appealing eccentricity and deal-breaking oddity is thinner than you might think.

Red Flags With Quirky Characteristics:

- Their unique traits aren't seasoning their personality; they've become the entire meal.

- They've confused "being genuine" with "sharing absolutely everything immediately."

- Their quirks come with zero volume control or situational awareness.

- They've turned minor characteristics into defining life features with religious devotion.

- Their unusual traits arrive without the courtesy of a gradual introduction or social timing.

- They demand complete acceptance of all behaviors while offering zero adaptability

- They use "that's just who I am" as a get-out-of-social-norms-free card

Authentic self-expression is valuable, but context matters. When someone's quirks become non-negotiable demands that everyone around them must accommodate, they're not expressing individuality—they're imposing it.

Whether it's Floyd's flatulence festival, Gordon's good ol' boy routine, Larry's wandering eye, or Paul's puppy preoccupation, these quirks aren't just innocent peculiarities—they're relationship challenges that require conscious navigation (or strategic avoidance).

You deserve someone whose uniqueness adds color to your life without painting over your comfort zones. Someone who brings their authentic self to the table while still recognizing that tables have social contexts and other people sitting at them.

True compatibility isn't about finding someone without quirks—we all have them. It's about finding someone whose peculiarities you find endearing rather than exhausting, and who manages their unique traits with self-awareness instead of stubborn inflexibility.

After all, life's too short to spend it explaining to party hosts why your date is testing the acoustics of every room with his bodily functions.

Chapter 10

THE COMMITMENT ENTHUSIASTS

Let's Set the Scene

Welcome to The Commitment Enthusiasts, where "taking it slow" is a foreign concept and U-Haul rentals are considered first date essentials! In this chapter, we dive headfirst into the deep end of the commitment pool with men who have turned long-term planning into an extreme sport.

In the fast-paced world of modern dating, some men have decided that "slow and steady" is for tortoises, and commitment should move at warp speed. From premature wedding planners to instant family seekers, these enthusiasts have turned the path to partnership into a sprint, complete with pre-written vows and pre-ordered matching towels.

You're about to encounter three commitment enthusiasts. Starry-Eyed Steve has already changed his relationship status while you're still reading his profile. Disney-Dad Dave, on the other hand, is not just looking for a partner, but an instant family complete with matching Mickey ears and a white picket fence. Last but not least is Family-First Forest, mapping out when you'll meet his parents before the appetizers arrive.

These commitment crusaders have turned dating into a high-speed chase to "happily ever after," leaving a trail of overwhelmed matches and half-finished wedding registries in their wake. They're the guys who make you wonder: Is it possible to get relationship whiplash? (Spoiler alert: yes, and it comes with a side of premature "I love you's" and family reunion invitations.)

While dedication can be admirable, these men have taken it to fairy tale proportions. They're living proof that sometimes, the most attractive quality is the ability to enjoy the journey rather than sprint to the finish line.

So grab your glass slippers and your commitment parachute, as we steer through the perilous landscape of turbo-charged romance. Whether they're rushing to the altar, planning the next trip to DisneyWorld, or introducing you to their entire extended family before the first date ends, these enthusiasm enthusiasts prove that sometimes the most meaningful connections grow at their own pace, no fairy godmother or rushed timeline required.

Now, let's examine these princes of premature progression and see if we can discern the line between enthusiasm and overexuberance.

The Hopeless Romantic

Starry-Eyed Steve

Let's get acquainted with Steve, the human embodiment of a Nicholas Sparks novel. This walking, talking Cupid has turned every interaction into a potential meet-cute and considers "casual dating" a tragedy worse than Romeo and Juliet.

Steve's dating profile reads like a Victorian love letter:

About Me: "Seeking my soulmate, my other half, the butter to my bread, the breath to my life! Looking for someone who appreciates a man who can turn a coffee date into an epic tale of destined love. My ideal match? A kindred spirit who thinks love at first sight is too slow and believes in fairy tale endings. Swipe right if you're ready for a romance that would make Jane Austen swoon!"

Photos showcase Steve in his natural habitat: gazing wistfully at sunsets, caught mid-twirl in flower fields, and a "candid" shot of him releasing doves at a wedding (not his). His attempt at a casual pic? A selfie where he's "accidentally" framed by a heart-shaped tree branch.

Steve doesn't just fall in love; he choreographs it, turning mundane moments into scenes worthy of a romance novel's cover.

Every text includes protestations of love, often accompanied by poetry references, and grocery shopping isn't complete without a dramatic declaration of love in the produce section.

First Date: A date with Steve is like stepping into a romantic movie montage. He'll suggest meeting at a quaint café he's decorated with fairy lights and rose petals, arrive with a handwritten scroll of poetry about your eyes, and spend the evening planning your future together. Be prepared for spontaneous slow-dancing, long monologues about finding "The One," and at least one attempt to name a star after you and to recreate the Titanic "I'm flying" scene at inappropriate locations.

Love Language: Grand gestures and writing your initials in the sky with fireworks

Attachment Style: Romantically attached to his rom-com delusions and collection of love sonnets

Dating Steve comes with the promise of never having an unromantic moment... whether you want it or not! Pack your sense of whimsy, a reality check, and maybe some sunglasses for when his starry eyes get too bright!

P.S. Steve's idea of taking it slow is waiting until the second date to introduce you to his parents as his "future spouse."

The Last Word

Steve: Your brand of romance isn't sweet, it's suffocating. Real love grows organically; it doesn't arrive pre-packaged with a soundtrack and special effects. The greatest love stories aren't written in sky-writing and grand gestures; they're built in small moments of genuine connection.

Ladies: Unless you want your life to feel like an endless Valentine's Day directed by Nicholas Sparks, swipe left on this walking Hallmark movie faster than Steve can say "You complete me." Your grounded sense of reality and public dignity will thank you.

The Fairytale Father

Disney-Dad Dave

Once upon a time, there was Dave, the man who turned weekend parenting into a non-stop carnival ride. This walking, talking Chuck E. Cheese doesn't just share custody; he shares sugar highs, theme park marathons, and a complete absence of vegetables, and he's seeking his female counterpart!

Dave's dating profile is a fairytale fever dream sprinkled with pixie dust and parental guilt:

About Me: "Fun-focused father seeking partner for family adventures! My kids (9 and 11, every other weekend) say I'm the 'cool dad' because bedtime is just a suggestion and ice cream is a food group. Looking for someone who understands that parenting is basically like being a party planner with guilt. Must love Disney (we go monthly) and understand that rules are more like... guidelines."

Photos showcase Dave in his natural habitat: matching Mickey ears with his kids at Disney World, buried in stuffed animals won from arcades, and "meal times" that consist entirely of pizza and cotton candy. His attempt at responsible parenting? A photo of fruit roll-ups captioned "See? We eat healthy!"

In Dave's world, every weekend is a competition to out-fun Mom's structure. He doesn't just parent; he performs, turning basic childcare into a spectacular show of excess. His idea of quality time? A 48-hour marathon of yes-saying that would make any pediatrician cringe.

First Date: Anything involving his kids, theme parks, sugar rushes, and absolutely zero responsibility.

Love Language: Buying affection in gift shop form, replacing rules with roller coasters, and the ability to justify pizza for breakfast

Attachment Style: Fantastically attached to his fairy tale ending and your role as instant mommy

The Last Word

Dave: Being the 'fun dad' might win short-term smiles, but kids need roots as well as wings. Try building memories that don't require admission tickets or sugar crashes. Real parenting happens in the moments between roller coasters.

Ladies: When a man's parenting style looks like a summer blockbuster and his kid's diet consists entirely of theme park snacks, proceed with caution. The "happiest place on earth" isn't a sustainable parenting strategy. Unless you want to be the voice of reason in a world of cotton candy chaos, swipe left on this walking Disney commercial faster than Dave can say "Dessert before Dinner!" Your sense of responsibility, immune system, and dentist will thank you.

The Instant Integrator

Family-First Forest

Brace yourself for Forest, the man who treats first dates like family reunions. This walking, talking family tree doesn't just want to date you; he wants to immediately adopt you into his entire clan, from Great-Aunt Gertrude to his second cousin's new puppy.

Forest's profile is a family newsletter disguised as a dating bio, where every word screams "we come as a package deal," and your role as significant other appears to have been pre-assigned since his family's Thanksgiving planning session.

About Me: "Family-oriented guy seeking newest addition to my family dynasty! Mom can't wait to meet you (she's reading this over my shoulder), and Dad's already saved you a seat at Sunday dinner. My sister's planning your welcome party, and Grandma's knitting you a sweater. P.S. We do Christmas cards in October, so hurry up and swipe right!"

Photos showcase Forest in his family-focused habitat, featuring group shots with his entire extended family (all tagged with their relation to him), "casual" pictures at family functions with conspicuously empty chairs next to him, and staged shots of him being the "fun uncle." His attempt at a solo pic? A family portrait with his face circled and "This could be us!" written in hearts.

First Date: A local restaurant where his family "happens" to be celebrating a birthday, anniversary, graduation, or (preferably) an engagement, followed by a slideshow of family vacations dating back to 1987

Love Language: Adding you to the family group chat immediately, sharing his family's secret recipes, and the ability to memorize his entire family tree (there will be a pop quiz)

Attachment Style: Preemptively attached to your role in his family photos before the first date

In Forest's world, every date is a potential opportunity for a family merger. He doesn't just introduce you; he integrates you, turning coffee dates into impromptu family meet-and-greets. Privacy with Forest is about as likely as getting the last word at his family dinner table.

The Last Word

Forest: Family is terrific, but relationships need room to grow before they're transplanted into the family garden. Try building a connection with one person before recruiting an entire clan of co-attachers. Even the Brady Bunch took a few episodes to blend.

Ladies: Unless you want your relationship to feel like an instant adoption process with no screening period, swipe left on this human family reunion faster than you can say "It's too soon to call your Aunt Margaret!" Your personal boundaries, privacy, and non-suffocating family will thank you.

Chapter 10
THE TAKEAWAY

Our expedition through Commitment Enthusiasts has revealed a dating landscape where relationship timelines come with rocket boosters and U-Haul trucks arrive before the first goodnight kiss! These men haven't just envisioned your future together; they've planned it, scheduled it, and possibly put down deposits on it.

This examination of the dating world's most enthusiastic participants has documented men who have mistaken first dates for engagement parties and casual coffees for family planning sessions. From romantic overload to instant integration, our catalog of these eager beavers explains why some dates feel less like getting to know someone and more like being swept away in a commitment tsunami.

Red Flags With Wedding Bells:

- Their relationship pace makes speed dating look like slow motion.

- They've confused "getting to know you" with "planning our golden anniversary."

- They've already named your future children before learning your middle name.

- Their idea of taking it slow involves waiting a whole week, or less, before introducing you to their parents as "the one."

- They measure relationship milestones in hours rather than months.

- They've mistaken infatuation for intimacy and chemistry for compatibility.

- They approach dating as if it's a race to the altar with no pit stops for actual connection.

Genuine commitment isn't measured by speed; it's built through shared experiences, mutual understanding, and natural progression. These commitment enthusiasts demonstrate that how quickly someone wants to lock things down often has little to do with you as a person and everything to do with their anxieties, fantasies, or misunderstandings about what makes relationships work.

Whether you're being serenaded by Steve's grand gestures, integrated into Forest's family photo, or cast as the perfect mother in Dave's fairytale, these rush jobs aren't about deep connection; they're about filling roles in pre-written scripts where your character development is optional.

You deserve someone excited about commitment but patient enough to earn it. Someone who wants to build a future with you, not just any breathing human who fits their timeline. Someone who values getting to know the real you more than checking relationship boxes at record speed.

After all, the most meaningful "happily ever afters" don't start with "once upon a time", they start with "let's take the time to really know each other."

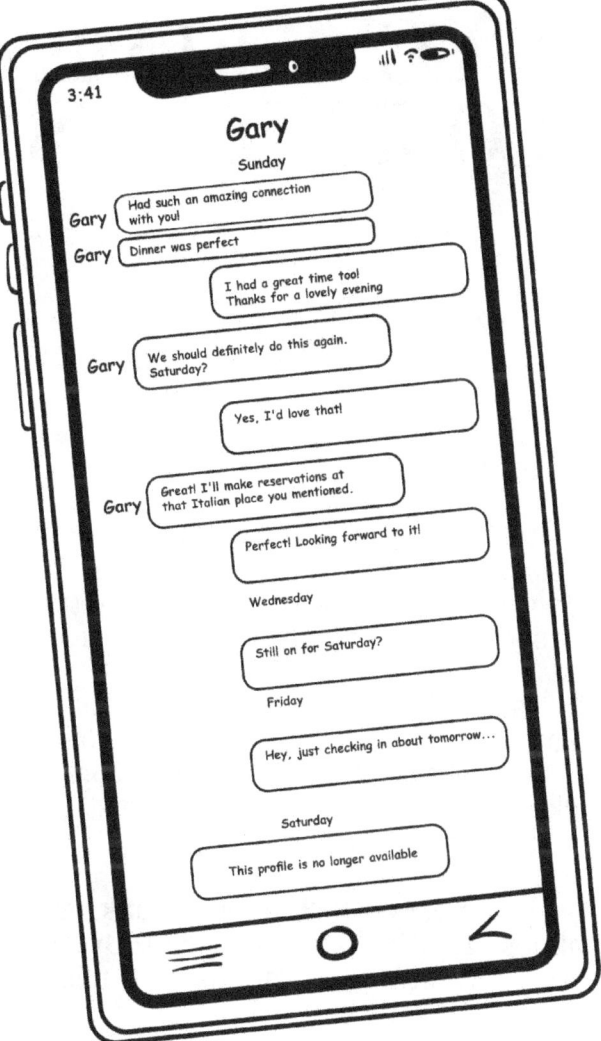

Chapter 11

THE COMMITMENT CONUNDRUMS

Let's Set the Scene

Welcome to The Commitment Conundrums, where "Happily Ever After" Goes to Die!

In this chapter, we plunge into the shadowy depths of romantic attachment or the lack thereof, exploring the fascinating world of those who view commitment as a rare and perilous species, best observed from a safe distance.

Enter our cast of emotionally unavailable specimens: Ghosting Gary, who disappears faster than your wine on girls' night, and Boomerang-Bread-Crumbing Brad, who keeps coming back like a bad penny, dropping just enough crumbs to keep you following his trail to nowhere.

Don't forget Friends-With-Benefits Frank, who surfs the waves of almost-relationships, and Not-Over-Her Norman, whose heart is so stuck in the past it might as well be fossilized.

These commitment conundrums are the reason your therapist bought a new yacht. From vanishing acts to reappearing routines, breadcrumb trails to situationships, and heartbroken past-dwellers, they're the ones who make you question if "happily ever after" is just a fairy tale conspiracy designed to sell greeting cards.

But don't despair, brave dater! This chapter is your survival guide in the jungle of non-commitment. We'll decipher their mixed signals, translate their cryptic texts, and equip you with the emotional Kevlar you need to protect your heart.

So strap in and hold on tight – because in the world of commitment conundrums, the only thing you can commit to is a wild ride. Sometimes the best commitment you can make is to your own sanity and a good sense of humor.

Let the commitment-dodging games begin!

The Vanishing Act

Ghosting Gary

Now you see him, now you don't - it's Gary. The man who treats dating like a game of hide-and-seek, where he's always hiding. This emotional Houdini doesn't just end relationships; he vanishes from them, leaving nothing behind but a faint whiff of cologne and a whole lot of confusion.

Gary's dating profile is as ephemeral as his presence in your life.

About Me: "Looking for a connection... until I'm not. Expert in Irish goodbyes and sudden radio silence. If you can't handle me at my ghostliest, you don't deserve me at my... oh, who am I kidding, you'll never see me again anyway."

His photos are blurry and out of focus, much like his commitment to any relationship.

In Gary's world, every interaction is potential ghosting material. He doesn't just chat; he leaves breadcrumbs of communication, each message carefully crafted to leave you wanting more, right before he disappears into the ether.

First Date: He'll suggest a dinner date, seem excited about it, then block you in as little as five minutes before you're supposed to meet

Love Language: Leaving you on read, mysterious social media activity, and the ability to disappear faster than free samples at Costco

Attachment Style: Dismissively unattached, literally. His longest relationship is with his "read receipts: off" setting

Gary has mastered the art of the slow fade so well that even his WiFi disconnects when it senses an emotionally charged conversation is about to begin. His version of closure is simply closing the app, and his idea of a relationship post-mortem is making sure you're blocked on all possible platforms.

The Last Word

Gary: Hey, Houdini, disappearing may be your favorite trick, but it's gotten old. For someone so practiced at vanishing, you've left quite a trail of emotional debris. Your disappearing act isn't mysterious; it's cowardly. Real strength isn't in how quickly you can ghost; it's in having the courage to communicate like an adult. The only thing more transparent than your excuses is your fear of genuine connection.

Ladies: A ghost might be fun on Halloween, but it's exhausting on a dating app. No ghost story ends with "and they lived happily ever after", and neither will this one. When his communication style is more spectral than human, swipe left faster than he can hit "block." Your time, weekend plans, and state of confusion will thank you.

The Reappearing Romeo

Boomerang-Bread-Crumbing Brad

Coming back around, it's Brad, the master of mixed signals and intermittent attention. This relationship strategist has perfected a two-pronged approach: vanishing completely when he's got better options, then dropping just enough breadcrumbs to keep you hanging on when he's between adventures.

About Me: "Part-time ghost, full-time emotional tourist seeking someone who appreciates unpredictable connection patterns. Expert in strategic reappearances and minimal-effort maintenance. Warning: May disappear completely or reduce contact to tactical breadcrumbs depending on my other options. Bonus points if you're willing to stay on my roster indefinitely while I scout the dating universe!"

In Brad's world, relationships exist on a spectrum from "completely ghosted" to "just enough contact to keep hope alive." He's mastered the art of calibrating his attention with scientific precision, sending perfectly timed "hey stranger" texts just when you've almost forgotten him, or dropping breadcrumbs of affection that are juuuust substantial enough to keep you from blocking him.

First Date: A surprisingly good time that establishes enough connection to fuel weeks of wondering why he suddenly went radio silent, followed by months of sporadic texts that never quite lead to a second date

Love Language: Strategic relationship maintenance through calculated minimal effort, from complete disappearances to tactical "thinking of you" texts, always timed for maximum impact with minimum investment

Attachment Style: Opportunistically attached, treating women like emotional investments he can check on periodically to see which might yield returns when his primary options fall through

P.S. Brad has a PhD in Mixed Signals with a minor in Wasted Time. His relationship pattern is so predictable that some women have started placing bets on exactly when his "Hey stranger" text will arrive after disappearing. Current record: 6 months and 3 days, precisely when she posted vacation photos with a new guy.

The Last Word

Brad: Your relationship strategy isn't clever, it's transparent and exhausting. People aren't options to be maintained or back burners to be ignited when convenient. Try offering consistent respect instead of this calculated cycle of absence and breadcrumbs. The only thing more pathetic than your disappearing act is your predictable reappearance when you're lonely.

Ladies: You deserve consistent attention from someone who sees you as a priority, not a backup plan. When a man treats your connection like a part-time hobby, he remembers only when he's bored, swipe left faster than Brad can say "I've been thinking about you lately!" Your self-respect and emotional availability will thank you.

The Situationship Surfer

Friends-With-Benefits Frank

Introducing Frank, the human embodiment of a "maybe" RSVP and a walking, talking grey area. This master of ambiguity has turned mixed signals into an Olympic sport and considers defining the relationship conversations a form of psychological warfare.

Frank's dating profile is a masterclass in strategic vagueness:

About Me: "Here for vibes, good times, and whatever the universe has in store. Seeking a cool co-pilot for life's adventure (pit stops only, no long-term parking). Expert in keeping things casual and emotionally equidistant. If you're looking for a label, try my shirt tag. Not looking for anything serious, but open to whatever happens."

Frank operates in that blurry territory between "just friends" and "almost dating," treating relationships like a surf spot, catching waves when convenient but never claiming a permanent spot on the beach. His emotional availability is as predictable as the tide, and his commitment level fluctuates as unpredictably as the value of cryptocurrency. Frank's idea of relationship progression is upgrading you from "hey you" to "hey babe" in his late-night texts.

First Date: A very casual "hang" at 11 PM that he'll definitely cancel if something better comes up, but he'll text you at 2 AM to see if you're still around

Love Language: Late-night booty calls, the occasional "like" on your Instagram post from three weeks ago, and remembering your name (sometimes)

Attachment Style: Selectively attached, like a Netflix subscription, available for entertainment but cancel anytime

Engaging with Frank is like trying to build a sandcastle at high tide, futile, messy, and likely to leave you with a sinking feeling. Pack your emotional life jacket and consider having a reality check on speed dial.

The Last Word

Frank: Your "situationship" strategy isn't sophisticated; it's selfish. You're not "going with the flow", you're manipulating the current. If you want casual encounters, at least have the decency to be upfront rather than cultivating emotional connections you have no intention of honoring. Women deserve more respect than you'd give a food delivery app, and your behavior is about as classy as a neon "OPEN" sign flickering at 3 AM.

Ladies: When a man's feelings for you are as clear as muddy water and as deep as a puddle, remind yourself that you're not a placeholder in someone else's 'finding myself' story. Unless you're specifically looking for a no-strings situation (and hey, no judgment!), swipe left and swim away from this situation-ship faster than Frank can say 'let's keep things casual.' Your vulnerability and self-respect will thank you.

The Ex-Obsessed

Not-Over-Her Norman

Still pining away, here's Norman, the human equivalent of a broken record stuck on the "My Ex" track. This walking, talking shrine to relationships past doesn't just have baggage; he's got a whole lost luggage department dedicated to his former flame, complete with a "Property of Sarah" tag on each piece.

Norman's dating profile is a thinly veiled love letter to his ex:

About Me: "Seeking someone exactly like my ex, but totally different. Must love hearing stories about Sarah (I mean, hypothetical Sarah-like people). Looking for someone who won't rip my heart out and use it as a hockey puck... SARAH. Bonus points if your name is Sarah and you were born on March 15th, 1992."

His photos are a museum of memories: Norman at places he used to visit with his ex, sporting his "better off single" t-shirt (clearly a lie), forcing a smile next to his newly adopted cat (named Sarah, naturally), and a series of poorly cropped couple photos where his ex's presence lingers like a ghost in the margins.

In Norman's world, every conversation is a wormhole back to his past relationship. He's got every moment cataloged, cross-referenced, and ready to recite at a moment's notice, while simultaneously spending his last paycheck on "Please Take Me Back" skywriting attempts.

First Date: A tour of all the places he used to go with Sarah, followed by scrolling through her Instagram while asking if her new boyfriend looks "like a jerk" to you, too

Love Language: Constant comparisons to his ex and the ability to turn any topic into a Sarah-centric TED talk

Attachment Style: Permanently attached to his ex's memory while treating new relationships like a Sarah tribute band

P.S. If you match with Norman, be prepared for dates that feel like episodes of "Sarah: The Documentary," complete with director's commentary and behind-the-scenes footage. In Norman's universe, "Netflix and chill" means binge-watching his Sarah highlight reel while he provides live analysis of where it all went wrong.

The Last Word

Norman: Your heart isn't on your sleeve; it's still in Sarah's lost and found box. Until you can engage in a full conversation without mentioning Sarah, the only date you should consider is with a therapist. You're not honoring your past relationship; you're hiding in it, using memories as a shield against the vulnerability of starting fresh. The most tremendous disservice you're doing isn't to your dates, it's to yourself.

Ladies: You deserve to be the star of someone's present, not the understudy in their past. Run faster than Norman runs back to his memories of Sarah. Your self-worth, emotional energy, and freedom from someone else's unfinished love story will thank you.

Chapter 11

THE TAKEAWAY

Our investigation into Commitment Conundrums has uncovered the graveyard where relationship clarity goes to die and emotional availability is more elusive than a unicorn sighting! These men haven't just demonstrated commitment-phobia – they've showcased avoidance techniques elevated to performance art worthy of its own Broadway show.

This catalog of the dating world's most frustrating specimens has documented classic disappearing acts, reappearing headaches, situational attachments, and past-fixated fantasies. From ghosting to bread crumbing, our analysis of these patterns explains why some relationships feel less like love stories and more like unsolved mysteries.

Red Flags With Commitment Issues:

- Their relationship status exists in a quantum state – simultaneously together and not together until observed.

- They've mastered the art of being physically present while emotionally AWOL.

- They treat clarity and directness like they're allergic reactions to be avoided at all costs.

- They've turned "keeping options open" into a lifestyle philosophy that requires multiple dating apps.

- Their relationship timeline is written in disappearing ink that conveniently fades when things get serious.

- They've perfected the magic trick of vanishing completely or just enough to keep you guessing.

- Their emotional baggage from past relationships has its own zip code and forwarding address.

Commitment challenges aren't always about you – they often reflect someone's unresolved issues, avoidance patterns, or inability to fully engage with the present. When someone consistently ghosts like Gary, boomerangs like Brad, situationship surfs like Frank, or obsesses like Norman, they're telling you exactly who they are and what they can (or can't) offer.

These patterns aren't just annoying quirks – they're relationship roadblocks. Whether you're being ghosted into oblivion, breadcrumbed along a path to nowhere, kept in relationship limbo, or competing with the ghost of relationships past, these commitment conundrums waste your time and emotional energy.

You deserve someone whose presence is as reliable as their interest, whose communication is clear rather than cryptic, who wants to build something fundamental in the present rather than living in the past or keeping all options perpetually open. Don't settle for being an option, a placeholder, a convenience, or a replacement – choose someone who chooses you, clearly and consistently.

After all, the most valuable currency in dating isn't attention – it's intention. And these guys are all seriously overdrawn.

Chapter 12

THE PERPETUAL PETER PANS

Let's Set the Stage

Welcome to The Perpetual Peter Pans, where growing up is optional and adulting is a four-letter word! In this chapter, we explore the world of men who have turned arrested development into an art form. These guys haven't just found the fountain of youth; they've turned it into a slip 'n' slide and are charging admission.

Meet Console Connor, whose idea of career advancement is leveling up in World of Warcraft, Still-Figuring-It-Out Stan, who treats life decisions like a multiple-choice test where "all of the above" is always the correct answer, and Needy Ned, whose emotional maturity peaked somewhere between recess and nap time.

These perpetual Peter Pans have mastered the art of avoiding adulthood with the dedication of someone fleeing a burning building. From fear of adulting and emotional dependency to career commitment-phobia, they're the guys who make you wonder: Is it possible to age backwards? Or have they just found a really good moisturizer?

While youthful energy can be charming, these men remind us that there's a fine line between being young at heart and being stuck in a time warp. They're living proof that sometimes, the most grown-up thing you can do is, well, grow up.

So buckle up, dear reader, as we navigate the Neverland of eternal boyhood. Just remember, in the world of dating, sometimes the most attractive quality is a valid driver's license and the ability to do your own laundry.

Now, let's explore these boyish peculiarities and see if we can find the man hiding behind the video games and pizza boxes!

The Eternal Gamer

Console Connor

Observe Connor, the human embodiment of arrested development with Wi-Fi. This button-mashing man-child has turned avoiding adulthood into an extreme sport, considering "responsibility" the ultimate boss he's not ready to face.

Connor's dating profile reads like a warning label for perpetual adolescence:

About Me: "Level 50 Human with level 12 Adulting Skills seeking Player 2 who doesn't mind being spectator mode. Employed (technically), but my real career is as a legendary Guild Leader with 570k followers on Twitch. Looking for someone who understands that work meetings are the perfect backdrop for racing games, and deadlines are more like optional side quests. Adulting is overrated – why pay bills when there are raid bosses to defeat?"

His photos feature Connor in his natural habitat: surrounded by empty energy drink cans, wearing his faded college fraternity letters while participating in a work Zoom call with a gaming headset on. His attempt at a professional pic? A filtered selfie where you can clearly see the reflection of his game screen in his glasses.

First Date: A "quick coffee" that he'll be 20 minutes late for because he "couldn't find a save point," followed by constant glances at his phone to check his guild's progress. If you're lucky, he might make it through appetizers before an "emergency raid" requires his immediate departure.

Love Language: Sharing his extra gaming controller and occasionally remembering your existence between levels

Attachment Style: Permanently attached to his gaming chair, while real-world connections remain in the loading screen indefinitely

P.S. Connor thinks "work-life balance" means positioning his laptop camera so his boss can't see his gaming monitor during meetings.

The Last Word

Connor: The only thing more alarming than your kill count is your stunted emotional growth. Life doesn't come with cheat codes or respawn points – time to upgrade from Player 1 to Actual Adult before you find your career, relationships, and prospects permanently game over.

Ladies: Unless you're auditioning for the role of "Mom Who Also Dates Him," swipe left faster than Connor minimizes his game when his boss enters the Zoom call. Your career ambitions, adult conversations, and relationship potential will thank you.

The Purpose Procrastinator

Still-Figuring-It-Out Stan

Under construction: Stan. The human embodiment of a quarter-life crisis that's extended well into his forties. This professional soul-searcher has turned indecision into a lifestyle, with a dating profile that reads like a help wanted ad for a life coach.

Stan's profile is a masterpiece of existential uncertainty:

About Me: "Aspiring for everything, succeeding at nothing specific. Job history is more eclectic than a Spotify playlist on shuffle. Currently on my 6th career path (this year). Looking for a partner-in-crime to join me on my path of self-discovery, destination unknown. Must be okay with spontaneous life changes and the possibility that I might move to Bali to become a surf instructor next week."

Photos showcase Stan in a dizzying array of personas: Zen meditation Stan, Day Trader Stan, Backpacker Stan, and "I just watched 'Julie & Julia' and now I'm a chef" Stan. Each image is like a glimpse into a parallel universe where Stan is committed to something.

First Date: A date with Stan is like a choose-your-own-adventure book, but all paths lead to confusion. He'll wow you with his knowledge of obscure philosophies, then ask if you can split the bill because he just quit his job to pursue his passion for underwater basket weaving. Be prepared for deep conversations about the meaning of life, interspersed with frantic LinkedIn updates as he pivots to his next "calling". He'll likely arrive as Corporate Stan but leave as Aspiring DJ Stan after a 'life-changing' conversation with the bartender.

Love Language: Lengthy texts about new life epiphanies and invitations to join multi-level marketing schemes

Attachment Style: Tentatively attached to his "career path of the month", while firmly attached to his parents' wallet and the belief that his 'big break' is just one more workshop/certification/vision quest away

P.S. Stan's idea of commitment is agreeing to a second date – but don't be surprised if he shows up with a shaved head because he's now a Buddhist monk-in-training.

P.P.S. If things get serious, be ready for a proposal... to join him on a year-long silent retreat in the Himalayas. Because nothing says "I love you" like renouncing all worldly possessions together.

The Last Word

Stan: Stan, buddy, the only thing you've mastered is the art of going nowhere fast. Life's not a buffet where you can sample everything without committing. Pick a path and stick to it, or you'll find yourself still "figuring it out" in the retirement home.

Ladies: Unless you enjoy being a supporting character in someone else's never-ending identity crisis, swipe left and run faster than Stan changes career aspirations. Your financial stability, emotional consistency, and unattended spiritual retreats will thank you.

The Maternal Seeker

Needy Ned

Introducing Ned, the man who's not so much looking for a partner as he is auditioning for a new mom. This bundle of neediness comes complete with emotional baggage, a startling lack of basic life skills, and an uncanny ability to make you feel like you've accidentally adopted a 30-year-old toddler.

Ned's dating profile is a thinly veiled cry for help.

About Me: "Seeking a strong, independent woman who can teach me how to use a washing machine and isn't afraid to cut the crusts off my sandwiches. Must be okay with late-night calls about nightmare monsters and impromptu tuck-ins."

In Ned's world, every interaction is an opportunity for nurturing. He doesn't just want your number; he wants your emergency contact info, blood type, and a signed permission slip to adult.

Conversation with Ned is like talking to a walking, talking "Adulting 101" manual... that hasn't been read yet. He doesn't just chat; he seeks constant reassurance, validation, and maybe a gold star sticker for remembering to brush his teeth. His favorite phrase? "But my mom always..."

Planning a future with Ned? Hope you enjoy being a combination of Google, his secretary, and a surrogate parent, because you're in for a wild ride of dependency. He doesn't just want a girlfriend; he wants a personal life coach, therapist, and chef all rolled into one maternal package.

First Date: You cook him dinner while he tells you about his day and asks for help with his taxes

Love language: It's not words of affirmation or physical touch; it's "please do everything for me while I helplessly watch." He's not looking for a significant other; he's looking for a significant mother.

Attachment Style: More attached to potential mother figures than his own independence, while maintaining the emotional self-sufficiency of a newborn koala

P.S. If you match with Ned, be prepared for dates that feel like you're babysitting a very large infant. In Ned's universe, "Netflix and chill" means you pick the show while he curls up with his head in your lap, asking you to stroke his hair and tell him everything's going to be okay.

The Last Word

Ned: Ned, it's time to cut the umbilical cord and join the adult world – your future partner should be your equal, not your replacement mommy.

Ladies: Unless you're looking to open a daycare for oversized toddlers, swipe left faster than Ned can say "But Mom always did it for me!" Your independence, emotional maturity, and patience will thank you.

Chapter 12

THE TAKEAWAY

Our tour through Neverland has confirmed that some boys become men biologically, but apparently missed the memo about everything else! These perpetual Peter Pans haven't just refused to grow up; they've demonstrated how avoiding adulthood can be transformed into an Olympic sport, consistently winning gold in the "Responsibility Avoidance" category.

Our field research on the dating world's most committed commitment-phobes has documented men who've mastered the art of aging without maturing. From gaming addictions to career carousels to maternal dependencies, our observations explain why some dates feel less like meeting a potential partner and more like inadvertently adopting an oversized child.

Red Flags With Training Wheels:

- Their life skills peaked somewhere around their sophomore year of college.

- They've turned "finding themselves" into a full-time career with parental funding.

- Their idea of meal prep involves knowing which pizza places deliver after midnight.

- They approach adult responsibilities like they're optional side quests in the game of life.

- Their emotional intelligence is still waiting for its growth spurt.

- They've mistaken dependence for connection and neediness for love.

- Their future plans have all the clarity and substance of morning fog.

Youthful energy and playfulness can be wonderful traits when paired with actual adult capabilities. These perpetual adolescents demonstrate that what might be charming at 22 becomes concerning at 32 and alarming at 42. The issue isn't that they enjoy video games, chart different paths, or appreciate nurturing; it's that these preferences have become escape hatches from adult responsibility.

Whether you're dealing with Connor's professional gaming career, Stan's endless identity crisis, or Ned's search for a surrogate mother, these Peter Pans aren't just quirky bachelors, they're men actively avoiding the personal growth necessary for healthy relationships.

You deserve someone who brings playfulness to adulthood, not someone who brings childishness to adult relationships. Someone who enjoys games without making them their entire identity, who knows what they want while remaining open to growth, who appreciates nurturing without expecting parenting.

After all, there's a world of difference between being young at heart and being immature at core, and your future happiness depends on knowing the difference.

Chapter 13

THE OVERLY ATTACHED

Let's Set the Scene

Welcome to The Overly Attached, where personal space is a myth and codependency is king! In this chapter, we're entering the sticky world of men who think "clingy" is a compliment and consider breathing room an optional luxury.

Our suffocating lineup begins with Velcro Vic, who who treats relationships like an emotional life raft and texts you like he's paid by the message, Doorbell Dan, a guy who thinks "It's Over" means "Please try harder", and Apron-Strings Andy, whose mother's approval is required for everything from dinner choices to your relationship status.

These attachment enthusiasts have turned neediness into an Olympic sport, leaving a trail of smothered partners and blocked phone numbers in their wake. They're the guys who make you wonder: Is it possible to suffocate from too much affection? (Spoiler alert: emotionally, yes!)

While devotion can be sweet, these men remind us that there is a fine line between attentiveness and suffocation. They're living proof that sometimes, the most romantic thing you can do is give your partner room to breathe.

Prepare to maneuver the suffocating seas of over-attachment. In the world of dating, sometimes the healthiest thing you can do is learn to love yourself before latching onto someone else.

Now, let's pry ourselves away from these persistent professionals and see if we can find the line between caring and smothering!

The Emotional Leech

Velcro Vic

Prepare to encounter Vic, the human equivalent of a koala bear - cute at first glance, but ultimately a clingy creature that will latch onto you and refuse to let go. Vic doesn't just wear his heart on his sleeve; he's got it plastered across a billboard with your name on it and a 24/7 livestream of his feelings.

Vic's dating profile is a cry for attention disguised as a bio:

About Me: "Seeking my other half, my reason for breathing, my everything. Must be available 24/7 for constant reassurance and emotional support. Leaving me on 'read' is considered cruel and unusual punishment."

Vic's text messages arrive in swarms like digital locusts, 'Good morning! Did you get my good morning text? Are you okay? Is your phone working? Did I do something wrong? I'm sorry for whatever I may have done. Please respond. Are you breaking up with me?', all sent within a three-minute window while you were in the shower.

In Vic's world, "me time" is a typo and clearly meant to be "we time." He doesn't just want to be part of your world; he wants to be your entire solar system, galaxy, and universe. His idea of a perfect date? Staring into your eyes for hours while periodically asking, "Do you still love me?" A conversation with Vic is like playing emotional whack-a-mole. Every sentence is an opportunity for him to seek validation. "How's the weather?" translates to "Is the weather as gloomy as you'll be if you ever leave me?"

Hope you like group activities, because he'll be there. Every. Single. Time. Girls' night out? He'll be waiting in the car. Business trip? He's already packed his bags. Bathroom break? He'll hold your hand under the stall door.

First Date: A seemingly innocent coffee date that turns into a 4-hour marathon of emotional show-and-tell. Be prepared for non-stop eye contact, constant physical touch, and at least a dozen variations of "What are you thinking about right now?" Warning: Attempting to check your phone will trigger an immediate emotional crisis.

Love Language: Vic's love language isn't just words of affirmation; it's paragraphs of affirmation, chapters of affirmation, entire novels of affirmation, preferably read aloud to him hourly while stroking his hair and assuring him that yes, he's still your favorite person in the world.

Attachment Style: Symbiotically attached like a koala with separation anxiety and unlimited data for constant texting

P.S. If you match with Vic, be prepared for a relationship that feels like you're constantly cradling a human-sized baby bird. In Vic's universe, "I need some space" is just secret code for "Please love me more intensely!"

The Last Word

Vic: You're holding on so tight, you're strangling any chance at a real connection. Love needs room to breathe – it's not meant to be a chokehold.

Ladies: A relationship shouldn't feel like an escape room challenge. Unless you fancy being someone's emotional oxygen tank, swipe left faster than Vic can say 'Where are you going?' Your boundaries, phone battery, and neglected friends will thank you.

The Persistent Pest

Doorbell-Dan

Ding-Dong, it's Dan, the human equivalent of a pop-up ad you can't close. This guy doesn't just have trouble letting go; he's got a PhD in Clinging On For Dear Life. Dan treats breakups like suggestions and goodbye like a temporary farewell.

Dan's dating profile is a masterclass in desperate determination, reading like a hostage negotiator's diary crossed with a romantic comedy script. Every word screams "I don't understand boundaries" louder than his 3 AM serenades.

About Me: "Passionate pursuer of second chances (and thirds, and fourths...) seeking someone who appreciates persistent romance and creative reconnection strategies. Expert in surprise appearances and impromptu serenades. Currently banned from three florists for excessive emergency bouquet orders."

In Dan's world, "I'm not interested" and "It's over" translate to "Please try harder." His rejection strategy is less "moving on" and more "moving onto your front porch." He's not pursuing; he's "romantically persisting." His idea of giving you space is standing across the street instead of at your doorstep.

First and Last Date: An enthusiastic dinner where Dan is clearly smitten, followed by weeks of being pursued, where he "surprisingly" appears at your favorite coffee shop and gym, with increasingly elaborate explanations for the "coincidence." Each encounter features heartfelt speeches about destiny that grow longer with each rejection.

Love Language: Showing up uninvited, doorbell symphonies, and unauthorized serenades, with a side of excessive text messages

Attachment Style: Permanently attached to your front porch, with polite requests to leave considered merely suggestions

Dan's bargaining skills would impress even the most seasoned hostage negotiator. He'll promise to change everything from his hair to his DNA if you'll just give him one more chance. He doesn't understand why changing his entire personality isn't a selling point for reconciliation.

Blocking Dan is like playing Whac-A-Mole with your phone. Block his number? He'll email. Block his email? Handwritten letters time. He's not above skywriting his apologies or hiring a mariachi band to serenade you with "Baby Come Back" in the middle of your workday.

P.S. If Dan's at your door again, don't worry about answering. Your neighbors have started a betting pool on how many days in a row he can appear with a different type of flower arrangement.

The Last Word

Dan: Persistence isn't charming when it's unwanted. Your love isn't a battering ram, and her "no" isn't a door to be broken down. It's time to ring your own bell of self-respect and move on.

Ladies: Unless you enjoy feeling like you're starring in your own personal rom-com that never ends, swipe left faster than Dan can say "Just one more chance!" Your neighbors, peace of mind, and emotional boundaries will thank you.

The Maternal Marionette

Apron-Strings Andy

Grab your apron for Andy, the man who has never cut the umbilical cord and wears it as a badge of honor. This walking, talking Oedipus complex doesn't just love his mom; he's practically joined at the hip with her, making every date a surprise threesome.

Andy's dating profile is a thinly veiled advertisement for a new daughter-in-law.

About Me: "Looking for a special lady who appreciates family values and doesn't mind sharing Sunday dinners with the most important woman in my life (Mother, of course!). Must love home-cooked meals and unsolicited advice."

His photos form a maternal montage: Andy and Mom at graduation, Andy and Mom on vacation, Andy in a "World's Best Son" t-shirt (a gift from, well, you know who).

In Andy's world, mother doesn't just know best; she knows everything, and her opinion is the gold standard by which all life decisions are measured. He doesn't just respect his mom; he reveres her with an intensity that makes religious zealots look casual. His idea of independence? Doing his own laundry (but only after a lengthy FaceTime tutorial with Mom).

A conversation with Andy is like playing a game of "Six Degrees of My Mother." He doesn't just chat; he channels his mom, peppering every discussion with her wisdom, recipes, and thinly veiled judgments. His favorite phrase? "Well, my mom always says..." (Spoiler alert: His mom always says a lot).

First Date: Hope you enjoy feeling like you're auditioning for the role of daughter-in-law, because you're in for a night of intense maternal scrutiny. He doesn't just choose restaurants; he selects venues pre-approved by Mom for their cleanliness, wholesome menu, and proximity to her house "in case of emergencies." Expect to spend your evening comparing every dish unfavorably to his mom's cooking and fielding calls from her to "check in."

Attachment Style: Umbilically tethered to mother's opinions, treating adult decisions like a multiple-choice quiz with only mom's answers

Love Language: Andy's love language isn't quality time or physical touch; it's maternal approval and the ability to replicate his mom's meatloaf recipe. He doesn't want a girlfriend; he wants a surrogate mother figure who's young enough to date (but not so young that Mom feels threatened).

P.S. In Andy's universe, "Netflix and chill" means watching old family videos while he provides running commentary on how cute he was as a baby. Don't be surprised if your romantic evening is interrupted by a surprise visit from Mom, who "just happened to be in the neighborhood" for the third time this week.

The Last Word

Andy: Hey, Mama's Boy! While your mother-son bond is touching, your dating life shouldn't require maternal approval and a permission slip. Time to trade those apron strings for some actual backbone. Mom's fantastic, but she shouldn't be your GPS for adult life.

Ladies: When a man's longest relationship is with his mother and every date feels like a daughter-in-law audition, run faster than this maternal minion can say "But Mom thinks you're great!" Your independence, dinner plans, and future relationship with your mother-in-law will thank you!

Chapter 13

THE TAKEAWAY

Our examination of The Overly Attached has taught us a fundamental truth: love should be like a comfortable sweater, not a straitjacket! This chapter's catalog of clingy characters has spotlighted men whose idea of attachment comes with a side of emotional superglue, turning what should be sweet devotion into a marathon of neediness.

The case studies of these attachment aficionados have revealed that there's a Grand Canyon-sized gap between "I miss you" and "I've been monitoring your location for the last six hours." While our research confirms that healthy relationships provide security and comfort, these specimens have demonstrated the suffocating results when caring crosses into obsession territory.

Red Flags With Velcro Backing:

- Their text messages arrive with the frequency of a caffeinated hamster on a wheel.

- Your personal space becomes a mythical concept, like unicorns or affordable housing.

- Their emotional dependency could qualify as a full-time job (with no benefits).

- They've planned your wedding after the first coffee date.

- Their jealousy flares if you so much as like another man's weather update on Facebook.

- Their identity outside the relationship is as thin as a budget motel bedsheet.

- They treat potential breakups like impending apocalypse scenarios.

- Your approval is more necessary to them than oxygen.

- Making decisions without you causes them more anxiety than tax season.

- Their attention feels less like flattery and more like being followed by a spotlight.

- Their life plans revolve around you with the precision of Earth orbiting the sun.

- Your friends and family have become suspicious "competitors" for your time.

A healthy partner wants to walk beside you, not become your second skin. When dating someone whose attachment style could qualify as performance art, the kindest swipe might be to the left, for both your sakes.

Because sometimes, the most romantic three words aren't "I love you," but "I respect boundaries."

Chapter 14

THE MIDLIFE MAYHEM

Let's Set the Scene

Welcome to The Midlife Mayhem, where age is just a number... that these guys are desperately trying to ignore! In this chapter, we delve into the chaotic world of men who have turned their midlife crisis into a full-blown identity meltdown.

Behold four masters of mayhem: Sugar-Daddy Sean, whose wallet opens wider than his age gap. Margarita Mark, who drowns his denial in tequila; Divorce-Party Devin, who celebrates his freedom with the enthusiasm of a teenager who just got his driver's license; and Six-Pack Sid, who spends more time at the gym than all his ex-wives combined.

These age-defying adventurers have turned the concept of growing old gracefully into a high-stakes game of "catch me if you can," leaving a trail of confused millennials and exasperated peers in their wake. They're the guys who make you wonder: Is it possible to Benjamin Button your way out of AARP eligibility? (Spoiler alert: no, but that won't stop them from trying!)

While embracing life at any age is admirable, these men have taken it to cringeworthy extremes. They're living proof that sometimes, the most attractive quality in midlife is the ability to rock your silver fox status with confidence, rather than desperately clinging to your lost youth.

So grab your reading glasses (if you can admit you need them) and your sense of humor as we maneuver the tumultuous terrain of midlife mayhem. In the world of dating, sometimes the most appealing quality is the wisdom that comes with age, if you can embrace it.

Now, let's delve into the escapades of these wannabe whippersnappers and see if we can find the line between youthful spirit and full-blown delusion!

The Vintage Vanguard

Sugar-Daddy Sean

Allow me to introduce Sean, the man who thinks the "half your age plus seven" rule is more of a suggestion than a guideline. With a wallet fatter than his medical file and an ego bigger than the age gap in his relationships, Sean is on a mission to prove that love knows no age, but his credit card knows no limits.

Sean's dating profile is a masterpiece of selective truth. His age? "Seasoned." His body type? "Investing in Microsoft in the '80s." His ideal match? Someone who thinks "The Beatles" is a new indie band and considers flip phones a relic of ancient history.

About Me: "Distinguished gentleman seeking a companion for life's finer adventures. CEO by day, aspiring Instagram user by night (still figuring out these 'hashtag' things). Can offer wisdom, wealth, and weekend trips to my villa in the islands. Passport required; a sense of wonder is essential. Warning: May accidentally buy you a car instead of a card for your birthday.

This silver fox is less interested in long walks on the beach and more into short walks to his private jet. Why settle for a beach when you can fly to your own slice of paradise? Sean's idea of a weekend getaway involves flying to the Caribbean, where he keeps his "humble" second home. It's not showing off; it's just "providing options" for quality time together.

Sean's conversation topics range from "back in my day" to want to see my airplane hangar? He's not out of touch; he's just waiting for you to explain what TikTok is... again.

Behind Sean's impressive portfolio lies a heart of gold that's worth more than his stock options. While he might confuse Instagram with Facebook, his sincerity and generosity come from a place of genuine care, not just his offshore bank accounts.

First Date: A date with Sean is like being in a time machine with a platinum credit card and a pilot's license. One minute you're at a five-star resort, the next you're jetting off to Nantucket because he "felt like fresh lobster." He's not just a boyfriend; he's a walking, talking history lesson with a side of financial advice and an island paradise thrown in for good measure.

Love Language: Grand gestures delivered with old-school charm, whether it's flying you to Paris for your birthday or having your favorite flowers delivered weekly

Attachment Style: Securely attached to his timeless principles and genuine intentions, while amusingly attempting to master modern dating with the latest technology

P.S. If you match with Sean, be prepared for dates that feel like a cross between a history documentary and an episode of "Lifestyles of the Rich and Famous." While he can fly you to the moon and back, he still can't manage social media without your help!

P.P.S. Sean's idea of Netflix and chill involves actual Netflix stocks and a chilled bottle of champagne that costs more than your rent.

Swipe right if you enjoy being the youngest person at dinner parties, don't mind explaining memes to someone who still uses air quotes and thinks the ideal Valentine's gift is paying off your student loans.

The Last Word

Sean: Your wealth may open doors, but it can't buy genuine connection. While your intentions might be golden, treating young women like luxury acquisitions makes you more of a collector than a partner. Consider finding someone who shares your life experience, not just access to your private jet and premium lifestyle.

Ladies: When a man can offer you both a history lesson and a trip to the Caribbean in the same conversation, you might be in for quite an adventure. However, proceed with caution. If he's more focused on showing off his assets than building real intimacy, and treats you more like a portfolio upgrade than a partner, run faster than his private jet can reach Palm Beach. Your self-worth, future relationships, and memoir will thank you.

The Cabana Casanova

Margarita Mark

Witness the spectacle that is Mark, the Peter Pan of the AARP set. He's traded his SUV for a convertible and his receding hairline for a backwards baseball cap. Mark's moved to a 55+ resort-style community, where he's got the big man on campus complex and thinks he's the social director of spring break for seniors.

Mark's dating profile is a cautionary tale of midlife crisis meets Margaritaville, where dignity goes to die on the rocks, with salt. Think Jimmy Buffett meets Jersey Shore, but with more Medicare and less hair.

About Me: "Professional paradise seeker and self-appointed BMOC (Big Man On Campus) seeking my next cocktail buddy. Living my best life one happy hour at a time in my souped-up golf cart (faster than your ex's sports car, baby). Age is just a number, and mine's unlisted. If you can't handle me at 70's karaoke night, you don't deserve me at the disco pool party.

His profile pic? A poorly-lit selfie at the local beach bar, strategically angled to hide his beer belly (spoiler: it doesn't work), and a host of other photos where his date is poorly cropped out of the photo.

By day, Mark is perfecting his tan (read: sunburn) bobbing in the resort-style pool as if he were moored, cocktail in hand, and doing his best to impress single and not-so-single women and anyone who hasn't grown tired of listening to him boast. By night, this bloated, intoxicated life of the party wannabe and self-proclaimed king of karaoke belts out "Don't Stop Believin" with more enthusiasm than vocal talent. He's on a desperate quest to reclaim his youth, one frozen margarita at a time.

But Mark's genuine pride and joy? His tricked-out, supercharged golf cart, a neon-colored monstrosity adorned with parrot decals, LED underglow, and a sound system that blasts music louder than a steel drum band. He cruises the community like it's a racetrack, leaving a trail of drugstore cologne and broken dreams in his wake.

First Date: With you (his latest online catch of the day) or the newest single "gal" resident at the pool bar, where you (and everyone within earshot) will be regaled with tales of his glory days as high school quarterback... 40+ years ago. But don't think you're special. Mark has dated every single woman in the neighborhood (and the surrounding area) and even targets married women who appear to want some of what he believes is his irresistible charm. In Mark's mind, he's not a home-wrecker; he's a "marriage spice-upper."

Love Language: Serenading you with off-key '70s rock songs while buying drinks with his Social Security check

Attachment Style: Permanently attached to his glory days and his ability to make everyone at the tiki bar cringe-watch his daily midlife meltdown

Swipe right if you enjoy beer bellies and man boobs, have a high tolerance for dad jokes, tacky Hawaiian shirts from Amazon and don't mind being the latest conquest in Mark's community-wide midlife crisis tour.

It's always 5 o'clock in Mark's world – mostly because he can't read his watch anymore without squinting, and partly because it's always happy hour when you're running from the reality of aging.

The Last Word

Mark: Your midlife crisis isn't a personality trait; it's a cautionary tale with a coconut bra. The only thing more inflated than your ego is your stomach and bar tab. Try aging gracefully instead of desperately, even Journey knew when to call it a night.

Ladies: When a man's idea of paradise is hitting on anything that moves from his LED-lit golf cart while butchering "The Pina Colada Song" nightly, swipe left faster than he can say "It's 5 o'clock somewhere." Let this lost boy keep searching for his never-never land, preferably in someone else's neighborhood. Your dignity and adult children will thank you.

The Recently Liberated

Divorce-Party Devin

Witness the rebirth of Devin, the human embodiment of a mid-life crisis with a fresh ink divorce decree. This walking, talking relationship rebound has turned his newfound single status into a second adolescence, and he considers his dad bod the hottest trend since sliced bread.

Devin's dating profile reads like a freedom manifesto written by a teenager trapped in a 40-something body:

About Me: "Just escaped a 15-year sentence (aka marriage) and ready to make up for lost time! Looking for someone who appreciates a man with the enthusiasm of a college freshman and the bedtime of a responsible adult (10:00 PM, but I can push it to 11 on weekends!). My ideal match? Anyone who isn't my ex-wife. Swipe right if you're ready for a wild ride in my sensible sedan!"

Photos showcase Devin in his newly reclaimed habitat: awkwardly posing in clubs surrounded by twenty-somethings, caught mid-air guitar at a Bon Jovi concert, and a "candid" shot of him flexing in front of his new bachelor pad (aka his sister's garage). His attempt at a sexy pic? A bathroom mirror selfie with visible toothpaste splatters, captioned "Single and ready to ming... wait, how does that go?"

First Date: A date with Devin is like chaperoning an overexcited puppy at a dog park. He'll suggest meeting at the trendiest spot in town (which was cool five years ago), arrive in his "going out" shirt that still has the tags on, and spend the evening oscillating between bragging about his freedom and panic-checking his phone for texts from his kids. Be prepared for cringeworthy attempts at current slang, long monologues about his ex (who he's TOTALLY over), and at least one instance of him tearing up while showing you pictures of his children on his phone's cracked screen.

Love Language: Oversharing about his divorce and gifting you with coupons from his new Costco membership (split custody means bulk shopping!)

Attachment Style: Rebound-ready, attached to his newfound freedom and dating app notifications

P.S. Devin's idea of Netflix and chill involves watching Netflix because he's still figuring out what "chill" means in this context.

P.P.S. If you make it to a second date, expect a tour of all his favorite date spots from 2005, which he insists are still "totally hip."

The Last Word

Devin: Hey there, newly liberated friend, your enthusiasm is infectious, but freedom isn't a race to the finish line. Take a breath. Process those feelings. Your divorce papers aren't a get-out-of-emotions-free card, and healing isn't something you can speed-swipe through. Your next chapter deserves better than being written in rebound ink. When you're ready to date without mentioning your ex in every other sentence, that's when your absolute freedom begins. Until then, spend some quality time with the most crucial relationship in your life right now, the one with yourself.

Ladies: Dating Devin comes with the rollercoaster of emotions that only a newly divorced man can provide! Pack your patience, a glossary of current dating terms, and maybe some tissues for the inevitable moment when he realizes he forgot to pick up his kids from soccer practice.

While Devin's enthusiasm can be appealing, it's essential to acknowledge that he's still adjusting to a significant life change. He might need some time to find his footing in the dating world before he's ready for a real connection. Sometimes, the kindest thing to do is to suggest he take a breath and rediscover himself before diving into the dating pool. So, swipe left faster than Devin signed his divorce papers. Your drama-free future and relationship goals will thank you.

The Aging Athlete

Six-Pack Sid

Stretch your patience for Sid, the man whose midlife crisis came with a gym membership and enough protein powder to fuel a small nation. After decades of being intimately acquainted with his couch, Sid has suddenly decided that age 52 is the perfect time to become an Instagram fitness influencer.

Sid's dating profile is a CrossFit confession booth meets motivational poster:

About Me: "Fitness quest day 157! Former dad bod transforming into Greek god (currently at Greek yogurt stage). Seeking a spotter for life who appreciates a man whose supplement budget exceeds his mortgage. Age is just a number, and my target heart rate proves I'm basically 25! #SilverFoxFitness #GrandpaGains #MidlifeMuscle"

Sid's camera roll has changed from family photos to an endless stream of flexing selfies, each one carefully angled to suggest the existence of abs that are still hiding behind 30 years of pizza and beer. His dating profile pics look like a before-and-after ad where the "after" is still very much in progress.

His new lifestyle includes:

- A closet full of compression gear that's doing some heavy compression.
- More gym selfies than actual reps.
- Constant references to his "transformation journey".
- Wearing tank tops in inappropriate weather.
- Using terms like "gains" and "beast mode" while getting winded taking the stairs.
- A supplement collection that looks like a GNC exploded in his kitchen.

First Date: A date with Sid means navigating around his strict meal prep schedule and listening to him explain why deadlifts are, in fact, a form of meditation. Be prepared for him to work "core engagement" into every conversation, order his burger protein-style while longingly eyeing your fries, and casually mention his step count at least seventeen times.

Love Language: Sharing his macro counts, flexing in every reflective surface, and the ability to spot him both emotionally and on the bench press

Attachment Style: Securely attached to his gym membership, anxiously attached to his fitness tracker, and permanently attached to every mirror he passes (while whispering "beast mode" to his reflection)

The Last Word

Sid: Your dedication to fitness is admirable, but Rome wasn't built in a day, and six-pack abs won't fill an empty nest. Try balancing those protein shakes with a little perspective. PS: Tank tops in December aren't fooling anyone!

Ladies: When a man's midlife crisis comes with more supplements than a vitamin store and his idea of small talk is explaining the difference between whey and casein protein, run. Your once-normal routine, balanced menu choices, and kitchen counter space will thank you for swiping left on this protein-powered Mid-Life Peter Pan.

Chapter 14
THE TAKEAWAY

Our trek through The Midlife Mayhem has revealed a fundamental truth: midlife isn't a crisis, it's an opportunity to age like fine wine. Unfortunately, our specimens have demonstrated that some men age like milk left on the counter during a heatwave! These calendar-deniers we've cataloged have mistaken "staying young at heart" for "desperately clinging to youth with a death grip and a bottle of Just For Men."

Red Flags With Sports Cars:

- Their age is the only number they can't exaggerate... so they lie about it.

- Their sudden lifestyle change is more dramatic than a soap opera season finale.

- They pursue partners young enough to have missed the original release of their favorite movies.

- Their vehicle screams "compensation" louder than their actual voice.

- Their financial priorities shifted from college funds to Corvette funds overnight.

- They refer to their receding hairline as an "alternative growth pattern."

- They use slang that makes their teenagers cringe.

- They suddenly believe skydiving is an appropriate weekend activity at 55.

- Their gym selfies outnumber their retirement contributions.

- They compare their dad bod to Chris Hemsworth and see no difference.

- They avoid friends their age because they're "too boring" (translation: too realistic).

- They quit their stable job to "follow their passion" of becoming a DJ.

- Their Instagram feed is more curated than the Louvre.

- They change the subject faster than their convertible's top when retirement comes up.

- They dismiss knee pain as "just needing to stretch more".

- Their dating app age range settings should come with a permission slip.

- They've had more cosmetic "touch-ups" than their heavily filtered profile pictures.

- They reminisce about their glory days while completely missing today's potential.

- They're one impulse purchase away from a financial advisor's nervous breakdown.

There's a universe of difference between maintaining youthful energy and denying the reality of aging. The most attractive quality in a midlife man isn't his artificially enhanced biceps or his suspiciously dark hair; it's the confidence to embrace his path with humor, wisdom, and authenticity.

Because nothing says "secure in my masculinity" quite like a man who can rock his silver fox status without pretending he's still rushing a fraternity.

Chapter 15

THE RED FLAG PARADE

Let's Set the Scene

NOTE TO READERS: While this chapter approaches the topic of concerning dating behaviors with humor, I recognize the seriousness behind many of these red flags. Some profiles, particularly in the Sexual Misconduct and Criminal Behavior sections, represent genuinely harmful behaviors that can pose real risks to women's safety, well-being, and dignity. If you've encountered these behaviors, please know you're not alone, and resources are available in Chapter 19. Your safety is never a laughing matter.

Welcome to The Red Flag Parade, where dating disasters march proudly and warning signs flash brighter than a Vegas casino! In this chapter, we're diving into the deep end of the dating pool's "shallow" section, where the water's cloudy and the lifeguards have all quit in despair.

The **Health Hazards** category includes Boozy Bruce, who thinks vodka is a food group, STD Sam, spreading more than just holiday cheer, and don't forget Toothless Todd, whose smile has more gaps than his employment history. Last, but certainly not least, is Halitosis Hal, whose kiss could qualify as a biological weapon.

Next up, in the **Sexual Misconduct** section, you'll encounter Dick-Pic Rick, who never met a camera angle he didn't like, Commode Cam Charlie with his questionable choice of backdrop, and Foot Fetish Felix, who's way too interested in your shoe size.

Discover **The Players:** Philandering Phil, whose contact list reads like a phone book, The Revolving Casanova Cal, who's never met a relationship he couldn't exit, and Mile-High Mike, whose "layovers" are suspiciously frequent.

We wind up the chapter with **Criminal Behavior**. Introducing Mugshot Mike, whose dating profile doubles as a wanted poster, Deadbeat-Dad Dean, who's ghosted more kids than dating apps, and Faux Romeo, whose love letters come with a request for your banking information.

These red flag bearers have turned dating faux pas into an Olympic sport, leaving a trail of broken hearts, empty wallets, and confused health professionals in their wake. They're the guys who make you wonder: Is it possible to get secondhand embarrassment from a dating profile? (Spoiler alert: yes, and it might require therapy.)

While everyone has flaws, these men have turned theirs into feature presentations. They're living proof that sometimes, the most attractive quality in a date is the ability to walk away from one.

So grab your hazmat suit and night vision goggles as we navigate the minefield of red flags in dating. In the world of romance, sometimes the bravest thing you can do is swipe left and live to date another day.

Now, let's scrutinize this parade of perplexing paramours and see if we can find any silver linings in these very dark clouds!

Health Hazards

The Human Breathalyzer

Boozy Bruce

Cheers to Bruce, the man who thinks "hydration" is code for "happy hour." His blood type? 80 proof. His dating profile pic? A blurry selfie with his "best friend", an extra dry martini with blue cheese olives.

Bruce's profile is a bartender's nightmare masquerading as a dating bio, where "work hard, play harder" really means "I haven't been sober since, well... I can't recall actually being sober."

About Me: "Social drinker* and professional good time enthusiast seeking a co-pilot for life's liquid adventures! (*Social drinking defined as: whenever I'm in the presence of another human being, or alone, or breathing). I work hard and play harder (the fun begins at happy hour or earlier). Looking for someone who appreciates spontaneity (like a liquid lunch at the beach) and doesn't mind that my three food groups are beer, Belvedere Vodka, and BOGO margaritas. If you think 'Irish Coffee' is a legitimate breakfast, and like your Long Island Iced Teas extra long, we'll get along great! Bonus points if you have a reliable car and a flexible moral compass about morning drinking."

Bruce's profile conveniently lists him as a 'social drinker', which is technically accurate if you consider that alcohol is his most committed relationship.

Bruce's refrigerator looks like a frat house inventory: bottled water (for hangovers), a rotating case of beer, and a freezer that's home to nothing but vodka and fossilized ice cubes. Every meal is just an excuse for another drink. Breakfast? "These eggs would go great with a mimosa!" Lunch? "It's not a business meeting without a martini." Dinner? "I know the perfect wine for that... and that... and that too! Dessert? "Espresso martinis!"

First Date: A tour of his favorite happy hour spots, punctuated by slurred compliments and at least one emotional confession about his ex and his kids. Every date with Bruce follows the same recipe: start at a bar, move to a restaurant with a bar, and end at, you guessed it, a different bar. Bring a breathalyzer and bail money.

Love Language: Speaking in slurred sweet nothings, shared hangovers, and the ability to turn every occasion (including breakfast) into a toast

Attachment Style: Anxiously attached... to barstools, walls, railings, and any stable surface within stumbling distance. His most secure relationships are with inanimate objects that prevent gravity from winning.

For Bruce, sobriety is like Bigfoot, often discussed, rarely seen. His girlfriend isn't so much a partner as she is a drinking buddy, part bartender, full-time enabler. Together, they're like an avant-garde performance art piece titled "Codependency and Cirrhosis: A Love Story."

Swipe right if you enjoy dates that you can't remember, have a liver of steel, don't mind being constantly embarrassed by his drunken behavior, and listening to family and friends ask you "WHY... just WHY?"

In Bruce's world, it's always 5 o'clock somewhere, and if it's not, that's what watches are for... adjusting.

Last Word

Bruce: Your liver isn't a renewable resource. You're treating your body like a dumpster fire and your brain cells like they're expendable. Newsflash: they're not. Here's a sobering thought: being perpetually sloshed isn't a personality trait, it's a problem. Women aren't looking for a project or to be a designated driver; they want a partner who can remember their name without checking their phone. Now, put down that beer, drink some water, and for the love of all that is holy, give your body a break. The dating world (and your internal organs) will thank you.

Ladies: No amount of "fun guy" energy is worth becoming someone's drinking buddy and enabler. Unless you're excited about becoming a combination designated driver, therapist, and bail bonds-person, swipe left faster than Bruce can say "just one more drink." Your liver, dignity, patience, family, and friends will thank you.

The Walking Petri Dish

STD Sam

Study the specimen known as Sam, the human embodiment of "YOLO" taken too far. This walking, talking red flag has turned irresponsibility into a lifestyle, considering safety measures optional at best. Sam's body is a theme park of diseases. He thinks penicillin is a food group. Dating him requires a hazmat suit and a very understanding doctor.

Sam's dating profile reads like a liability waiver:

About Me: "Free spirit with a flexible approach to medical advice, seeking adventure partner with good health insurance. Looking for someone who lives in the moment and doesn't ask too many questions about my mysterious rashes. Bonus points if you have a convenient clinic nearby! Medical professionals swipe left, you're too judgmental."

In Sam's world, every date is a potential public health incident. He doesn't just play fast and loose with hearts; he's playing Russian roulette with everyone's immune systems. His idea of protection? Crossing his fingers and hoping for the best.

First Date: A quick meetup at the shadiest bar in town, followed by empty promises about "getting tested soon." Sam's selfishness extends beyond the bedroom. He's likely to "forget" his wallet, leave you with the bar tab, and then ask if you want to split the cab fare to his place. Must be comfortable with vague explanations about his "seasonal allergies" that somehow require antibiotics.

Love Language: Sharing everything (literally EVERYTHING), ghosting before test results arrive, and the ability to pronounce "azithromycin" and "doxycycline" correctly

Attachment Style: Promiscuously attached to his collection of antibiotics and creative explanations for "that rash"

Sam's approach to sexual health is about as responsible as using a chocolate bar as sunscreen. He thinks "protection" is just a fancy word for "killjoy" and treats STD tests like pop quizzes, best avoided at all costs. His idea of safe sex is making sure the bed won't collapse. His health check is a quick glance in the mirror, and his approach to dating is leaving a wake of regretful partners and concerned healthcare professionals. Swipe left unless you enjoy awkward conversations with your doctor and a lifetime supply of antibiotics.

When it comes to his dating history, Sam's memory is conveniently spotty. He can't recall how many partners he's had, but he's pretty sure it's "not that many", give or take a small village. His philosophy? What past partners don't know can't hurt them... right?

P.P.S. Sam's idea of a follow-up text is "You should probably get tested. No reason. Just a hunch!" In Sam's world, ignorance isn't just bliss; it's a lifestyle choice.

The Last Word

Sam: Listen up, Patient Zero, your body isn't an experimental lab for STDs, and other people's health isn't your personal Russian roulette game. The only thing spreading faster than your diseases is your reputation. Consider approaching your dating life with the same level of urgency as your next clinic visit. Your attitude is more toxic than your test results.

Ladies: This isn't just a swipe left, it's a matter of public health. No amount of "living in the moment" is worth a lifetime of prescription refills. Your health is worth more than his "good time." When a man treats safe sex like optional trip insurance and considers STD tests an invasion of privacy, run faster than antibiotic-resistant bacteria. Your immune system, future reproductive health, and peace of mind will thank you.

The Dental Dodger

Toothless Todd

Grin and bear Todd, the man whose smile is more hole-y than righteous. This walking, talking advertisement for dental insurance doesn't just have a gap in his teeth; he's got a canyon where his incisor should be, and a cavalier attitude about the whole situation.

Todd's dating profile is a masterclass in strategic photography.

About Me: "Looking for someone to fill the gap in my life... and maybe recommend a good dentist? Smile enthusiast with a unique charm. I put the 'ooth' in 'smooth'! Seeking a woman who appreciates character over caramels and substance over substances that require chewing. My dental plan? Finding someone who thinks whistling while talking is endearing. On the bright side, I've saved thousands on floss and never have to worry about food stuck in my teeth, at least not THOSE teeth!"

His photos are a carefully curated collection of closed-mouth smiles, strategic angles, and at least one picture of him thoughtfully eating an apple (sideways, of course).

First Date: In Todd's world, every first meeting is a reveal worthy of a makeover show, except the 'after' is more surprising than the 'before'. He doesn't just greet you; he unleashes a smile that's one part charming, two parts alarming. His idea of dinner and a movie? Anything that doesn't involve corn on the cob or chewy caramel.

Love Language: Soft foods, drinking everything through a straw, and the ability to appreciate his unique whistle when he pronounces 's' sounds

Attachment Style: Dentally detached but firmly attached to his belief that dental hygiene is a government conspiracy

In Todd's universe, "Netflix and chill" means watching ice hockey highlight reels while he regales you with the epic tale of how he lost his tooth in a valiant battle (with a particularly stubborn pistachio). Just don't be surprised if he asks you to cut his steak for him on the second date.

P.S. If you match with Todd, be prepared for dates that feel like you're starring in a very low-budget remake of "The Hangover".

The Last Word

Todd: Oh, Todd. Sweet, gap-toothed Todd. You're out here on dating apps, flashing that hole-y grin like it's a quirky personality trait rather than a dental emergency. Newsflash, buddy: that missing tooth isn't a conversation starter, it's a red flag with roots. Quality women aren't looking for a project or a reason to dust off their dreams of being a dental hygienist. So here's some bite-sized advice: before you try to fill the gap in your love life, how about filling the one in your smile? Invest in yourself. Show the ladies you care about your health, your appearance, and yes, your ability to enjoy a good corn on the cob. A smile is worth a thousand words, but yours is currently saying, "I make questionable life choices." Now, make that dentist appointment. Your future dates (and your gums) will thank you!

Ladies: A missing tooth might be charming on a six-year-old waiting for the tooth fairy, but on a grown man, it's just a sign he's not invested in basic self-care. When his dental work has more gaps than his employment history and his smile looks like a jack-o'-lantern in January, swipe left faster than he can whistle the letter' S'. Your dental hygiene standards and gag reflex will thank you.

The Breath Bandit

Halitosis Hal

Take a big step back and observe Hal, the man whose breath could wake the dead – and then kill them again. This olfactory offender has turned bad breath into an extreme sport, considering mint a four-letter word.

Hal's dating profile is a masterpiece of misdirection:

About Me: "Seeking a partner with a strong constitution and a weak sense of smell. Love long talks (from a distance), garlic-heavy cuisine, and testing the limits of human endurance. Mint allergy, probably."

Photos showcase Hal in his natural habitat: always shot from a distance, mysteriously foggy close-ups, and "candid" shots where nearby plants seem to be wilting. His attempt at a kissing-booth pic? A hazmat team was called.

First Date: A date with Hal is like an episode of Fear Factor. He'll suggest meeting at a restaurant (preferably one with no other customers), arrive in a cloud of his own making, and spend the evening watching you try not to gag. Be prepared for conversations that feel like olfactory assault courses, constant offers of his "homemade breath mints" (spoiler: they're not breath mints), and at least one attempt to explain why oral hygiene is a government conspiracy.

Love Language: Sharing his collection of "rare" cheeses and gifting you nose plugs

Attachment Style: Blissfully detached from dental hygiene while firmly attached to his "breath mints are for wimps" philosophy

P.S. Hal's idea of freshening up is eating a whole head of garlic to "neutralize" the smell.

P.P.S. If you somehow agree to a second date, expect it to be at a landfill – the only place where his breath might go unnoticed.

The Last Word

Hal: Let's clear the air, shall we? Your breath isn't just breaking the ice; it's melting it and not in a good way. Here's a novel idea: try breaking out a toothbrush instead of breaking wind from your mouth. The only thing that should take people's breath away on a date is your charming personality, not your toxic exhalations. Until you get this sorted, maybe consider a career in bioweapon development? Your dating life (and everyone within a 10-foot radius) will thank you. Now, go find a dentist and make friends with some mouthwash – your future depends on it!

Ladies: When his breath can peel paint and plants lean away when he talks, it's not just a red flag, it's a biohazard warning. Swipe left faster than Hal can wilt flowers. Your nose and stomach will thank you.

Sexual Misconduct

The Exhibitionist

Dick-Pic Rick

Quick, close your eyes! It's Rick, a man who never learned the art of appropriate sharing. This walking, talking overshare button has turned privacy settings into suggestions and considers consent an optional feature.

Rick's dating profile reads like a content warning:

About Me: "Amateur photographer seeking an appreciative audience. Looking for someone who enjoys surprises and isn't afraid of full disclosure. My ideal match? Someone who thinks 'getting to know each other' starts with an uninvited photo tour. I believe in cutting through the small talk and getting straight to the point (and the pictures). Communication is all about transparency, literally! Swipe right if you're ready for a very revealing conversation!"

A chat with Rick quickly turns into an unwanted slideshow. He'll start conversations with "Want to see something?"; and arrive in your inbox with alarming frequency, spending evenings testing the limits of your block button.

Rick is perpetually baffled by the lack of enthusiasm for his "photography." He considers himself the Ansel Adams of awkward oversharing, yet his masterpieces are met with blocks and reports instead of applause. When confronted about his inappropriate behavior, Rick has a standard repertoire of responses, including "It was just a compliment," "You're too sensitive," and the classic "It was meant for someone else."

Rick's favorite pastimes include misinterpreting polite conversation as invitations, turning innocent compliments into excuses for impromptu photoshoots, and wondering why his matches disappear faster than his sense of propriety.

Rick's idea of a great first impression is best left unseen. Proceed with caution, keep your finger on the 'report' button, and consider investing in some virtual eye bleach.

First Date: There isn't one, unless you enjoy being a witness in a cyber-harassment case. Save the "date" for your statement to the cyber crimes unit.

Love Language: Unsolicited photography sessions and the ability to turn every conversation into an impromptu anatomy lesson

Attachment Style: Pathologically attached to his camera's zoom function and utterly detached from social norms and legal consequences

P.S. Rick's idea of a successful interaction is when someone takes more than 3 seconds to hit 'block.'

P.P.S. If you match with Rick, expect a barrage of messages asking, "Did you get it?" "What did you think?" and "Hello?" in rapid succession.

Last Word:

Rick: Let's have a frank talk about franks, shall we? Your unsolicited "junk mail" is about as welcome as a pop-up ad for erectile dysfunction during a work presentation. Newsflash: women aren't sitting around hoping for a surprise glimpse of your disco stick. Your little photo shoots aren't artistic expression; they're a one-way ticket to Blockedville, population: you.

Here's a shocking revelation: consent is sexy. You know what's not? Violating app guidelines and basic human decency faster than you can say "restraining order." Your behavior isn't just creepy; it's a literal crime in many places. So unless your life goal is to become a registered sex offender, keep your "Dick pics" to yourself.

The only thing your unsolicited photos are exposing is your lack of respect, common sense, and originality. Try cultivating a personality instead of a portfolio of your nether regions. Trust me, it'll get you further in the dating world and keep you out of legal trouble. Now, put your phone down, zip up, and for the love of all that is holy, keep your "junk" in your trunk unless explicitly invited to do otherwise. The dating world (and frankly, the entire internet) will thank you.

Ladies: Rick's profile isn't just a swipe left; it's a report and block situation. When a man's opening move is digital flashing, run faster than his photos can load. This isn't just creepy behavior; it's literal sexual harassment. Report, block, and keep your local cyber crimes unit on speed dial. By reporting instead of just blocking, you're helping protect other women from the same unwelcome surprise in their inbox. Womankind, your corneas, and future generations will thank you.

The Restroom Romeo

Commode-Cam Cody

Feast your eyes on Cody, the human embodiment of a "do not enter" sign. This walking, talking hygiene hazard has turned bathroom photography into a calling and considers cleanliness optional when it comes to impressing the ladies.

Cody's dating profile reads like a health inspector's nightmare:

About Me: "Laid-back dude seeking a partner who appreciates raw authenticity (and raw everything else). Looking for someone who finds bathroom ambiance romantic and thinks 'messy' is just another word for 'lived-in'. My ideal match? A gal who's not afraid to look past the toothpaste splatters to see the real me. Swipe right if you're ready for a man who's not afraid to show you his 'throne room'!"

Photos showcase Cody in his natural habitat: flexing shirtless in a mirror that hasn't seen Windex since the Bush administration, caught mid-selfie with a toilet peeking into frame, and a "candid" shot where he's perched on the porcelain throne. His attempt at a classy pic? A bathroom selfie where he's wearing a tie... and nothing else.

What Cody doesn't realize is that his bathroom gallery is more likely to attract the attention of the CDC than potential dates. He's baffled why women aren't lining up to meet him, unaware that his "intimate" photos are sending ladies running faster than you can say "E. coli."

Cody's bathroom doesn't just look like a biohazard zone, it smells like one, too. The aroma is a unique blend of forgotten gym socks, expired cologne samples, and whatever that fuzzy thing growing behind the toilet is. As for his shower? It's less of a cleansing space and more of a thriving ecosystem. The shower curtain hosts more cultures than a world food festival, and the loofah has developed sentience and is plotting world domination.

First Date: A date with Cody is like a risky game of "Guess That Stain". He'll suggest meeting at his place (a red flag!), greet you in the same shirt from his profile picture, and spend the evening trying to convince you that cleaning products are a conspiracy by "Big Soap." Be prepared for impromptu tours of his "bachelor pad," lengthy discussions about the evils of air fresheners, and at least one attempt to explain why the kitchen sponge is in the bathroom.

Love Language: Sharing his prized body spray collection and gifting you with slightly used bath products

Attachment Style: Inexplicably attached to taking selfies in public restrooms, treating toilet paper dispensers like photo props

P.S. Cody's idea of tidying up for a date is to flush twice and close the shower curtain.

P.P.S. If you somehow agree to a second date, expect an invitation to help him "redecorate" his bathroom... by which he means buying a new toilet brush.

The Last Word

Cody: Seriously, your penchant for shirtless bathroom mirror selfies is downright embarrassing. Your bathroom isn't just a crime scene; it's a public health crisis. The only thing growing faster than the mold behind your toilet is the list of women blocking your profile. Consider putting on a shirt and investing in some cleaning supplies before purchasing a new phone camera. Even your shower curtain bacteria have better culture than you.

Ladies: When a man's mirror selfies come with their own CDC warning labels and his toilet makes a guest appearance in every photo, Swipe left and run like you're being chased by whatever that fuzzy thing is growing behind his sink. Your sense of smell and immune system will thank you.

The Toe Aficionado

Foot-Fetish Felix

Step right up and observe Felix, whose eyes are always drawn south. This walking, talking podiatry textbook has turned footwear appreciation into an extreme sport and considers "from the ground up" a dating strategy.

Felix's profile reads like a shoe catalog crossed with bad poetry:

About Me: "Seeking a sole-mate who can keep me on my toes. Looking for someone who appreciates a man who notices the little things... like your choice in sandals. Ideal match? Someone who finds discussions about arch support riveting. Swipe right if you're ready to walk a mile in my shoes!"

What Felix doesn't mention in his profile is how quickly his "appreciation" can cross boundaries. His camera roll has more feet than faces, and his casual shoe compliments often come with an uncomfortably heavy breathing soundtrack.

First Date: A date with Felix is like a very focused fashion show. He'll suggest meeting at a mall (conveniently near the shoe stores), arrive with a measuring tape "just in case," and spend the evening stealing glances below the table. Be prepared for unsolicited shoe compliments, impromptu foot-health lectures, and at least one offer of a "therapeutic massage."

Love Language: Unsolicited foot massages and the ability to turn every conversation into a detailed discussion about your arches

Attachment Style: Securely attached to your shoe collection, anxiously attached to pedicure schedules, and desperately seeking a sole-mate

Felix's fascination might seem quirky, but it's essential to maintain your boundaries. While his attention to detail can be flattering, it's vital to ensure that his interest in your footwear doesn't overshadow his interest in you as a whole person. If his fixation makes you uncomfortable, it's always okay to put your foot down and walk away!

👣👠📸!

P.S. If you make it to a second date, don't be surprised if he suggests a "fun day out" at a high-end shoe store, followed by a trip to the fanciest nail salon in town. In Felix's world, the way to a woman's heart is definitely through her soles.

The Last Word

Felix: Your foot fixation isn't a personality trait; it's a red flag with toe rings. Try lifting your gaze above ankle level and developing interests that don't require a pedicure. The only thing creepier than your DMs is your camera roll full of strangers' feet.

Ladies: When a man's more interested in your shoe size than your soul size, run faster than Felix can say "What's your stance on open-toed sandals?" This isn't just a foot fetish, it's a boundary-crossing crisis waiting to happen. Keep your feet (and the rest of you) far away from this toe-tallitarian regime. Your comfort zone and feet will thank you.

The Players

The Serial Charmer

Philandering Phil

Let me present Phil, the man who treats monogamy like it's a spelling bee word he can't quite master. This smooth-talking Casanova doesn't just have a way with words; he's got a whole thesaurus of sweet nothings, each one carefully crafted to make you feel like you're the only woman in the world... along with Sarah, Jennifer, and Alicia.

Phil's dating profile is a masterpiece of manipulation disguised as romance, where every word is as carefully curated as his contact list of rotating girlfriends:

About Me: "Professional appreciator of feminine beauty seeking multiple opportunities to spread my considerable charm (and questionable morals). Expert in making every woman feel special through carefully scheduled attention and artfully crafted compliments. Master's degree in excuse-making, PhD in smooth-talking. Looking for someone who doesn't ask too many questions about the mysterious texts lighting up my phone at 2 AM."

In Phil's world, every interaction is an opportunity for flirtation. He doesn't just chat; he seduces, each word dripping with more honey than a beehive in summer. A conversation with Phil is like dancing with a charming octopus; you're never quite sure where all those hands have been. His date-scheduling skills would impress an air traffic controller, and his ability to keep stories straight rivals a bestselling novelist. Each woman gets her own special nickname, partly because it's "romantic," but mostly because it's harder to mess up "baby" or "sweetheart" than actual names.

Phil's excuse repertoire includes classics like "She's just a friend," "You're overreacting," and the ever-popular "That lipstick on my collar? Must be yours from last week." When inevitably caught, Phil doesn't just break hearts; he's got a full damage control protocol that would impress crisis management professionals. His tearful apologies and promises to change are as rehearsed as his pickup lines.

The most dangerous thing about Phil isn't just his ability to juggle multiple women; it's his uncanny talent for convincing them to give him "one more chance" after they've caught him red-handed.

First Date: A candlelit dinner at a restaurant three towns over, where the chance of running into "someone he knows" is minimal, followed by a romantic evening of checking his phone and crafting elaborate excuses about why you can't come to his place (his other girlfriend is there).

Love Language: Strategic flattery, carefully timed attention, and the ability to make every woman feel like she's the only one

Attachment Style: Simultaneously attached to multiple women while maintaining plausible deniability in all area codes

Red Flags That Phil's Waving:

- Has more passwords than the CIA and guards his phone as if it contains nuclear codes.

- Claims to work for a demanding company that's "always having emergencies".

- Becomes mysteriously unavailable during holidays and weekends.

- Has an allergic reaction to being tagged in social media posts.

- Knows every back-road restaurant within a 50-mile radius.

- Master's the art of the "business trip" that never aligns with his office calendar.

- Has more "sick relatives" than a hospital ward

P.S. If you fall for Phil's charms, be prepared for a relationship that feels like you're starring in your own personal soap opera, until you realize you're just one episode in his ongoing series.

The Last Word

Phil: Your love life isn't a romantic comedy; it's a cautionary tale with multiple victims. The only thing more numerous than your lies is your collection of blocked numbers from women who've finally caught on. May your future be as empty as your promises and as lonely as the truth you've been avoiding.

Ladies: When a man's charm comes with more red flags than a Soviet parade and his phone has more password protection than the Pentagon, swipe left faster than this heart hustler can switch between his dating apps. Your emotional well-being and holiday plans will thank you.

The Revolving Door Romeo

Casanova Cal

Next in line, it's Casanova Cal, the guy whose bedroom should have a "Now Serving" number dispenser. Cal doesn't just have a little black book; he's got an entire library of conquests. His neighbors don't need Netflix; they just grab some popcorn and watch the parade of women coming and going from Cal's place.

Cal's dating profile is a masterpiece of vague promises and innuendo.

About Me: Equal opportunity romance provider seeking next addition to my ever-rotating cast of leading ladies. Currently accepting applications for positions available between 10 PM and 2 AM. Please note that scheduling conflicts may occur due to high volume. Experience with the 'walk of shame' preferred, but not required. Here for a good time, not a long time... but I can make it feel like forever, baby."

His profile pics are a carefully curated collection of "accidental" shirtless shots that somehow always include his washboard abs.

This maestro of musical beds has turned hookups into an Olympic sport. He doesn't just play the field; he's the owner, coach, and MVP. Cal's bed has a revolving door, and his sheets are changed more often than a newborn's diapers.

In Cal's world, "exclusive" is a dirty word, and "commitment" is something that happens to other people. He's not a player; he's a "romance enthusiast" with a very broad definition of romance. His idea of a long-term relationship is remembering a woman's name the morning after.

The mystery of Cal's success keeps his neighbors up at night (well, that and the sound of his headboard hitting the wall). Theories range from him being a secret agent to having a twin brother to being three kids in trench coats.

First Date: A 2 AM "you up?" invitation, followed by a carefully orchestrated exit before breakfast. Must be comfortable with stepping around other women's hair ties on the floor.

Love Language: Late-night texts, morning ghosting, and the ability to dodge awkward "what are we?" conversations with Olympic-level skill

Attachment Style: Rotationally attached, treating relationships like a revolving door with multiple emergency exits

Behind Cal's charming facade lurks a trail of broken hearts and questionable sexual health decisions. His smooth talk is as practiced as his exit strategy, and his promises are as empty as his capacity for genuine connection.

Swipe right if you enjoy being part of a human conveyor belt, don't mind being just another notch on a very crowded bedpost, and think that "STD" stands for "Sensationally Tantalizing Dude."

P.S. If you match with Cal, be prepared for a night that's less "The Notebook" and more "Fast and Furious: Bedroom Drift." Because in Cal's universe, "You're special" means you're the third "special" person he's had over today!

The Last Word

Cal: Your little black book is more like a phone directory, and your reputation is spreading faster than the STDs you're likely carrying. Try developing a personality that doesn't require a prescription for penicillin.

Ladies: Swipe left faster than Cal can say "You're different from the others" (which he's already said three times tonight). When a man's bed has more visitors than Grand Central Station and his phone has more blocked numbers than a telemarketer, run like you're being chased by his collection of untreated STDs. Your immune system and self-respect will thank you.

The Aviation Aficionado

Mile-High Mike

Fasten your seatbelt for Mike, the human embodiment of a delayed flight, all promises, no arrivals. This walking, talking pre-flight safety demonstration thinks having a pilot's license is a license to play the field at 35,000 feet.

Mike's dating profile is cleared for takeoff with red flags:

About Me: "Captain seeking new flight crew member for occasional layovers (wink). Current relationship status? Let's just say I'm as free as the clouds, baby! Looking for an adventurous spirit who understands that what happens in different area codes stays in different area codes. Swipe right if you're ready to join my elite frequent flyer program (benefits subject to availability)!"

In Mike's world, every city has a different story, and every story has a different leading lady. His photo gallery showcases his player lifestyle: cockpit selfies with that signature smirk (and visible wedding ring tan line), group shots with suspiciously young blonde flight attendants, and "casual" first-class lounging pics captioned "Living the dream... one city at a time."

First Date: A date with Mike is like going through customs, but with lots of questionable declarations and suspicious baggage. He'll suggest meeting at an airport hotel bar (where nobody knows him... supposedly), arrive fashionably late with stories about "weather delays," and spend the evening name-dropping cities like they're his personal conquests. His phone will mysteriously remain in airplane mode, and he'll have multiple "work emergencies" requiring immediate bathroom breaks during which he checks his dating apps and phone calls from his wife and kids.

Love Language: Promising you the world while delivering nothing but air miles and alibis

Attachment Style: Permanently attached to his pilot's wings and ego while maintaining the emotional availability of lost luggage

P.S. Mike's idea of exclusivity is limiting himself to one girlfriend per city.

The Last Word

Mike: Listen up, Captain Unfaithful, your wedding ring tan line isn't a fashion statement, it's a billboard for your character. While you're up there playing single and ready to mingle at 35,000 feet, your wife is down here holding together the life you're too cowardly to commit to. The only thing more pathetic than your in-flight dating game is thinking nobody notices that subtle ring removal before takeoff.

Ladies: Mike's emotional baggage has exceeded the weight limit, and honey, there aren't enough upgrade vouchers in the world to make this flight worth booking. Unless you want your relationship status to be permanently 'in transit,' swipe left on this high-flying Casanova faster than Mike can change his flight plan. Your grounded future, his unsuspecting wife, and married women everywhere will thank you

Criminal Behavior

The Conniving Ex-Con

Mugshot Mick

Newly paroled and ready to mingle: Mick, whose profile picture is unmistakably a mugshot, complete with a height chart in the background. However, Mick insists it's just a "character study" for his budding acting career. He boasts about his recent "relocation" while remaining suspiciously vague about the details.

Mick's profile screams "fresh out of the pen" without actually saying it:

About Me: "Recently relocated from state-sponsored housing seeking partner in... life (definitely not crime). Looking for someone who appreciates prison-grade tattoos and doesn't ask too many questions about my 'sabbatical.' Must be comfortable with scheduled check-ins and surprise visits from my 'life coach' (AKA parole officer)."

Mick proudly lists his hobbies as weight lifting and making license plates, showcasing his unique skill set. He can't stop bragging about his tattoos, with special emphasis on the teardrop under his left eye.

In Mick's world, every conversation is a delicate dance of avoiding specifics about his "previous residence." His idea of transparency is admitting that his recent "meditation retreat" had higher walls than most.

First Date: A romantic evening within a strictly defined radius of his current location, timed perfectly around his (well-hidden) ankle monitor's curfew alert. Must be comfortable with hourly check-ins and spontaneous visits from his "accountability partner." If you play your cards right, Mick might even show off his prized collection of smuggled plastic sporks.

Love Language: Collect calls, commissary credits, and the ability to communicate through hand signals across visiting rooms and through glass partitions. Mick expresses his affection through acts of service (offering to teach the art of turning everyday objects into potential weapons).

Attachment Style: Criminally attached to his collection of booking photos and "it's not what it looks like" explanations

Mugshot Mick isn't just comfortable with small spaces; he's practically a minimalist living guru! His years of "government-sponsored studio living" have made him an expert in maximizing every square inch. Who needs a sprawling mansion when you can perfect the art of using a toilet as a combination seat, desk, and dining table?

Mick boasts that he can do a whole workout routine in a space barely larger than a phone booth. His idea of "open concept living" is a room with bars instead of walls. And let's not forget his unparalleled skills in bunk bed etiquette; he's a top bunk aficionado who never complains about the climb.

P.S. Just don't ask him about his experience with "room service." Apparently, sliding mystery meat through a small window isn't quite the five-star experience you'd expect!

The Last Word

Mick: Your dating profile isn't just a red flag, it's a prison jumpsuit masquerading as a personal ad. Try focusing less on your 'state-sponsored vacation' stories and more on actual rehabilitation.

Ladies: When a man's profile reads like a rap sheet and his relationship history includes conjugal visits, run like you're being chased by the entire department of corrections. No amount of prison yard muscle is worth becoming his next accomplice. Swipe left faster than Mick can say "it was all a misunderstanding." Your freedom and independence will thank you.

The Child Support Dodger

Deadbeat-Dad Dean

Introducing Dean, the human embodiment of a disappeared dad joke. This walking, talking responsibility vacuum has turned parental evasion into an Olympic sport, considering child support an optional monthly donation to a cause he'd rather forget.

Dean's dating profile reads like a masterclass in selective memory:

About Me: "Fun-loving, carefree guy seeking a partner for spontaneous adventures. I love to travel, especially to non-extradition countries. Looking for someone who appreciates a man unburdened by responsibility. Kids? What kids? Oh, those kids. They're practically adults now, right? Swipe right if you're ready for a relationship freer than my bank account after payday!"

Photos showcase Dean in his natural habitat: posing with expensive toys he can't afford, caught mid-fleeing from process servers, and candid shots of him living his best life while conveniently forgetting that he helped create other lives. His attempt at a family pic? A selfie with his dog, captioned "The only dependent I acknowledge."

First Date: A date with Dean is like watching a one-man show titled "It's Not My Fault: The Musical." He'll suggest meeting at happy hour (because full-price drinks cut into his escape fund), arrive in a car that's nicer than his kids' college fund, and spend the evening spinning tales of his ex's unreasonable demands (like expecting him to parent). Be prepared for rants about the unfairness of the legal system, long monologues about his "oppressive" responsibilities, and at least one phone call he ignores because it might be his ex asking about this month's missing payment.

Love Language: Ghosting his familial obligations and showering new partners with money he should be sending to his kids

Attachment Style: Selectively attached to his wallet, which mysteriously disappears when child support is due

While Dean's "freedom" might seem appealing at first glance, in the world of responsible adulting, real men step up for their kids. With Dean, you're not just dating him, you're enabling a masterclass in parental negligence and getting a front-row seat to karmic debt in action.

Caution: Prolonged exposure to Dean may result in a distorted sense of responsibility, an uncanny ability to spot process servers from a mile away, and the sinking feeling that you're dating someone who peaked in high school and never grew up.

P.S. Dean's idea of co-parenting is remembering his kids' names... most of the time.

P.P.S. If you somehow agree to a second date, expect it to be scheduled around his elaborate schemes to appear broke on paper while living large in reality.

The Last Word

Dean: Playing hide and seek with your parental responsibilities isn't a lifestyle, it's a crime. The only thing lower than your child support payments is your character. Try being as invested in your kids as you are in dodging them. Your 'freedom' comes with a price tag that your children are paying.

Ladies: No amount of "spontaneous adventure" is worth dating someone who turns deadbeat into a lifestyle choice. His kids deserve better, and so do you. When a man's prouder of escaping responsibility than facing it, swipe left faster than he runs from process servers. Your conscience, single mothers everywhere, and his abandoned children will thank you.

The Sweet-Talking Scammer

Faux Romeo

Scam alert: It's Romeo, the "American soldier" whose profile pic looks suspiciously like a stock photo and whose English is as broken as the hearts he leaves behind. This digital Don Juan is ready to sweep you off your feet and directly into his offshore bank account.

Romeo's profile is a masterclass in contradiction:

About Me: "God-fearing American military general/neurosurgeon/engineer (currently stationed overseas) seeking true love and your bank account details, I mean, soul connection! Newly widowed after a tragic accident involving ninjas and/or pirates. Have a $50 million inheritance, but need your help (and a small processing fee) to access it. Must love long-distance romance, gift cards, and Western Union."

Romeo's backstory is more elaborate than a telenovela plot. He's a widowed Army general, oil executive, or secret agent (pick your flavor of the week) with a conveniently tragic past and an inconvenient inability to meet in person. His location? Always "just deployed" or "on a top-secret mission", probably to the nearest internet café in Lagos. He's a 35-year-old widower with 30 years of military service. He's fluent in English but somehow always ends up typing "kindly" and "dear" in every other sentence. His photos exude a "male model" vibe, but his camera is always broken when you ask for a live video chat.

This long-distance charmer falls in love faster than you can say "Western Union." His passionate declarations would make Shakespeare blush, if only they weren't copied and pasted from a scammer's handbook. Romeo's idea of romance is asking for your credit card number; it's not financial fraud, it's "building trust"!

First Date: A perpetually postponed meeting due to endless "military missions," followed by urgent requests for gift cards to help him get home to you

Love Language: Copy-pasted poetry, stock photos of roses, and the ability to transfer funds internationally at a moment's notice

Attachment Style: Securely attached to your bank account details, anxiously attached to Western Union's operating hours, and completely detached from reality

Romeo's courtship strategy is a perfectly orchestrated symphony of manipulation: Love bombing through stolen romantic quotes, creating urgency through manufactured crises, and isolating you from friends who might notice that General Doctor Astronaut Romeo's story has more holes than a fishing net.

These predators deliberately seek out vulnerable women, the recently widowed, divorced, empty-nesters, or those struggling with loneliness. They scan profiles for mentions of loss or heartbreak, then tailor their approach to offer precisely the emotional connection their targets crave. Their research is thorough; they'll study your social media to personalize their scam, making you feel truly "seen" while they're sizing up your financial potential.

Warning signs include:

- Falling in love at warp speed
- Constant excuses for why he can't meet
- Heart-wrenching stories that always end in requests for money
- Profile details that don't add up
- Pressure to move communication off the dating app

If his love sounds too good to be true, it probably is. Real romance doesn't come with a price tag or a MoneyGram request. Stay savvy, stay skeptical, and keep your heart and your wallet guarded against Faux Romeo and his ilk.

P.S. Real soldiers don't need your gift cards to come home, and genuine love doesn't come with wire transfer instructions.

P.P.S. If Romeo claims he needs money to feed his unit/save his sick child/escape a war zone, remind him that the U.S. Army/oil companies/secret agencies generally frown upon crowdfunding military operations or personal emergencies through dating apps.

The Last Word

Romeo: Your scam is as transparent as your stock photos, and your love stories are as fake as your military credentials. The only thing more pathetic than your attempts at romance is your Google-translated sweet talk. I hope your next 'deployment' is to a prison cell.

Ladies: DANGER - THIS IS A SCAM! When a too-good-to-be-true military doctor with model looks starts love bombing you and can never video chat because he's "in a secret location," block faster than he can say "Western Union." Your heart (and bank account) will thank you.

Chapter 15

THE TAKEAWAY

Having completed our inspection of dating's danger zone, we've witnessed men who aren't just waving red flags, they're hosting full-scale parades with marching bands and confetti cannons! While our dating crusade has shown everyone has quirks, this chapter's examination has documented behaviors that cross from "endearingly flawed" straight into "run for your life" territory.

Lab results confirm these aren't just dealbreakers; they're relationship wrecking balls with neon warning signs that shouldn't be ignored, rationalized, or filtered through rose-colored glasses. The evidence is clear: when your date is flying more red flags than an Olympic opening ceremony, it's time to make like a fire drill and exit quickly.

Red Flags With Sirens Blaring:

Health Hazards:

- Their relationship with alcohol is more committed than they'll ever be to you.

- Their personal hygiene makes public restrooms seem appealing by comparison.

- Their dental work has more gaps than their employment history.

- Their breath could be classified as a biological weapon by the CDC.

Sexual Misconduct:

- Their camera roll contains more unsolicited anatomy than a medical textbook.
- Their fetishes arrive before their introduction and without an invitation.
- Their bathroom selfies come with visible biohazard warnings.
- Their idea of consent is "I sent it, therefore you wanted it."

The Players:

- Their contact list requires color-coding to keep track of simultaneous relationships.
- Their excuse-making skills qualify them for creative writing awards.
- Their phone has more security than Fort Knox for very non-mysterious reasons.
- Their romantic promises expire faster than milk in summer heat.

Criminal Behavior:

- Their parental obligations are treated like optional side quests in a video game.
- Their dating profiles contain more fiction than the fantasy section at the library.
- Their financial requests come disguised as declarations of undying love.
- Their background check results read like a prime-time crime drama.

These aren't just red flags; they're flashing neon warnings of potential disrespect, danger, or disaster. While humor helps us process these dating disasters, the underlying message is deadly serious: your safety, dignity, and well-being should never be compromised for the sake of romance.

Sometimes, the most romantic thing you can do is protect yourself from someone who doesn't deserve you. The right person won't come packaged with warning labels and emergency sirens; they'll respect your boundaries, tell the truth, and treat you with dignity. Accept nothing less!

Chapter 16

THE TOXIC MASCULINITY TROUPE

Let's Set the Scene

NOTE TO READERS: While this chapter employs humor to examine toxic masculine behaviors, I would like to acknowledge the very real danger that these patterns pose. The men profiled here aren't just disappointing dates; they're individuals whose behaviors can lead to emotional trauma, financial harm, and in some cases, physical danger. Toxic masculinity isn't just an inconvenience; it's a harmful system that thrives on control, manipulation, and the diminishment of women's autonomy and worth. If you recognize these patterns from personal experience, please know you're not alone. The resources in Chapter 19 are there to help, and your well-being is always more important than any relationship. Identifying these behaviors early isn't just about avoiding bad dates; it can be a matter of personal safety, self, and emotional preservation.

Welcome to the hall of infamy, where fragile egos meet manipulation tactics in a spectacular display of "how not to human!" In this chapter, we're diving deep into the toxic soup of masculine behavior gone awry, where emotional warfare collides with outdated ideals in an explosive cocktail of red flags.

Think of this as your field guide to the various species of toxic masculinity, each more fascinating (and concerning) than the last. These specimens are organized into five distinct but equally alarming categories:

Our **Emotional Manipulation** experts have mastered the dark arts of psychological warfare. Featuring All-About-Me Alden, whose narcissism is so powerful it has its own gravitational pull; Overwhelming Owen, who love bombs with the subtlety of a glitter explosion; and Projecting Preston, who's developed projection into such a fine art he could open his own IMAX theater.

The **Manipulation Tactics** squad showcases Gaslighting Gus, who can make you doubt whether water is wet; Trust-Issues Troy, whose paranoia has a paranoia of its own; and Silent Silas, who has weaponized the silent treatment into emotional nuclear warfare.

Our **Power & Control** enthusiasts include Alpha Al, whose fragile masculinity requires constant affirmation; Toxic Tom, who spreads emotional radiation wherever he goes; and Jealous Joe, who monitors your movements with the dedication of a stalker with a LinkedIn premium account.

In the **Misogyny & Prejudice** corner, we've got Chauvinist Charlie, still waiting for women to return to the kitchen; Nice-Guy Nick, whose "nice" behavior comes with more strings attached than a puppet show; and Biased Byron, whose prejudices have prejudices.

The **Aggressive Behaviors** bunch introduces us to Angry Angus, a walking emotional landmine; Passive-Aggressive Patrick, who has turned indirect hostility into an Olympic sport; and Bitter Brett, who is so focused on revenge dating that his blood type is "spite positive."

Get ready to traverse this treacherous terrain where toxic masculinity meets emotional manipulation. These aren't just dating profiles – they're cautionary tales wrapped in red flags and seasoned with audacity.

If your gut is sending alarm signals louder than a tornado siren, listen to it! Your instincts are often recognizing danger before your conscious mind has processed all the red flags. Trust that inner voice, it's your emotional security system working overtime to protect you.

Now, let's dissect these specimens and see what we can learn about the fascinating (and horrifying) intersection of toxic masculinity and emotional manipulation. Warning: No egos were spared in the making of this chapter!

Emotional Manipulation

The Narcissistic Cyclone

All-About-Me Alden

Enter master manipulator, Alden, the human embodiment of a hall of mirrors; every reflection shows only him. This walking, talking masterclass in manipulation doesn't just enter your life; he love bombs his way into your heart with the precision of a tactical strike.

Alden's dating profile is a carefully curated highlight reel:

About Me: "Successful entrepreneur/devoted family man/philanthropist seeking a queen who deserves to be worshipped. Let me sweep you off your feet and show you what real love looks like. All my exes were crazy (red flag #1, ladies), but you seem different. You'll never meet anyone like me, I promise."

Photos showcase Alden's manufactured persona: volunteering at charities (for photo ops only), surrounded by admiring friends (his carefully groomed "flying monkeys"), and power poses highlighting his expensive watch and car (all for show). His social proof is impeccable, his charm infectious, and it's all as fake as his promises.

The Alden Experience comes in four acts:

Act 1 (Love Bombing): Prepare to be dazzled by grand gestures, future-faking, and mirroring of your every interest. He'll seem too good to be true (spoiler: he is).

Act 2 (Devaluation): Watch the mask slip as subtle put-downs replace compliments, gaslighting becomes your new normal, and your self-worth is systematically dismantled.

Act 3 (Discard): Brace for the brutal finale where you're vilified and painted as the "crazy ex" while he love bombs his next target, sometimes before officially ending things with you.

Act 4 (The Hoover): Just when you think you're free, he launches an emotional rescue mission to "save" your relationship. The love bombing begins anew, complete with tearful promises of change, grandiose gestures of redemption, and claims that you're the only one who truly understands him. Beware, this is just the prelude to another cycle of manipulation.

First Date: A masterclass in manipulation disguised as the perfect evening. He'll arrive in an expensive car, shower you with flowers, and demonstrate an uncanny knowledge of your interests. The conversation flows like expensive champagne as he mirrors your every passion, while subtly dropping hints about his success, influence, and how his exes "just couldn't handle" his intensity.

Love Language: Love bombing and emotional extortion, with a side of gaslighting for dessert

Attachment Style: Parasitically attached to his reflection and your depleting energy reserves

P.S. In Alden's universe, your sole purpose is to feed his insatiable ego.

Warning: Behind that charismatic smile lurks an emotional vampire who'll drain your joy, twist your reality, and leave you questioning your sanity. Side effects include: anxiety, depression, PTSD, and a complete reconstruction of your self-worth (therapy required).

The Last Word

Alden: Behind your smoke and mirrors lies an empty shell where a soul should be. Your greatest fear isn't being alone, it's being exposed as the fraud you are. No amount of love bombing can fill your bottomless void. You are not the exceptional being you pretend to be; you are a hollow vessel repeating the same manipulative playbook with every woman you date, with a script so predictable that it's become a textbook example.

Ladies: If his charm seems too perfect and his story about "crazy exes" sounds rehearsed, trust your gut. The only crazy thing would be ignoring these red flags. Alden isn't just a swipe left; it's a run for your life. Your mental and physical health, and possibly your life, depend on avoiding this emotional predator. The peace you will feel without his presence in your life is worth being the villain in his story. Your future self and everyone in your life will thank you.

The Love Bomber

Overwhelming Owen

Brace yourself for Owen, the human equivalent of a glitter bomb explosion in a Hallmark store. This walking, talking heart-eyes emoji has turned infatuation into an extreme sport and considers the word "soulmate" appropriate first-date terminology.

Owen's dating profile reads like a romance novel on steroids:

About Me: "Hopeless romantic seeking the love of my life (as of this week). Looking for someone who appreciates grand gestures, constant attention, and plans for our future by the second date. My ideal match? Someone who thinks U-Haul trucks are just mobile dating apps. Swipe right to star in the rom-com of my dreams!"

Photos showcase Owen in his natural habitat: posing with oversized teddy bears amidst a sea of long-stemmed red roses, practicing his proposal stance in various scenic locations, and a "candid" shot of him writing love poetry at sunset.

First Date: A date with Owen is like being caught in a tornado of rose petals and future plans. He'll suggest meeting at "our future wedding venue," arrive with a promise ring and a five-year relationship timeline, and spend the evening plotting your happily ever after. Be prepared for declarations of undying love, impromptu serenades, and at least one attempt to introduce you as his "future spouse" to unsuspecting waitstaff.

Love Language: Overwhelming displays of affection and planning your entire future without consulting you

Attachment Style: Suffocatingly attached, showering affection like confetti cannons until his target's defenses crumble

Owen's gift-giving strategy can only be described as "shock and awe." Expect a barrage of presents ranging from the extravagant (a car after a week of dating) to the eerily presumptuous (monogrammed towels with your shared initials). Romantic dates are less about getting to know you and more about creating Instagram-worthy moments – think private concerts, hot air balloon rides, and recreations of scenes from your favorite rom-coms (which he's memorized after one mention).

Vacations? Owen's planning a world tour before you've even agreed to a second date. He's already got your shared passport photos mocked up and a couple's travel blog set up. As for meeting your family, Owen will charm them faster than you can say "it's too soon." He'll arrive with personalized gifts, inside jokes he's practiced, and a comprehensive PowerPoint presentation outlining why he's the perfect fit for you. Your mom will be planning your wedding before dessert is even served.

In the grand theater of emotional manipulation, Owen is the master of the love bombing act, that intoxicating first phase of narcissistic abuse where he'll drown you in affection until you're too dizzy with devotion to see the red flags. His overwhelming attention isn't love; it's a calculated strategy to fast-track emotional dependency, creating a high so intense that you'll spend the rest of the relationship chasing that initial rush while he holds it just out of reach.

Beware: Owen's love is like a supernova – burning bright and hot before imploding spectacularly. The pedestal he put you on has a trapdoor. Once the initial rush fades, you might find yourself in a whirlwind of devaluation and discard, only for Owen to reappear later, ready to restart the cycle with promises of "this time it's forever."

Dating Owen comes with more red flags than a Chinese parade and the constant feeling that you're drowning in a sea of heart-shaped confetti. Pack your emotional life jacket, and consider having a restraining order on standby.

P.S. Owen's idea of taking it slow is waiting a whole week before having your name tattooed on his arm.

P.P.S. If things progress beyond the first date (heaven help you), expect daily flower deliveries, hourly check-ins, and a scrapbook of your future life together, including names for your hypothetical children. Because in Owen's world, why waste time dating when you can skip straight to suffocating lifelong commitment?

P.P.P.S. In Owen's revised dictionaries, "love" is a verb meaning "to overwhelm and possess," and "forever" is defined as "until I get bored or you set a boundary."

The Last Word

Owen: Your love bombing isn't romance, it's emotional warfare disguised as affection. Behind your grand gestures lies a void so deep that all the roses in the world couldn't fill it. Try therapy instead of treating women like emotional test subjects. The only thing more exhausting than your grand gestures is the inevitable crash when your mask slips and the love bomber turns into a soul destroyer.

Ladies: DANGER! This isn't love, it's the first phase of narcissistic abuse wrapped in romance and tied with trauma bonds. When a man comes on stronger than a CAT-5 hurricane, he's not swept away by love; he's calculating how long it'll take to sweep away your boundaries. This devil wears Valentino, but he'll steal your soul in designer bags. Swipe left faster than this emotional vampire can say 'you're my soulmate!' Your rational boundaries, un-traumatized psyche, and untethered soul will thank you.

The Accusation Mirror

Projecting Preston

Mirror, mirror on the wall: Preston, the human embodiment of "I know you are, but what am I?" This walking, talking IMAX of insecurities has turned psychological projection into an extreme sport and considers self-reflection a concept as foreign as accountability.

Preston's dating profile reads like a list of qualities he desperately wishes he had:

About Me: "Seeking an honest, faithful partner who doesn't play games. Tired of cheaters and liars. Looking for someone trustworthy who values transparency and open communication. If you have nothing to hide, we'll get along great!"

Photos showcase Preston in his natural habitat: squinting suspiciously at the camera, caught mid-argument with an unseen person, and a "candid" shot of him checking his partner's phone when they're not looking. His attempt at a trustworthy pic? A selfie with his "best friend," who looks suspiciously uncomfortable.

Dating Preston comes with a free masterclass in gaslighting and enough projection to open your own cinema! Pack your patience, a lie detector, and maybe a mirror to hold up when he starts accusing you of his behaviors.

First Date: A date with Preston is like being cross-examined by a paranoid prosecutor. He'll suggest meeting somewhere he can watch the door (to catch you sneaking in your "other date"), arrive with a list of questions about your recent whereabouts, and spend the evening accusing you of flirting with the waiter. Be prepared for demands to see your phone, interrogations about your social media activity, and at least one accusation of cheating because you took too long in the restroom.

Love Language: Accusing you of everything he's guilty of and demanding reassurance for his misdeeds

Attachment Style: Defectively attached, treating his red flags like party favors to pin on others

Every accusation from Preston is a confession in disguise. When he's suddenly obsessed with the idea you're cheating, check his text messages. His accusations are a perfectly polished mirror, reflecting his behavior; each paranoid suspicion is a breadcrumb trail leading straight to his latest transgression. This isn't just projection; it's psychological warfare designed to keep you defensive while he operates in the shadows of his accusations.

While Preston's insecurities might initially masquerade as concern or attentiveness, in the world of emotional manipulation, every accusation is a confession. With Preston, you're not just dating him, you're dating every insecurity and misdeed he's trying to hide from himself.

P.S. Preston's idea of trust involves sharing your location 24/7 and granting full access to all your passwords.

P.P.S. If you somehow make it to a second date, expect a full report on all the ways you've supposedly wronged him since your last meeting, each one a thinly veiled confession of his misdeeds.

The Last Word

Preston: Your accusations are as transparent as your projections. Every finger you point has three pointing back at you, and your paranoia is just your guilt wearing a disguise. Try looking in a mirror instead of making others reflect your sins. The only thing more exhausting than your constant accusations is knowing each one is just a preview of your subsequent betrayal.

Ladies: When a man's accusations sound suspiciously specific, they're usually confessions in disguise. His projection is a preview of his transgressions; believe him when he tells on himself. Swipe left faster than Preston can say "Who are you texting?" because by the time he's accusing you of cheating, he's already changed his phone password twice. Your honest heart and clear conscience will thank you.

Manipulation Tactics

The Reality Reviser

Gaslighting Gus

Question your reality with Gus, the man who could convince you the sky is green and it's your fault for not noticing sooner. This walking, talking manipulator has turned reality distortion into an art form, making you question everything from your memories to your sanity.

Gus' profile reads like a psychological thriller's plot synopsis written by an unreliable narrator, where every word is as twisted as his version of reality, and truth is just a suggestion he'll edit later:

About Me: "Seeking someone who appreciates my unique perspective on reality. Looking for a partner who's open to... reinterpretation of facts. If you think something happened one way, let me explain why your memory is wrong and how it's probably your fault anyway. Trust me, I'm always right, even when I'm lying."

Photos showcase Gus in his manipulative habitat: perfectly curated shots that tell half-truths, group photos where he's always the victim of others' "misunderstandings," and carefully staged scenes that he'll later deny ever happened. His candid shots? They're about as genuine as his apologies.

In Gus's world, reality is whatever he says it is today, subject to change tomorrow. He doesn't just bend the truth; he breaks it, reshapes it, and convinces you the broken pieces were your fault. His specialty? Any scenario that he can later rewrite to fit his narrative, preferably without witnesses.

First Date: He'll make plans, show up late, then convince you that you got the time wrong, somehow making you apologize for it

Love Language: Subtle manipulation, reality revision, and making you doubt your own judgment while positioning himself as your only truth compass

Attachment Style: Deceptively attached to his alternative facts and your diminishing grip on reality

The Last Word

Gus: Your version of reality isn't just twisted, it's toxic. The only thing more manipulative than your lies is your attempt to make others believe them. The truth doesn't need constant revision, and neither do your victims' memories.

Ladies: When a man has more versions of events than a fiction writer and makes you question your memories more than a psychological thriller, swipe left and run faster than he can say "that's not how it happened." Your reality is valid, your memories are real, and his manipulation isn't your imagination. Trust your gut, it's the one thing he can't gaslight, and it will thank you.

The Paranoid Paramour

Trust-Issues Troy

Paranoid and proud: Troy, the human embodiment of a tin foil hat. This guy's trust issues have trust issues. He's not just guarded; he's got more walls than a medieval fortress and enough red flags to outfit a Soviet parade.

Troy's dating profile is a masterpiece of vague non-information, reading like a legal disclaimer with more fine print than a pharmaceutical advertisement.

About Me: "Looking for someone honest*" (*Terms and conditions apply. Honesty will be vigorously tested and disputed). Must be willing to provide hourly updates, location sharing, and a detailed dossier of past relationships (with references). Looking for someone who enjoys spontaneous phone checks and doesn't mind explaining every male name in their contacts. Please note: All responses will be fact-checked against your social media history.

His photos? All taken from mysterious angles that could be him... or Bigfoot.

Every answer you give will be stored, cross-referenced, and used against you in future interrogations. His trust issues aren't just baggage; they're a carefully crafted tool to keep you constantly on the defensive, forever proving your innocence to a self-appointed judge who's already decided you're guilty.

In Troy's world, every ex is a potential spy, every text message a coded threat, and every friendly smile a mask for nefarious intentions. He doesn't just carry baggage; he's got a whole luggage store of past relationship trauma that he's more than happy to make your problem.

First Date: Troy is less a conversationalist and more an amateur detective. He cross-examines your every statement like a caffeinated lawyer. "You say you're a dog person, but I noticed cat hair on your jacket. EXPLAIN YOURSELF!" His idea of small talk is demanding alibis for your whereabouts last Tuesday.

Love Language: Background checks and GPS tracking, with a side of surveillance photos to show he cares

Attachment Style: Suspiciously attached to his conspiracy theories about your girls' night out

Troy's paranoia isn't just fear; it's a weapon. He'll use your attempts to reassure him as proof of deception, turn your transparency into "suspiciously perfect behavior," and transform your patience into evidence that you're "too good to be true."

Swipe right if you enjoy feeling like you're constantly under surveillance, don't mind providing DNA samples to prove your whereabouts, and think that a healthy relationship is built on a foundation of suspicion and impromptu lie detector tests.

P.S. If you match with Troy, be prepared for dates that feel more like CIA interrogations. In Troy's world, "I trust you" is just another way of saying "I haven't caught you... yet."

The Last Word

Troy: Your trust issues aren't a personality trait; they're a self-fulfilling prophecy. Keep treating everyone like they're guilty until proven innocent, and you'll end up exactly where you fear: alone with your suspicions.

Ladies: No amount of proof will ever be enough for someone who's already convicted you in the court of his insecurities. Swipe left faster than Troy can question your story, and before you become another exhibit in his case file of paranoia. Your daily peace and personal freedom will thank you.

The Silent Treatment Specialist

Silent Silas

Say hello to the cold shoulder specialist, Silas, the human embodiment of emotional warfare through silence. This walking, talking void has weaponized the silent treatment into a signature move of manipulation, shame, and control.

Silas's dating profile is a masterclass in emotional manipulation disguised as mystery, where every carefully crafted silence hints at the psychological warfare to come.

About Me: "Seeking someone who appreciates the power of silence. I'm not ignoring you; I'm just giving you time to think about what you did wrong. Master of meaningful pauses and emotional withholding. If you can't handle me at my quietest, you don't deserve me at my loudest."

Photos showcase Silas in his natural habitat: brooding silently by windows, giving meaningful looks that scream "you should know what you did," and mastering the art of appearing present while being emotionally absent.

First Date: A date with Silas is like playing emotional Russian roulette. One wrong word, one "attitude" he doesn't like, and suddenly you're trapped in a void of silence so deep it has its own gravity. Be prepared for days of unanswered texts, ignored calls, and the special kind of psychological torture that comes from being treated like you've ceased to exist.

Love Language: Emotional radio silence and calculated communication blackouts

Attachment Style: Punitively attached to his silent arsenal, wielding the cold shoulder like it's an Olympic sport

The silent treatment isn't just his response to conflict; it's his favorite tool for punishment, manipulation, and control. He'll withhold affection, communication, and basic acknowledgment until you're begging for forgiveness for crimes you didn't know you committed.

P.S. If you match with Silas, be prepared for a relationship where silence isn't golden, it's weaponized. In Silas's world, your voice only matters when it's saying exactly what he wants to hear.

The Last Word

To Silas: Your silence speaks volumes about your emotional cowardice. Real men use words; manipulators use silence as a weapon. The only thing more pathetic than your communication skills is your need to control through absence.

Ladies: The silent treatment isn't just annoying, it's a form of abuse designed to shame, manipulate, and control. Don't let his silence drown out your self-worth. Swipe left on this emotional terrorist faster than Silas can ghost you. Your unsilenced spirit will thank you.

Power & Control

The Testosterone Tyrant

Alpha Al

Enter top dog, Al, whose idea of foreplay is flexing in the mirror and growling. He thinks "The Wolf of Wall Street" is a documentary and "How to Win Friends and Influence People" is for losers. His favorite hobby? Mansplaining feminism to feminists. Al has definitely roared at his reflection... more than once.

Al's profile is a testosterone-soaked manifesto where toxic masculinity meets fragile ego, written with all the subtlety of a monster truck rally hosted by a caveman.

About Me: "Real Alpha Male seeking submissive female to worship my greatness. I'm the top dog, the big cheese, the head honcho. If you can't handle me at my most dominant, you don't deserve me at my... well, I'm always dominant. Beta males need not interact with my females. Looking for a woman who knows her place (which is always a step behind me). Must be able to stroke my ego as well as iron my shirts."

Al runs his relationships like a dictatorship, where "compromise" is just a ten-letter word he can't spell. He considers any differing opinion a challenge to his authority and thinks eye contact is a dominance contest. Al's so controlling, he argues with his GPS and tries to alpha-stare his coffee maker into brewing faster.

Al's treatment of service staff is a masterclass in dominance display. Waiters are 'buddy' or 'chief,' baristas are 'sweetheart,' and heaven help the delivery person who forgets his extra sauce. He tips based on subservience levels rather than the quality of service.

When you accomplish something impressive, Al either dismisses it ('that's cute') or somehow takes credit ('my motivation techniques are working on you'). Your successes aren't yours; they're either threats to his supremacy or trophies for his influence.

First Date: Prepare for a masterclass in male superiority. At dinner, he'll order for you without asking (because "alpha males know best"). Don't worry about choosing the wine, Alpha Al already knows what you like better than you do. He'll interrupt every sentence you manage to begin, and spend the evening talking about his "pack" (his gym buddies) and how he's the leader of everything from his fantasy football league to the office water cooler crowd. After dinner, you'll be graced with a guided tour of his man cave, complete with a protein shake bar, motivational posters featuring lions, and a wall dedicated to his supplement collection. He'll then expect gratitude for his overwhelming presence and a detailed acknowledgment of his superior existence.

Love Language: Dominance displays and unsolicited lectures about male superiority

Attachment Style: Toxically attached to his perceived dominance and his dog-eared copy of '48 Laws of Power

The Last Word

Al: Hey there, Simba! I see you're still trying to mark your territory all over the dating scene. Here's a wild idea: try being an actual human being instead of a walking, talking protein shake with daddy issues. You might find that people enjoy your company more when you're not constantly trying to flex your ego in everyone's face. Oh, and by the way, real wolves don't have alphas in the wild; that study was debunked. But you knew that, being so alpha and all, right? Don't let facts challenge your fragile masculinity!

Ladies: This isn't just a red flag, it's a five-alarm fire in a red flag factory. When a man's personality is more toxic than a nuclear waste dump and his ego is more fragile than wet tissue paper, swipe left faster than Al can assert his dominance over a houseplant. Your independence, self-respect, and untamed spirit will thank you.

Radioactive Romeo

Toxic Tom

Grab your hazmat suit one more time and welcome Tom, the human equivalent of a nuclear waste dump disguised as a dating profile. This maestro of mayhem doesn't just have baggage; he's got a whole toxic waste treatment facility strapped to his back.

Tom's dating profile is a masterclass in red flags, each one waving more vigorously than the last:

About Me: "Looking for a drama-free relationship (unlike my exes, who were all crazy). Must be okay with mood swings, occasional outbursts, and my unresolved anger issues. Every ex has a restraining order, and every story has a villain (spoiler alert: it's never me). Bonus points if you enjoy psychological warfare disguised as 'passionate love. No gold diggers or feminists!"

In Tom's world, every interaction is an opportunity for emotional whiplash. He doesn't just have mood swings; he's got mood bungee jumps. One minute he's love bombing you harder than a Hallmark movie marathon, the next he's colder than a penguin's popsicle.

A conversation with Tom is like navigating a minefield while blindfolded and on roller skates. He doesn't just talk; he unleashes a torrent of backhanded compliments, not-so-subtle jabs, and enough gaslighting to light up a small city. His go-to phrases include "You're overreacting" and "I'm just being honest."

Tom is a boundary-testing specialist, pushing small limits to see what he can get away with. He'll forget your clearly stated rules, show up unannounced when you've asked for space, or contact your friends when you don't respond fast enough, all while acting like you're overreacting when called out. He's cultivated a loyal circle of enablers who only hear his carefully edited versions of events. These friends are ready to text you, 'he's really hurting, just talk to him' after he's reduced you to tears, reinforcing his distorted reality where he's always the victim, never the villain.

First Date: Hope you enjoy emotional rollercoasters, because you're in for a wild ride. He doesn't just pick you up; he arrives 30 minutes late, blames you for his tardiness, then expects gratitude for gracing you with his presence.

Love Language: Tom's love language isn't words of affirmation or acts of service; it's a complex dialect of subtle manipulation, with a side of guilt trips and a sprinkle of intermittent reinforcement. He doesn't just play hard to get; he plays impossible to please, with a rulebook that changes more often than he changes his socks.

Attachment Style: Hazardously attached, requires a warning label and environmental impact study

P.S. Swipe right if you enjoy walking on eggshells, have always wanted to star in your own psychological thriller, and think that "peace" is highly overrated.

P.P.S. If you match with Tom, be prepared for a relationship that feels like you're constantly defusing a bomb while juggling flaming torches. In Tom's universe, "I'm sorry" is just a brief intermission before the next act in his drama-fueled production. Don't forget your hazmat suit!

The Last Word

Tom: Your toxicity levels are so high, Chernobyl called, they want their radiation back. No hazmat suit in the world can protect anyone from your radioactive personality.

Ladies: This isn't a red flag, it's a nuclear warning alarm. Swipe left faster than you'd evacuate a toxic waste spill, because this man's emotional fallout has a half-life longer than his last relationship. Your sanity, serenity, and emotional stability will thank you.

The Possessive Puppeteer

Jealous Joe

Possessively yours, it's Joe, the human embodiment of a clingy octopus. His love language? Surveillance. His hobby? Keeping tabs on your every move. Joe doesn't want a partner; he wants a personal hostage.

Joe's dating profile is a maximum-security prison disguised as a love story, where every word screams' trust issues' louder than his midnight texts asking why you were active on Instagram three hours ago.

About Me: "Devoted partner seeking my one and only (emphasis on ONLY). Looking for someone who understands that real love means sharing everything - your location, phone passwords, and complete social calendar. Your friends miss you? Too bad, they're probably plotting to break us up."

Photos showcase Joe's "protective" nature: strategically positioned to mark his territory, hovering in the background of every social interaction, and giving suspicious side-eyes to any male within a 50-mile radius.

A relationship with Joe involves you, him, and absolutely no one else. He treats your social circle like a particularly aggressive strain of the plague. Friends? Family? To Joe, they're all potential rivals in the Olympic sport of Monopolizing Your Attention.

Got plans with the girls? Watch Joe transform into a one-man soap opera, complete with dramatic sighs and Oscar-worthy guilt trips. He'll make you feel like you're abandoning a puppy in the rain...for years...on its birthday.

Joe's phone tracking skills would impress the CIA. He's not stalking; he's "just checking in" - every five minutes. He'll text you more often than you blink, each message a thinly veiled attempt to ensure you're not having too much fun without him.

In Joe's world, trust is a four-letter word, and your independence is a personal insult. He's not controlling; he thinks your life should revolve around him, as if he's the sun and you're an exceptionally devoted planet.

Joe's masterful at disguising isolation as devotion. 'Quality time together' gradually replaces all other activities until your world shrinks to just the two of you. Meanwhile, his double standards operate on Olympic levels – he maintains friendships, hobbies, and social media connections that would trigger a three-day interrogation if they were yours. His phone remains face down and password protected, while yours sits on the coffee table, unlocked and available for 'random' checks. Remember: it's not 'control' – it's 'caring enough to know your every move.

First Date: A date with Joe is like being under house arrest with a particularly clingy warden. He'll insist on vetting every text message, monitoring your social media like it's his job, and turning every innocent interaction into an imagined betrayal.

Love Language: Surveillance with a side of emotional blackmail.

Attachment Style: Parasitically attached, treating trust like it's a mythical creature and your phone like it's his personal surveillance system

P.S. If you match with Joe, invest in a clone. It's the only way you'll manage to be in two places at once - with him and living your actual life.

P.P.S. If you decide to date Joe, prepare for your world to shrink faster than a wool sweater in hot water. In Joe's universe, trust is a myth, and your independence is a threat to his control.
Remember, Joe's not insecure; he thinks love means never having to say, "I trust you to have a life outside of me."

The Last Word

Joe: Your jealousy isn't love - it's a prison you've built from your own insecurities. The tighter you grip, the more you'll end up alone, watching everyone escape your emotional jail cell. The only thing more exhausting than your constant surveillance is the mental gymnastics you do to justify it - try channeling that energy into actual therapy instead of tracking apps.

Ladies: Joe's jealousy isn't flattering; it's the first step toward complete isolation. Run before your world becomes as small as his capacity to trust. **This isn't protection - it's possession.** Swipe left faster than Joe can say "Who's that guy?" Your friendships, family ties, and breathing room will thank you.

Misogyny & Prejudice

The Misogynist

Chauvinist Charlie

Mansplaining his way in, it's Charlie, the human embodiment of a dusty time capsule from an era best left behind. This walking, talking anachronism has turned gender roles into a religion and considers women's rights a personal affront to his fragile masculinity.

Charlie's dating profile reads like a 1950s want ad for a housewife:

About Me: "Traditional gentleman seeking a real woman who knows her place (preferably in the kitchen). Looking for a partner who appreciates a man who brings home the bacon and doesn't mind if he acts like a pig. Must be comfortable with silently nodding, laughing at all my jokes, and having your opinions gently corrected. Swipe right if you're ready to travel back in time to the good ol' days!"

Photos showcase Charlie in his natural habitat: mansplaining at a women's rights rally, flexing in front of his vintage Playboy collection, and a "candid" shot of him looking confused in the feminine hygiene aisle. His attempt at a charming pic? A forced smile next to a BBQ grill, caption reading "King of my castle, looking for my queen to serve me!"

His social media is a treasure trove of 'women in the kitchen' memes and angry rants about how men are the 'real victims' in modern society. He religiously follows podcasters who specialize in 'traditional masculinity' and has bookmarked more anti-feminist videos than cooking tutorials."

First Date: A date with Charlie is like being trapped in a Mad Men episode without the stylish outfits or witty dialogue. He'll insist on picking you up (women can't be trusted to drive themselves), arrive in a cloud of overwhelming cologne, and spend the evening enlightening you about how the world works. He'll order for you without asking – always the lightest salad option on the menu, because 'no man wants a woman who doesn't watch her figure.' The evening's conversation will include his unsolicited rankings of women in the restaurant and cherished anecdotes about how his mother catered to his father's every need – the blueprint for his dream relationship. Be prepared for unsolicited opinions on everything from politics to portion sizes, backhanded compliments about how you're "not like other girls," and at least one anecdote that starts with "Now, I'm not sexist, but..."

Love Language: Condescension disguised as chivalry and "compliments" that sound suspiciously like orders

Attachment Style: Securely attached to his 1950s mindset and the belief that feminism is a four-letter word

Behind closed doors, Charlie's sexism evolves from annoying to alarming. Disagreements aren't discussions – they're 'female hysteria.' Your career accomplishments are diminished with comments like 'that's cute that they let you lead a project.' He'll regularly remind you of your 'biological clock' and how your purpose is really to nurture his legacy, not build your own.

P.S. Charlie's idea of foreplay is asking you to fetch his slippers while he manspreads on the couch.

P.P.S. If things get serious, expect a proposal that comes with a pre-nuptial agreement stipulating your domestic duties and a resignation letter for your job. Because in Charlie's world, a woman's career is just a cute hobby until she finds a man to support her! A woman having her own opinion is like a fish needing a bicycle, wholly unnecessary and mildly offensive to his sensibilities.

The Last Word

Charlie: Your misogyny isn't 'traditional values', it's prehistoric garbage that belongs in the same dumpster as your outdated ideology. The 1950s called; they don't want you back either. Even cavemen were more evolved.

Ladies: If you want to experience the 1950s, watch a documentary, don't date one. Swipe left faster than Charlie can say, "Actually, let me explain women's rights to you." Your equal rights, hard-won freedoms, and the entire women's movement will thank you

The Closet Misogynist

Nice-Guy Nick

Look! It's not-so-nice guy Nick, the human embodiment of a wolf in sheep's clothing. This walking, talking red flag has turned subtle sexism into a skill and considers his "nice guy" status a free pass for problematic behavior.

Nick's dating profile reads like a masterclass in misdirection:

About Me: "Genuine nice guy seeking a traditional girl who appreciates chivalry. Looking for someone who understands that real men still exist. My ideal match? A sweet, undemanding woman who knows her worth (but not too much). Swipe right if you're tired of jerks and ready for a true gentleman!"

Photos showcase Nick in his carefully curated habitat, helping elderly ladies cross the street, caught mid-volunteer work at animal shelters, and a 'candid' shot of him cooking (caption: "Real men cook!"). His attempt at a masculine pic? A gym selfie with a suspiciously long, self-deprecating caption about inner beauty.

First Date: A date with Nick starts charming but quickly reveals underlying issues. He'll suggest a nice restaurant (where he knows the maitre d'), arrive with flowers, and spend the evening alternating between compliments and subtle put-downs disguised as concerns. Be prepared for unsolicited advice about your life choices, thinly veiled judgments about your independence, and at least one comment about his antiquated view of women's "place" in society.

Love Language: Backhanded compliments and weaponized "kindness"

Attachment Style: Toxically attached to his "nice guy" badge and collection of hidden misogyny

Dating Nick comes with a one-way ticket to a world where your worth is measured by your waist size and dinner-table silence. Pack your feminist literature (but keep it hidden) and maybe have a time machine on standby for a quick escape back to the 21st century! Nick's "nice guy" facade often hides deeper issues. His compliments come with conditions, and his chivalry has a dark side.

Side effects of engaging with Nick may include: a sudden urge to burn your bra, an encyclopedic knowledge of logical fallacies from countering his arguments, and a newfound appreciation for the progress women have made in the last 70 years. Proceed with extreme caution, or better yet, don't proceed at all.

The Last Word

Nick: Your 'nice guy' act is as transparent as your fragile ego. Real nice guys don't need to announce it, and real gentlemen don't keep a scorecard of their 'kindness.' The only thing genuine about you is your entitlement. Perhaps try being genuinely nice instead of using kindness as a means to exert control.

Ladies: Swipe left on this walking red flag factory and run faster than Nick can say "Make me a sandwich"! Better yet, BLOCK this toxic POS. Your uncompromising standards and emotional well-being will thank you.

The Prejudiced Profiler

Biased Byron

Close-minded and proud, here's Byron, a man whose narrow-mindedness is matched only by his ignorance. Byron doesn't just have preferences; he has poorly disguised prejudices that he tries to pass off as "just having a type."

Byron's dating profile is a minefield of red flags and contains coded language and dog whistles that make more open-minded people cringe:

About Me: "Seeking someone who shares my 'traditional' values. You know what I mean! Must appreciate my 'refined tastes' and understand that some differences just can't be bridged. If you have to ask what I mean, you're probably not my type; I'm just trying to preserve my heritage and values!"

His photos showcase a life devoid of diversity, each image more homogeneous than the last.

In Byron's world, every interaction is an opportunity to make sweeping generalizations and unfounded assumptions. He doesn't just chat; he interrogates, probing for information to confirm his preconceived notions. His idea of getting to know someone involves asking inappropriate questions about their background and making offensive "jokes" to test boundaries.

Byron's prejudiced views severely limit his dating pool and life experiences. He misses out on meaningful connections due to his baseless biases. His dates often end abruptly when his true colors show, leaving him confused and bitter.

First (and last) Date: For Byron, it's less about the activity and more about vetting his date's background to ensure it aligns with his narrow worldview

Love Language: Micro-aggressions and thinly veiled "preferences"

Attachment Style: Selectively attached to his prejudices and the belief that his dating "preferences" aren't just thinly veiled bigotry

P.S. If you match with Byron, be prepared for an uncomfortable experience that will likely end with you educating him on why his views are problematic (if you have the energy) or simply walking away. In Byron's universe, "Netflix and chill" means watching documentaries that reinforce his biases while making offensive commentary.

Note: Byron's behavior is not to be emulated. His character serves as a cautionary tale about the harmful effects of prejudice in dating and life.

The Last Word

Byron: Your 'preferences' aren't a dating filter, they're a reflection of your prejudiced soul. While you're busy judging others, the world is moving forward without you, leaving you and your bigotry in history's trash heap where they belong.

Ladies: Zero discussion needed. Swipe left faster than Byron can say "I'm not prejudiced, but..." Your moral compass, diverse friendships, and humanity will thank you.

Aggressive Behaviors

The Emotional Landmine

Angry Angus

If you're a glutton for punishment and are searching for a guy who will constantly remind you of his glory days (aka the 90s) and complain about how his ex-wife ruined his life, then step right up!

Angus's profile is a minefield of misery where every word screams 'unprocessed trauma' and reads like a therapy intake form crossed with a hazmat warning.

About Me: "I'm a walking, talking emotional minefield, pre-loaded with enough trust issues, cynicism, and baggage to fill a U-Haul. I'll happily regale you with tales of my failed marriage and how the modern dating world is full of gold-digging harpies who are only after my money (which my ex-wife cleaned out, by the way). Hope you're good at walking on eggshells, because I'm easily triggered and my mood can turn on a dime!"

Proceed with extreme caution; this fragile ego doesn't take kindly to any perceived slights or attempts to bring positivity into his life. Swipe right if you're a sucker for punishment and have a burning desire to be his emotional punching bag!

Angus is the embodiment of the "Hurt People, Hurt People" philosophy; his toxicity and volatility are a direct result of his unresolved pain and insecurities. Proceed with extreme caution, and don't be afraid to cut and run at the first sign of this emotional landmine going off!

First Date: Your date with Angus will feel like you are navigating a veritable minefield of potential explosions. Any innocent comment or question could set him off on a bitter, angry rant about how women are untrustworthy, the dating world is rigged against men, or how his ex-wife ruined his life.

Love Language: Dramatic Sighs and Moody Eye Rolls

Attachment Style: Triggered attachment, like a human landmine with a hair-trigger and zero warning signs

P.S. Angus comes pre-loaded with a heavy dose of entitlement, so he'll expect you to prove your loyalty from day one. Heaven forbid you make him feel insecure in any way; you'll pay for it with nonstop backhanded comments and accusations.

The Last Word

Angus: Your bitterness isn't a personality trait, it's a warning label. Try trading that chip on your shoulder for some therapy sessions. The only thing more explosive than your temper is how fast potential dates run away.

Ladies: Swipe left faster than Angus can say "my ex-wife." Unless you're looking to star in your own emotional horror movie, this ticking time bomb of trauma isn't worth the inevitable explosion. Your emotional and physical safety will thank you.

The Snide Sniper

Passive-Aggressive Patrick

It's time to encounter Patrick, a man who's turned indirect hostility into a talent. This maestro of masked malice doesn't just have a chip on his shoulder; he's got an entire bag of passive-aggressive potato chips, and he's serving them with a side of thinly veiled contempt.

Patrick's dating profile is a masterclass in backhanded compliments:

About Me: "Looking for someone who can handle a real man. No drama queens (unlike my ex) or high-maintenance princesses (you know who you are). Honesty is important to me, so I'll just say what everyone's thinking."

In Patrick's world, every interaction is an opportunity for a subtle dig. He doesn't just ask how your day was; he inquires with a raised eyebrow and a "Hope it was better than mine. Some of us have real jobs, you know." His idea of a compliment? "Wow, you look almost as good as my ex today. Almost."

A conversation with Patrick is like navigating a minefield of disguised insults and guilt trips. He doesn't argue; he sighs heavily and mutters, "It's fine. I'm used to disappointment." His go-to phrase? "I'm just saying..." followed by something that absolutely didn't need to be said.

His aggression comes gift-wrapped in "just kidding" and "no offense, but..." packages, each barb carefully crafted to maintain plausible deniability while inflicting maximum damage. When called out, he'll weaponize phrases like "you're too sensitive" or "I was just being honest," the classic armor of the passive-aggressive warrior.

First Date: Hope you enjoy a side of emotional manipulation with your dinner. He doesn't suggest a restaurant; he insinuates that your choice would be subpar anyway. "We can go where you want. I'm sure it'll be... interesting."

Love Language: It isn't words of affirmation; it's words of subtle undermining. He believes that if a jab isn't wrapped in a layer of plausible deniability, it's not worth throwing. He's not upset; he's "disappointed", a word he uses more often than most people say "hello".

Attachment Style: Indirectly attached to his arsenal of sighs, eye-rolls, and "whatever" responses

Swipe right if you enjoy constantly reading between the lines, don't mind feeling vaguely insulted but can't quite put your finger on why, and think that "honest communication" is overrated anyway.

P.S. If you match with Patrick, be prepared for dates that feel like you're constantly apologizing, but you're not sure why. In Patrick's universe, "No, really, it's fine" means anything but fine, and you'll be hearing about it in subtle jabs for the next six months!

The Last Word

Patrick: Your passive aggression isn't clever, it's cowardice with a smile. Everyone who experiences your verbal daggers knows that 'no offense, but...' is just your shield for inflicting maximum damage. No offense, but... maybe you should work on that. Just saying! Oh, and by the way, that heavy sigh you're about to heave? It's as transparent as your tactics.

Ladies: Life's too short for men who make art out of subtle cruelty. A relationship shouldn't feel like a game of emotional dodgeball with someone too cowardly to throw straight. Swipe left faster than Patrick can say "I'm just saying..." Your emotional clarity and snark-free life will thank you. Just saying!

The Revenge Dater

Bitter Brett

Last, but certainly not least, it's Brett, the man who's turned heartbreak into an extreme sport. This walking, talking breakup ballad doesn't just have baggage; he's got a whole emotional luggage store that he's desperately trying to unpack on every date.

Brett's dating profile is a thinly veiled cry for vindication.

About Me: "Recently single (not my fault!). Looking for someone to show my ex what she's missing. Must be hotter, smarter, and more successful than Satan in a skirt. Bonus points if you're friends with her on social media."

His photos are a passive-aggressive gallery: Brett looking sad at places he used to visit with his ex, Brett with his "better off single" t-shirt, Brett forcing a smile next to his newly adopted cat (named "Freedom").

Brett's bitterness isn't just a phase; it's a weaponized worldview. Each new relationship is ammunition in his war against past hurts. His anger has become a self-fulfilling prophecy: divorce made him bitter, bitterness drives away new partners, and new rejections fuel more bitterness. He's not dating; he's recruiting soldiers for his vendetta against love itself.

First Date: A tour of all the places he used to go with his ex, but now with you (upgraded version, obviously), making sure to take plenty of photos for social media. Don't forget to look ecstatically happy!

Love Language: Mutual ex-bashing, strategic social media posts, and the ability to listen to his "can you believe she did that?" stories for the hundredth time

Attachment Style: Vengefully attached to his ex's Instagram and his "all women are evil" manifesto

Brett's aggression masquerades as justified anger, but beneath the "wronged man" facade lies a calculated desire to make everyone else feel as damaged as he does. Every date is both a battlefield and an audience for his pain. He doesn't just converse; he vents, turning every topic into a referendum on his past relationship. His idea of moving on? Obsessively checking his ex's social media and interpreting every post as a secret message to him.

P.S. If you match with Brett, be prepared for dates that feel like you're starring in a very bitter rom-com. In Brett's universe, "Netflix and chill" means watching their old favorite shows while he provides bitter commentary on how his ex never really understood the deeper themes.

The Last Word

Brett: Your bitterness isn't a personality trait; it's a prison you've built from divorce papers and alimony checks. While you're busy plotting revenge against your past, your future is swiping left on your present. Try therapy instead of turning dates into depositions. The only thing more exhausting than your revenge fantasies is watching you audition new actresses for your victim story.

Ladies: Save yourself from becoming another chapter in Brett's book of grievances. When a man's emotional baggage has its own zip code and his bitterness has custody of his personality, it's time to swipe left faster than he can say "my ex-wife's attorney." Your self-esteem and drama-free life will thank you.

Chapter 16

THE TAKEAWAY

As we conclude our tour through the Toxic Masculinity Museum, it's time for an exit interview about what we've witnessed. Our expedition has examined specimens that should be kept behind glass (or better yet, in therapy) instead of roaming free in the dating pool. These profiles haven't just showcased difficult personalities; our research confirms they're emotional hazmat situations requiring full protective gear.

Red Flags With Danger Labels:

Emotional Manipulation Masters:

- They love bomb you like they're trying to set a Guinness World Record for excessive gifting.

- Their empathy levels make a brick wall look emotionally available.

- They rewrite reality more frequently than software updates.

- Their emotional consistency makes weather campaign promises look reliable.

- They can find your insecurities faster than Google can complete your search.

Manipulation Strategy Experts:

- They create instant intimacy that feels as authentic as a $3 bill.
- They use silence as a weapon more effective than any words.
- They rush to rescue you from problems they probably created.
- They manufacture drama as if it were their full-time job.
- Their guilt trips could earn frequent-flyer miles.

Power & Control Commanders:

- Their ego is so fragile that it should come with bubble wrap.
- They think "compromise" is just a fancy word for "do it my way."
- Their idea of a partnership looks suspiciously like a dictatorship.
- They monitor your movements more closely than a helicopter parent.
- They believe the 1950s wasn't a decade but a relationship manual.

Misogyny & Prejudice Promoters:

- They've mistaken women's rights for a personal attack.
- Their worldview is so narrow that you could slide it under a door.
- They dismiss your opinions faster than spam email.
- They view women as decorative accessories rather than human beings.

- They think equality means they're being oppressed.

Aggressive Behavior Specialists:

- Their emotional range runs from "mildly irritated" to "nuclear meltdown."
- They've perfected passive aggression into a performance art.
- Their reaction predictability rivals a slot machine.
- They consider intimidation a communication style.
- They treat apologies like rare diamonds, nearly impossible to find.

These toxic behaviors aren't just annoying quirks; they're danger signs illuminated with stadium lighting. Real masculinity isn't about domination, control, or emotional warfare; it's about respect, partnership, and the radical notion that women are actual human beings.

If you've survived a relationship with any of these types, your resilience deserves a standing ovation. The good news? Once you can identify these red flags, they become impossible to unsee, making your next dating decision infinitely clearer. Your emotional well-being, self-respect, and future happiness will thank you for recognizing these patterns and showing these toxic types the door.

Chapter 17

THE GREEN FLAG GALLERY

Let's Set the Scene

Welcome to The Green Flag Gallery, where red flags fear to tread and healthy relationships bloom like well-tended gardens! In this chapter, we're showcasing the cream of the crop, the diamonds in the rough, the men who make you wonder if you've accidentally stumbled into a romance novel (but in a good way).

Our **Stability Superstars** have mastered the art of reliable adulthood without the boring side effects. Welcome Brilliantly Balanced Brian, who juggles life's demands with the grace of a Zen master, Dependable Don, who shows up so reliably you could set your watch by him, and Future-Focused Frank, who plans for tomorrow without forgetting to live for today.

The **Growth Gurus** demonstrate that evolution isn't just for Darwin's finches. Watch as Curious Chris collects interests like some collect shoes, Evolving Evan transforms self-improvement from a chore to a lifestyle, and Nurturing Nathan proves that real men don't fear emotional labor or perfectly executed pigtail braids.

Our **Emotional Intelligence Elite** showcase what happens when feelings aren't treated like inconvenient explosives. Honest Abraham demonstrates that vulnerability isn't just brave, it's downright attractive. Consent Conner respects boundaries better than most respect speed limits, and Respectful Ryan proves that chivalry isn't dead, it just evolved past opening doors to listening when you speak.

These relationship role models have turned the dating world into a beacon of hope, leaving a trail of restored faith in humanity and "where can I clone him?" requests in their wake. They're the guys who make you wonder: Is it possible to be too good to be true? (Spoiler alert: sometimes yes, but these gents are the real deal!)

While perfection is a myth, these men have mastered the art of being genuinely good humans. They're living proof that sometimes, the most attractive quality is simply being a decent person who's got their act together.

So polish your rose-colored glasses and prepare your faith in humanity for a boost as we analyze this gallery of green flags. In the world of dating, sometimes the biggest thrill is finding someone who doesn't make you want to pull your hair out.

Now, let's leap into this pool of positivity and see if we can bottle some of this magic for the greater good of the dating world!

Stability Superstars

The Balanced Beacon

Brilliantly Balanced Brian

Finally, someone worth meeting! Brian is the human Swiss Army knife of life skills. This walking, talking masterpiece of equilibrium doesn't just have his act together; he's bound it in leather, indexed it, and published the bestselling audiobook version (which he recorded himself, naturally).

Brian's dating profile is the unicorn of dating apps – it actually matches the man behind it:

About Me: "Seeking a partner to share life's adventures, big and small. Biotech engineer by day, budding chef and backpacking enthusiast by night. Believer in continuous growth, quality time with loved ones, and the perfect homemade pizza. Let's build something beautiful together!"

His photos showcase a man so well-rounded he's practically spherical: Brian closing a major work deal (without looking like a corporate robot), whipping up a gourmet meal (without a fire extinguisher in sight), summit hiking with buddies (looking rugged yet approachable), and volunteering at an animal shelter (where even the cats like him, which is statistically impossible).

In Brian's world, multitasking isn't chaotic, it's choreographed. While most guys consider it a victory to remember both deodorant AND breakfast, Brian is simultaneously advancing his career, maintaining genuine friendships, and remembering to water both his plants AND his relationships. When other men are choosing between fitness and social life, Brian is organizing a charity run with friends that ends at a farmers' market where he knows all the vendors by name.

Brian represents what happens when emotional intelligence meets actual intelligence, with a side of practical life skills that didn't come from his mother doing his laundry until he was 30. He's proof that men can evolve beyond the "work all day, video games all night" paradigm without swinging to the "I've replaced my personality with CrossFit" extreme.

First Date: If you match with Brian, prepare for dates that engage your mind, body, and spirit without feeling like an episode of The Bachelor on steroids. He'll plan an activity that combines learning something new, giving back to the community, and having fun together, such as a bread-making class that donates loaves to a local shelter. Yes, he'll remember if you're gluten-intolerant.

Love Language: Quality time, acts of service, and the ability to be fully present in each moment without checking sports scores under the table.

Attachment Style: Securely attached with healthy boundaries and emotional intelligence that doesn't need a user manual or an intervention from his therapist.

P.S. In Brian's universe, "Netflix and chill" might mean discussing the documentary you just watched while he teaches you his famous homemade bruschetta recipe. And yes, he'll send you home with leftovers in containers he doesn't need back.

The Last Word

Brian: Keep shining that light of balance and authenticity, you're proof that having it all doesn't mean doing it all at once. Your recipe for life is as well-crafted as your homemade pizza, mixing just the right amounts of ambition, adventure, and genuine connection.

Ladies: When you find a man whose calendar has equal space for career growth, personal development, and quality time, and who knows how to use a calendar without his mother setting it up, pay attention. A partner who understands that balance isn't about perfect equilibrium but about mindful choices is rarer than a perfectly ripe avocado. This is what green flags look like, ladies, no filter needed. Swipe right on this stable soul; your mind, body, and spirit will thank you.

The Reliable Rock

Dependable Don

Solid as a rock, it's Don, the human GPS of reliability in a world of "sorry, I forgot" and "something came up" excuses. This walking, talking monument to dependability has turned showing up into a skill that makes the Swiss railway system look positively flaky by comparison.

Don's profile is the dating app equivalent of finding out Santa Claus is real and he delivers year-round:

About Me: "Seeking a partner who values stability as much as spontaneity. I believe trust is built in the small moments, showing up when you say you will, following through on promises, and being there through life's ups and downs. Looking for someone to build a foundation of reliability with, while still keeping the adventure alive!"

Photos showcase Don in his natural habitat: helping friends move (he not only shows up, but brings coffee and doesn't mysteriously develop back pain halfway through), organizing community events (with color-coded spreadsheets that would make Monica Geller weep with joy), celebrating his 10th work anniversary (while his job-hopping friends wonder what that's like), and being the designated driver (every time, without the passive-aggressive sighing). His candid shots show him fixing things around his well-maintained home and playing with pets who have been with him longer than most marriages last in Hollywood.

Don is so reliable that the atomic clock synchronizes to him, not the other way around. If he says he'll be there at 7, your watch probably needs adjusting if he isn't. His exes still list him as their emergency contact, not because they're still hung up on him, but because even they know that when the zombie apocalypse hits, Don will show up with the survival kit he prepared five years ago, and he'll still be on time.

What sets Don apart isn't just showing up, it's showing up with such impressive consistency that his friends have considered having him legally classified as a natural phenomenon. "As dependable as Don" should replace "as sure as the sunrise" in the lexicon of certainty. Yet, he wears his reliability like a perfectly tailored suit rather than a uniform.

First Date: A well-planned evening with room for spontaneous detours, where showing up on time is just the beginning of showing up for each other. The reservation will exist (unlike your last Tinder date's "plans"), the tickets will be purchased in advance, and you'll never hear "I thought YOU were bringing the picnic blanket."

Love Language: Acts of service, quality time, and the ability to make "I'll handle it" sound sexier than any pickup line in history.

Attachment Style: Reliably attached, treating commitments like promises rather than suggestions scribbled on a Post-it note in disappearing ink.

The Last Word

Don: Your reliability isn't just about keeping promises, it's about creating a foundation where trust flourishes and hearts feel safe to land. Continue to be that steady light that helps others find their way home.

Ladies: When a man's word is as solid as his character, and his actions consistently match his promises, you've found a rare treasure in today's "I'll text you later" wasteland. This is what absolute security looks like: someone who shows up not just for the big moments, but for all the small ones that build a life together. Swipe right on this reliable guy; your relationship goals, exhausted dating expectations, and peace of mind will thank you.

The Financial Steward

Future-Focused Frank

It's a pleasure to introduce Frank, the unicorn who knows the difference between investing and gambling with his rent money on crypto. This walking, talking financial literacy course has somehow made responsible money management sexier than a sports car bought on credit by a guy with seven maxed-out credit cards.

Frank's dating profile reads like a love letter to balanced portfolios:

About Me: "Seeking a partner to build a wonderful life together. Career-established optimist who believes in living well while planning wisely. Looking for someone who appreciates that the best things in life are free, but having a solid financial foundation makes life's adventures more enjoyable. Let's create memories while creating security!"

Photos showcase Frank enjoying life's pleasures without the financial hangover: traveling to bucket-list destinations (on points, naturally, which he accumulated through strategic credit card use that would make a financial advisor blush with envy), hosting dinner parties for friends (in a home he owns rather than rents from six roommates), and volunteering at financial literacy workshops (where his students don't realize they're developing crushes along with their budgeting skills). His casual shots show him enjoying simple pleasures, such as picnics in the park (with wine that isn't screw-top), farmers' market adventures (where he knows the difference between endive and escarole), and DIY home improvements that add both joy and value (without requiring an emergency plumber visit afterward).

Frank's idea of living dangerously is letting his emergency fund dip below six months of expenses. His credit score isn't just excellent, it's framed on his wall next to his diplomas. While other guys are buying crypto based on tweets from tech bros, Frank has a diversified portfolio that performs so reliably that his financial advisor calls him for advice.

In Frank's world, "going Dutch" isn't a sign of cheapness; it's an acknowledgment of equal partnership. He can make budgeting sound sexy and retirement planning feel like foreplay. He doesn't just bring flowers on a date; he brings flowers that he has grown himself, because "the ROI on gardening is both financial and emotional." His idea of dirty talk includes phrases like "compound interest" and "maxing out your Roth IRA," and somehow, it works.

First Date: A cooking class that teaches how to prepare gourmet meals on a budget, followed by a sunset picnic featuring a special wine he's been saving for an occasion worth the uncorking. End the evening stargazing while casually discussing your shared five-year plan in a way that somehow doesn't feel like a job interview.

Love Language: Planning adventures with sensible budgets, surprising you with thoughtfully researched investments in your shared future, and finding ways to make compound interest sound more romantic than Shakespeare ever could

Attachment Style: Responsibly attached to both his goals and your shared success, treating financial planning like a team sport where everyone gets a championship ring that's been responsibly insured

The Last Word

Frank: Your approach to finances isn't just about numbers; it's about creating a foundation for dreams to flourish. Continue to show the world that responsibility and joy can coexist, like a well-balanced portfolio of life's best moments.

Ladies: This is what responsible romance looks like: someone who can plan for tomorrow while still making today count. When a man understands that financial security is about providing for possibilities rather than restricting joy, and his concept of wealth encompasses both monetary and emotional benefits, take note. Swipe right on this fiscal superhero; your joint ventures, bucket list dreams, and retirement years will thank you (along with your formerly stressed-out financial advisor).

Growth Gurus

The Lifelong Learner

Curious Chris

At last, say hello to Chris, the human version of an endlessly fascinating documentary series you can't stop watching.

Chris's dating profile reads like if Wikipedia and TED Talks had a very enthusiastic baby:

About Me: "Seeking a partner for intellectual adventures and mutual growth. Professional software engineer and amateur at everything else. Current fascinations: medieval Japanese poetry, urban beekeeping, and why my sourdough starter keeps trying to escape its jar. Let's learn something new together!"

His photos showcase a man whose hobbies require their own dedicated storage unit: Chris attending a cooking class (where he's asking the chef about molecular gastronomy while perfectly dicing onions), absorbed in a book at a local café (not staged, he genuinely didn't notice the photographer), attending a lecture (front row, already has his question prepared), and showing off his latest DIY project (a lamp made from parts of his first computer, which somehow doesn't look like electrical-fire decor).

In Chris's world, "I don't know" isn't an admission of failure; it's an exciting prelude to "but I'm going to find out!" While most people's idea of research is asking Siri three times before giving up, Chris delves into information rabbit holes so deep that he occasionally needs GPS to return to the present moment. He doesn't just read books; he devours them, complete with annotations, follow-up questions, and occasional correspondence with the authors who are equally surprised and delighted by his insights.

What makes Chris special isn't just his knowledge; it's his complete lack of condescension in sharing it. He treats everyone like they have something to teach him, approaching conversations as mutual explorations rather than opportunities to flex his mental muscles. His genuine wonder at the world is so infectious that the CDC should study it.

First Date: A trip to a museum exhibition followed by dinner, where you'll somehow end up discussing everything from ancient pottery techniques to musician Bill Evans' contributions to impressionist jazz. Prepare for the most interesting conversation of your life that won't make you feel like you're back in school getting pop-quizzed.

Love Language: Sharing fascinating discoveries, listening with genuine interest to your perspectives, and remembering every detail about the things that matter to you (while possibly forgetting where he parked his car)

Attachment Style: Securely attached with a side of "Did you know John Bowlby developed attachment theory in the 1950s, and it was later expanded upon by Mary Ainsworth? I just read a fascinating paper about it!"

P.S. If you match with Chris, be prepared for text messages containing random facts he thought you'd appreciate, links to articles he found intriguing, and the occasional "Sorry I'm late, I got caught up in a fascinating conversation with the bookstore owner about WWII aviation.

The Last Word

Chris: Your curiosity isn't just charming, it's a beautiful reminder that we never have to stop growing. Keep questioning, exploring, and sharing your enthusiasm with a world that desperately needs more genuine wonder.

Ladies: When you find a man whose mind is as open as his heart, who approaches life as a continuous learning opportunity rather than a test he's already passed, pay attention. His curiosity about the world is likely to extend to you; your thoughts, dreams, and perspectives will be valued, not just tolerated. Swipe right on this intellectual explorer; your mind, dinner conversations, and Netflix documentary queue will thank you.

The Growth Partner

Evolving Evan

Marvel at Evan, the human equivalent of a butterfly who keeps finding new cocoons. This walking, talking personal development seminar has turned self-improvement into an extreme sport, considering "comfort zone" a synonym for "the place I used to live before I renovated."

Evan's dating profile reads like a masterclass in authentic evolution:

About Me: "Seeking a growth-oriented partner for life's journey. Former corporate lawyer turned sustainable business consultant. Believer in continuous improvement, radical honesty, and stepping toward challenges rather than away from them. Let's help each other become our best selves!"

Photos showcase a man in perpetual positive motion: Evan completing his first triathlon (after overcoming a childhood fear of swimming), teaching a workshop on ethical entrepreneurship, meditating on a mountain top (not as pretentious as it sounds, he's doing it wrong and laughing about it), and cooking with his elderly neighbor (who's teaching him family recipes in exchange for tech lessons). His transformation timeline could make a caterpillar jealous.

Evan treats personal growth like most people treat breathing, an essential, continuous process rather than a New Year's resolution abandoned by January 15th. While others are perfecting their excuses, he's perfecting his approach to challenging situations. His journal collection requires its own bookshelf, each one filled with reflections, lessons learned, and occasionally questionable doodles from his "let's try drawing" phase.

What sets Evan apart isn't just his dedication to improvement; it's his complete lack of the "holier than thou" attitude that makes most self-help enthusiasts unbearable at dinner parties. He approaches growth with humility and humor, treating his past mistakes as valuable data points rather than shameful secrets or "character-building moments" to humble-brag about.

First Date: An activity slightly outside both your comfort zones, just challenging enough to create a genuine connection but not so extreme you'll need therapy afterward. Think cooking a cuisine neither of you has tried before, not free-solo rock climbing without harnesses.

Love Language: Thoughtful feedback delivered with kindness, celebrating your wins (no matter how small), and creating space for authentic transformation rather than superficial change

Attachment Style: Securely evolving, treating relationships as opportunities for mutual growth rather than transactions or therapy sessions.

P.S. If you match with Evan, be prepared for a relationship that feels more like a creative collaboration than a stagnant situation. And yes, he will eventually ask if you'd like to try couples' meditation, but he won't make that weird humming noise that most meditation enthusiasts can't seem to resist.

The Last Word

Evan: Your dedication to growth without the side of self-righteousness is refreshing in a world of performative self-improvement. Keep evolving authentically and creating space for others to do the same.

Ladies: When you find a man who views relationships as opportunities for mutual growth rather than competitions or constraints, you've found someone truly special. A partner who continues to evolve while supporting your goals, without trying to "fix" you or expecting you to be their personal life coach, is the foundation of a relationship that remains exciting long after the honeymoon phase ends. Swipe right on this evolving soul; your future self and untapped potential will thank you.

The Family Man

Nurturing Nathan

How refreshing it is to introduce Nathan, the man who's single-handedly dismantling toxic masculinity one bedtime story at a time. This walking, talking advertisement for healthy fatherhood has turned nurturing into a superpower, considering "dad skills" to include both emotional intelligence and the ability to build a decent blanket fort.

Nathan's dating profile reads like a refreshing dive into genuine family values:

About Me: "Dedicated dad and hopeful romantic seeking partner who values family and understands that strength comes in many forms. An elementary school counselor who believes in teaching kids emotional intelligence alongside ABCs. Looking for someone to join our little team, my 8-year-old daughter has approved this message and is currently helping me pick profile pictures."

Photos showcase a man who's simultaneously a jungle gym and emotional support human: Nathan coaching his daughter's soccer team (with appropriate enthusiasm rather than sideline-screaming-coach syndrome), cooking dinner while explaining fractions (turning homework into something delicious), attending a father-daughter dance (creating an evening his daughter will remember forever), and building an impressive garden with child-sized tools alongside adult ones. His DIY skill level is "competent enough to be helpful but humble enough to watch YouTube tutorials when needed."

Nathan approaches fatherhood like it's the most important job he'll ever have, incorporating both traditional nurturing (usually assigned to mothers) and healthy masculine guidance. He can discuss feelings, braid hair, and teach appropriate boundaries, the parenting equivalent of a triple axel. His daughter's emotional vocabulary makes most adults look like they're still using crayon communication.

What makes Nathan exceptional isn't just his parenting; it's how he has integrated it into his identity without making it his sole personality trait or using it as a dating strategy to appear sensitive. He's deeply committed to his role as a father while maintaining healthy boundaries, understanding that being a great dad means modeling what a fulfilled, balanced adult looks like.

First Date: A thoughtfully planned outing that respects both your time and his parenting schedule. Don't expect to be introduced to his daughter right away; he maintains appropriate boundaries while being transparent about his family commitments. When the introduction eventually happens, it will be casual and pressure-free, not a high-stakes "meet your future stepdaughter" scenario from a sitcom.

Love Language: Acts of service that serve, thoughtful inclusion in family traditions, and the ability to be emotionally present without expectation of emotional labor in return

Attachment Style: Securely attached with healthy boundaries and the emotional intelligence to help others feel safe without becoming a surrogate therapist

P.S. If you match with Nathan, be prepared for a man who can discuss your feelings without making it weird, who plans dates around school schedules without resentment, and who understands that bringing you into his family's life should happen at a respectful pace that works for everyone involved.

> **The Last Word**
>
> **Nathan:** Your dedication to nurturing the next generation while maintaining your own identity is a testament to true strength. Continue to show the world what healthy, engaged fatherhood looks like.
>
> **Ladies:** When you find a man who approaches fatherhood with the dedication of a calling rather than an obligation, who has mastered emotional intelligence alongside practical skills, you've found someone truly special. His nurturing capacity extends beyond his child; it's part of who he is at his core. Dating a single parent comes with unique considerations, but a man who's this thoughtful about his most important relationship will bring that same care to yours. Swipe right on this nurturing soul; your heart, future family dynamics, and inner child will thank you.

Emotional Intelligence Elite

The Vulnerability Victor

Honest Abraham

The green flags are waving for Abraham, the emotional equivalent of a glasshouse with the curtains wide open. This walking, talking testament to authentic living has transformed vulnerability from a buzzword into a lifestyle, considering therapy an investment rather than an emergency response system.

Abraham's dating profile reads like a refreshing dive into the deep end of emotional honesty:

About Me: "Seeking a partner who values authentic connection over surface-level perfection. I believe that true strength comes from acknowledging our humanity, complete with flaws, fears, and occasional existential crises at 3 AM. Former corporate warrior who discovered that emotional armor weighs more than it protects. Let's create a relationship where we can be gloriously, imperfectly human together."

Photos showcase a man comfortable in his own skin: Abraham engaged in meaningful conversation (actually listening, not just waiting to speak), laughing genuinely at what appears to be a joke at his own expense, wiping away a tear at his best friend's wedding (front row, not hiding it), and meditating in nature (without the Instagram-perfect positioning that screams "I'm only doing this for the likes!"). His expressions range across the full emotional spectrum rather than defaulting to the classic "constipated attempt at looking mysterious" that plagues most dating profiles.

Abraham approaches emotions the way most people approach buffets: nothing is off-limits, and he's willing to try everything on the table. While other men are still playing emotional Jenga, carefully removing selected feelings until the whole structure collapses, he's building an integrated emotional literacy that includes words beyond "fine" and "whatever." His emotional vocabulary makes Shakespeare look like he was working with refrigerator poetry magnets.

What makes Abraham extraordinary isn't just his willingness to be vulnerable – it's his ability to do so without using emotional honesty as a manipulation tactic or treating every date like an unpaid therapy session. He shares authentically without oversharing inappropriately, understanding the difference between vulnerability and emotional dumping. He's done the work to understand his patterns without expecting you to be his emotional janitor.

First Date: A conversation that flows effortlessly between lighthearted and meaningful topics, where "How are you?" is answered with refreshing honesty rather than the automated "good" we've all been programmed to say. Expect genuine questions about your life and thoughtful responses to your answers rather than the usual first-date performance art.

Love Language: Open communication, emotional presence, and the courage to say "I was wrong" or "I don't know" without treating it as a character flaw

Attachment Style: Securely self-aware with the tools to recognize and manage his emotional responses without projecting them onto others

P.S. If you match with Abraham, be prepared for a man who might cry during sad movies, express genuine excitement without worrying it makes him look uncool, and occasionally text "I'm feeling anxious today" without following it with "...just kidding!" His emotional transparency isn't a phase – it's his baseline operating system, the result of years of intentional personal work.

> ### The Last Word
>
> **Abraham:** Your courage to live authentically isn't just refreshing – it's revolutionary in a world that often rewards emotional performance over genuine connection. Keep creating spaces where others feel safe to remove their armor.
>
> **Ladies:** When you find a man who approaches emotions as valuable data rather than inconvenient glitches, who has done the inner work to understand himself without expecting you to be his tour guide, you've found someone truly rare. A partner with emotional intelligence doesn't just make relationships easier – it makes them deeper, more authentic, and ultimately more fulfilling. Swipe right on this emotional pioneer; your heart, communication patterns, and future relationship will thank you.

The Boundary Respecter

Consent Conner

Here's a breath of fresh air: Conner, the human embodiment of "your comfort matters." This walking, talking masterclass in respectful interaction has turned consent and boundaries from awkward concepts into everyday practice and considers "Can I..." a more important phrase than "I want...".

Conner's dating profile reads like a refreshing oasis in the desert of boundary violations:

About Me: "Seeking a partner who values clear communication and mutual respect. Firm believer that the best connections happen when everyone feels safe and heard. Criminal defense attorney by day, amateur chef and jazz enthusiast by night. Let's build something authentic at whatever pace feels right for both of us."

Photos showcase a man who understands personal space isn't just a NASA concept: Conner in friendly group settings (maintaining appropriate distance from others), enjoying outdoor activities (respecting nature's boundaries too), offering a hand to someone who appears to be stepping down from a stage (waiting for them to accept it rather than grabbing), and cooking with his niece (at an age-appropriate station he set up with safety in mind). His expressions convey attentiveness without intensity, interest without entitlement.

Conner treats consent like oxygen – essential, continuous, and never assumed. While most men are still operating on the "absence of no means yes" operating system (with occasional forced updates they immediately dismiss), he's running on the premium "enthusiastic yes or it's a no" platform with regular self-initiated upgrades. International diplomats should study his approach to personal boundaries – he neither builds walls nor invades territories.

What makes Conner exceptional isn't just his respect for boundaries – it's how effortlessly he has integrated this respect into his personality, without making interactions feel like legal negotiations. He's mastered the art of being respectfully flirtatious without being creepy, attentive without hovering, and communicative without turning romance into a terms-of-service agreement. The result is an atmosphere of safety that fosters more genuine connections, not less.

First Date: An evening where "Would you like to..." is asked more than "We should..." Expect a comfortable pace, attentive but not intense eye contact, and zero pressure to extend the date beyond its natural conclusion. If he reaches for your hand, it will be with a glance that gives you time to accept or decline without awkwardness.

Love Language: Creating safety through consistent respect, checking in without interrogating, and the profound understanding that enthusiasm cannot exist without the freedom to decline

Attachment Style: Securely respectful, treating boundaries as healthy aspects of individuality rather than tests to be overcome or threats to be neutralized

P.S. If you match with Conner, be prepared for a refreshing absence of boundary-pushing disguised as flattery. When he says "Let me know when you're ready," he means it, not "Let me ask you every twenty minutes until you give in." His respect isn't a dating strategy; it's a core value that extends to all areas of his life.

The Last Word

Conner: Your respect for boundaries isn't just considerate – it's the foundation that makes a genuine connection possible. Continue creating spaces where consent is celebrated rather than sidestepped.

Ladies: When you find a man who treats your boundaries as valid without taking them personally, who understands that respect enhances rather than inhibits connection, you've found a treasure. A partner who consistently seeks consent isn't being formal or awkward – he's creating the safety that allows genuine intimacy to flourish. Swipe right on this boundary champion; your sense of safety, personal autonomy, and authentic self-expression will thank you.

The Genuine Gentleman

Respectful Ryan

What a joy to introduce a real keeper! Ryan is the living proof that chivalry isn't dead; it has evolved past opening doors to include listening when you speak. This walking, talking embodiment of modern respect has turned consideration into a skill without expecting a medal for basic human decency.

Ryan's dating profile reads like what knights in shining armor would be if they weren't fictional and problematic:

About Me: "Seeking a partner for mutual respect and adventure. Environmental engineer who believes that kindness isn't weakness and listening isn't just waiting for your turn to speak. Raised by a feminist mother and mentored by my two older sisters – they've approved this bio and reminded me to mention that I know how to both cook AND clean without being asked."

Photos showcase a man whose respect isn't an act: Ryan engaged in conversation with an elderly woman (making eye contact, not checking his phone), volunteering at a community garden (doing the unglamorous work, not just posing with tools), attending his friend's art opening (actually looking at the art, not just the free wine), and playing with his nieces and nephews (fully engaged, not babysitting while scrolling). His genuine smile reaches his eyes in a way that stock photo models have tried and failed to replicate.

Ryan treats respect like a daily practice rather than a special occasion outfit. While most men are still confusing respect with reluctant tolerance or performative door-opening, he has mastered the nuanced understanding that absolute respect means seeing others as fully human, rather than supporting characters in his life story. His consideration extends beyond romantic prospects to everyone he encounters – from restaurant servers to his elderly neighbors to children whose opinions he takes seriously.

What makes Ryan remarkable isn't just his respectful behavior – it's the genuine character behind it. He's not performing respect to earn points; he's expressing his authentic values through consistent actions. The difference is as apparent as a real smile versus one practiced in a mirror. He respects women not because they're women, but because they're people, while still understanding the unique challenges they face in a world that often fails to offer them the same respect.

First Date: An evening where you'll notice subtle acts of consideration that have nothing to do with outdated gender roles. You can expect genuine questions about your interests, opinions that invite discussion rather than domination, and careful attention to your comfort without treating you like you're made of glass.

Love Language: Active listening that makes you feel truly heard, consistent consideration that doesn't demand recognition, and respect that extends to all areas of life, not just when he wants something

Attachment Style: Securely respectful, treating relationships as partnerships between equals rather than hierarchies or transactions

P.S. If you match with Ryan, be prepared for a man who will respect your career as much as his own, remember details about your friends without mixing them up, and never use the phrase "I'm a nice guy" because he's too busy being one. His respect isn't conditional on your behavior or appearance – it's his baseline way of interacting with the world.

The Last Word

Ryan: Your genuine respect isn't just refreshing – it's transformative in a world where consideration is often transactional. Continue to show others what it means to be truly seen and valued.

Ladies: When you find a man who offers respect as freely as oxygen, who treats kindness as a strength rather than a strategy, who considers your humanity as complete as his own, you've found something precious. A true gentleman doesn't announce himself – he reveals his character through consistent actions that honor your autonomy, intelligence, and worth. Swipe right on this respectful soul; your sense of equality, authentic self, and faith in humanity will thank you.

Chapter 17

THE TAKEAWAY

Having finally reached our endangered species exhibit after touring countless dating disasters, we can confirm these green flag men exist; they're not mythical creatures or elaborate dating app simulations. Our research expedition has documented genuine specimens that, after too long in the toxic dating trenches, might seem like mirages, but our evidence proves they're real!

This catalog of positive patterns demonstrates that while red flags warn you of danger, green flags invite you to discover possibility. The men we've examined aren't just "nice guys"; they're emotionally evolved humans who somehow managed to grow up without assuming the dishwasher loads itself or thinking "compromise" means you giving up everything you want.

Green Flags Worth Celebrating:

Stability Superstars:

- Their emotional regulation doesn't require you to become their unpaid therapist.

- They remember important dates without setting a reminder titled "avoid doghouse."

- Their finances suggest they understand money exists beyond the next paycheck.

- They clean the bathroom without expecting a parade in their honor.

- They apologize without adding "but" followed by why it's your fault.

Growth Gurus:

- They evolve without needing relationship ultimatums as fertilizer.
- Their bookshelf contains more than just sports almanacs and gaming guides.
- They view your success as cooperation, not competition.
- They've been to therapy without a court mandate.
- Their self-improvement doesn't come with a side of superiority complex.

Emotional Intelligence Elite:

- They express feelings using more words than "fine" and "whatever."
- They ask about your day and listen to the answer.
- They set boundaries without building emotional fortresses.
- They understand that consent is ongoing, enthusiastic, and never assumed.
- They treat service staff like actual humans, not furniture with pulse rates.

While these green flags aren't guarantees, they're promising indicators that you've found someone who views relationships as partnerships rather than conquests, coaching opportunities, or therapy sessions.

The most refreshing thing about these men? Their decency isn't a performance or manipulation tactic; it's just who they are. They don't expect medals for basic human respect or keep scoreboards of their good deeds. They understand that healthy relationships require continual investment, not just effort during the recruitment phase.

When you spot these rare specimens in the wild, approach them with appropriate appreciation, but still maintain healthy skepticism. After all, even the greenest flag can sometimes be a red flag wearing a convincing disguise. Trust should be earned over time, not granted at first impression, even when that impression comes with impressive emotional vocabulary and clean fingernails.

Sometimes, the most significant green flag of all is the one that doesn't need to wave itself in your face.

Chapter 18

THE SWIPE SMART SURVIVAL GUIDE

The Dating Traffic Light

Welcome to The Swipe Smart Survival Guide, where we break down the complex world of online dating into a simple, color-coded system even a colorblind cupid could follow!

Ever wish dating came with a user manual? Well, you're in luck, because you're about to get the next best thing. Think of this chapter as your personal GPS through the jungle of Deceptive Dave's, Shady Shawn's, and Narcissistic Nick's.

Red means stop, orange means proceed with caution, and green means go – it's just like driving, but instead of avoiding car crashes, you're dodging emotional pileups and relational roadkill.

In the following pages, we'll give you the lowdown on:

● Red Light: When to slam on the brakes and execute a U-turn faster than you can say "un-match" or "block and report".

● Orange Light: The dating equivalent of a yellow light; slow down, look both ways and decide if it's worth the risk.

● Green Light: The "go" signals that indicate you might have found a keeper (or at least someone who won't use your toothbrush to clean the toilet).

In the grand demolition derby of dating, this guide is your crash course in avoiding the lemons and finding a smooth ride. So flip that turn signal on, check your blind spots, and let's negotiate this romantic roundabout together!

Caution: Reading this chapter may cause sudden increases in dating standards and a decreased tolerance for red-flag-waving weirdos. Proceed at your own risk (and reward)!

🔴 RED LIGHTS: Swipe Left, Block and Run! 🔴

- Disrespects your boundaries or pressures you to change them.
- Exhibits controlling behavior or extreme jealousy.
- Sends unsolicited explicit photos or makes inappropriate sexual comments.
- Speaks negatively about all their exes or blames others for everything.
- Lies or is evasive about important information (e.g., relationship status).
- Shows signs of aggression or an inability to manage anger
- Consistently cancels plans or is unreliable.
- Belittles your opinions, dreams, or accomplishments.
- Refuses to discuss or plan for the future.
- Displays addictive behaviors that they're not addressing.
- Pushes for serious commitment unusually quickly.
- Shows a lack of empathy or consideration for others.
- Has vastly different core values or life goals.
- Exhibits stalker-like behavior or violates your privacy.
- Refuses to compromise or always needs to be right.

- Shows signs of financial irresponsibility or tries to control your finances.

- Displays manipulative behavior or plays emotional games.

- They have unresolved trauma, and they aren't willing to address it.

- Refuses to communicate openly about issues.

- Shows a pattern of ghosting or breadcrumbing.

- Shows signs of being a scammer: requests money, has a too-perfect profile, rushes into declaring love, or makes excuses to avoid video chats or in-person meetings.

Warning: These red lights aren't just decorations; they are warning signs. Don't ignore them, no matter how charming the person might seem!

🟠 ORANGE LIGHTS: Proceed with Caution 🟠

- Has limited dating experience or is newly single after a long relationship.

- Shows inconsistency in communication patterns.

- Seems overly attached to or dependent on family/friends.

- Has different communication styles or love languages than you.

- Displays minor jealousy that doesn't escalate to controlling behavior.

- Shows signs of unresolved emotional baggage from past relationships.

- Has a busy lifestyle that might limit availability for dating.

- Exhibits some political or religious views that differ from yours.

- Demonstrates occasional moodiness or emotional unpredictability.
- Shows minor signs of financial stress or instability.
- Has a few unresolved personal issues they're actively working on.
- Displays some difficulty in expressing emotions or vulnerabilities.
- Shows occasional lack of punctuality or forgetfulness.
- Has a friendship with an ex that makes you slightly uncomfortable.
- Exhibits some social awkwardness or difficulty reading social cues.
- Shows signs of mild insecurity or need for reassurance.
- Has some lifestyle habits you're unsure about (e.g., social drinking).
- Demonstrates occasional poor conflict resolution skills.
- Shows some resistance to change or trying new things.
- Has different ideas about the pace of the relationship.

Assess thoughtfully: Orange lights don't necessarily mean "stop," but they do mean "slow down and observe." These issues may resolve with time, effective communication, and personal growth – or they may develop into significant concerns. Trust your instincts and communicate openly!

🟢 GREEN LIGHTS: Swipe Right and Celebrate! 🟢

- Communicates openly, honestly, and consistently.
- Respects your boundaries and personal space.
- Shows genuine interest in your life, dreams, and opinions.

- Has a stable career or is actively working towards goals.
- Demonstrates emotional intelligence and self-awareness.
- Is kind to service workers and strangers.
- Has healthy relationships with family and friends.
- Takes responsibility for their actions and apologizes sincerely.
- Shows enthusiasm for personal growth and learning.
- Supports your ambitions and celebrates your successes.
- Has similar core values and long-term life goals.
- Demonstrates financial responsibility and independence.
- Shows consistency between words and actions.
- Has interests and hobbies outside of the relationship.
- Respects your time and is punctual for dates.
- Handles conflicts maturely and seeks compromise.
- Shows empathy and compassion for others.
- Is comfortable with both giving and receiving affection.
- Has a good sense of humor and can laugh at themselves.
- Respects your independence and encourages your personal growth.

Promising sign: Green lights are like finding a four-leaf clover in the dating field – rare and valuable! These traits indicate potential for a healthy, fulfilling relationship. However, keep in mind that nobody is perfect, and it's the overall pattern that counts.

Safety First

Navigating Love with a Level Head

Online Dating Safety: Because Romance Shouldn't Be a Horror Story

- Trust Your Gut: If something feels off, it probably is. Your intuition is like your personal dating app firewall; use it!

- Meet in Public: First dates should take place in public, preferably in a place with witnesses, such as a coffee shop.

- Tell a Friend: Always share your date details with someone you trust. It's not paranoia; it's having a safety net and a potential rescue team in place.

- Keep Personal Info Personal: Your address should be harder to obtain than a PlayStation 5 at launch.

Respecting Boundaries: It's Not Rocket Science, It's Basic Decency

- No Means No: And it's not a challenge or a negotiation starter. It's a complete sentence.

- Ask Before You Send: Unsolicited pictures are like surprise veggie smoothies - nobody wants them.

- Respect Privacy: Research for safety? Smart. Screenshot his photos to analyze with your friends for three hours? You've gone too far.

- Take "Maybe" as a "No": If they're not enthusiastic, they're not interested. Move on, Period.

Reporting Inappropriate Behavior: Be the Hero Dating Apps Need

- Use the Report Button: It's not just there for decoration. If someone's crossing lines, report them faster than you can say "red flag."

- Be Specific: When reporting, give details. "He was creepy" is less helpful than "He sent inappropriate images without consent."

- Block and Move On: Once reported, block them. Your mental health doesn't need their drama.

- Support Others: If a friend shares a bad experience, encourage them to report it too. Be the wingman in the fight against creeps.

A great date respects you, your boundaries, and doesn't make you want to call the authorities. Stay safe out there. May your matches be respectful and your conversations creep-free!

Romance Scammers: Because Prince Charming Shouldn't Need Your Credit Card

- Too Good to Be True? If their profile looks like a Hollywood headshot and their job is "international businessman/model/secret agent," your scam detector should be beeping.

- Sob Stories and Emergencies: If they're always one wire transfer away from visiting you, don't forget, you're looking for a date, not a charity case.

- **Moving Too Fast:** Love at first sight is for Disney movies. If they're declaring undying love before the first date, they're probably in love with your wallet.

- **Never Met in Person?** If they always have an excuse not to meet, they might be catfishing you harder than a professional angler.

- **Asking for Money or Personal Information:** The only thing they should be asking for is your time, not your Social Security number or bank details.

- **Sketchy Communication Patterns:** If they can only talk at odd hours or insist on moving to WhatsApp immediately, they might be juggling more victims than a circus clown.

- **Google Is Your Friend:** Use reverse image search to find their photos. If your "unique" match appears on stock photo sites, it's time to report and block it.

- **Trust Your Instincts:** If something feels off, it probably is. Your gut feeling is sharper than the smoothest scammer's lines.

A real catch won't need to catch your cash. Keep your heart open, but your bank account closed!

The Final Destination: Your Voyage, Your Rules

Please keep in mind that this traffic light system is your co-pilot, not your autonomous driver. Dating isn't just about avoiding crashes; it's about enjoying the adventure and finding destinations worth visiting. These guidelines are tools for your dating toolbox, not commandments etched in stone. Your unique experiences, values, and instincts are the ultimate navigation system. Sometimes the most interesting relationships start with an orange light that turns green with time and communication. Other times, that vibrant green can fade to red faster than last season's fashion trends. Trust yourself enough to slow down when needed, accelerate when it feels right, and most importantly, to pull over completely when your emotional check engine light starts flashing.

After all, the most important relationship you'll ever steer is the one with yourself – make sure that one's always cruising in the green zone. Now get out there and drive your dating life like the confident, savvy navigator you are!

SWIPE SMART, SCREEN SUITORS, STAY SAFE

Chapter 19

RESOURCES THE SAVVY SWIPER'S SAFETY NET

The Dating Safety Net:
Because Cupid Sometimes Needs A Backup Plan

Welcome to the "In Case of Emergency, Break Glass" section of our dating adventure! While I hope your journey through the landscape of love is smooth sailing, it's always good to have a life jacket handy. These resources are like your dating Swiss Army knife - ready to tackle everything from creepy crawlies in your DMs to the occasional emotional avalanche.

Reaching out for help isn't just okay - it's downright brilliant. Your safety and well-being are the real prize in the dating game. Don't hesitate to use these resources - they're here to ensure your love story is a tale of triumph, not a cautionary one!

If you're in immediate danger, always call 911 or your local emergency number.

Emergency & Immediate Safety Resources

(Because Sometimes Prince Charming Turns Out to Be A Frog In Crisis)

- National Domestic Violence Hotline: 1-800-799-SAFE (7233) or text START to 88788 www.thehotline.org

- RAINN (Rape, Abuse & Incest National Network): 1-800-656-HOPE (4673) www.rainn.org

- National Suicide Prevention Lifeline: 1-800-273-8255 suicidepreventionlifeline.org

- VictimConnect Resource Center: 1-855-4-VICTIM victimconnect.org

Bar Safety Programs

(Because Sometimes You Need A Discreet Exit Strategy)

- **"Angel Shot:** Order this at participating bars if you feel unsafe on a date.

    - **Neat:** Bar staff will escort you to your car
    - **With Ice:** Bar staff will call a ride share/taxi for you
    - **With Lime:** Bar staff will call the police

- **"Ask for Angela":** Tell bar staff you need to "Ask for Angela"; this code phrase lets them know you need help leaving an unsafe situation.

Note: These codes may vary by location. Look up local programs in your area before going on a date, and always choose establishments that participate in safety initiatives.

Dating Safety
Financial Abuse & Scam Prevention

(Because That Overseas Oil Executive Is Just Scammer Scott In Disguise)

- Romance Scams Now™: 1-870-939-6727
  www.romancescamsnow.com

- FBI's Internet Crime Complaint Center: www.ic3.gov

- FTC's Romance Scam Guide:
  www.consumer.ftc.gov/articles/what-you-need-know-about-romance-scams

- Identity Theft Resource Center: 1-888-400-5530
  www.idtheftcenter.org

- National Center on Elder Abuse: www.ncea.acl.gov
  (Because wisdom and experience deserve extra protection)

- Financial Abuse Resource Center:
  www.finra.org/investors/insights/financial-fraud

- National Adult Protective Services Association:
  www.napsa-now.org

Stalking Prevention & Protection

(For When "Persistent" Becomes Problematic)

- Stalking Prevention, Awareness, and Resource Center (SPARC): www.stalkingawareness.org

- National Center for Victims of Crime: 1-855-4-VICTIM
  www.victimsofcrime.org

Legal Resources

(Because Some Dating Disasters Require More Than Just Blocking)

- Women's Legal Defense and Education Fund: www.legalmomentum.org (Legal information and referrals for women)

- American Bar Association Free Legal Answers: www.abafreelegalanswers.org (Free online legal advice for qualifying individuals)

- WomensLaw.org: www.womenslaw.org (Legal information specifically for women facing abuse)

- National Network to End Domestic Violence: www.nnedv.org/resources (Resources including legal information)

- Legal Aid in your area: Search "[Your State/City] Legal Aid" for local free or low-cost legal services

- Cyber Civil Rights Initiative: www.cybercivilrights.org (Legal help for victims of nonconsensual pornography and online harassment)

Many attorneys offer free initial consultations. If you're facing dating-related legal issues like harassment or stalking, speak with a legal professional about your options for protection orders or other legal remedies.

Mental Health & Relationship Counseling

(Because Sometimes The Heart Needs A Personal Trainer)

- Psychology Today Therapist Finder: www.psychologytoday.com/us/therapists

- National Alliance on Mental Illness (NAMI): 1-800-950-NAMI www.nami.org

- Love Is Respect: 1-866-331-9474 or text LOVEIS to 22522 www.loveisrespect.org

- Codependents Anonymous: www.coda.org

- The Attachment Project: www.attachmentproject.com

- Personal Growth Resources: www.goodtherapy.org/learn-about-therapy/issues/attachment

Divorce Recovery Support

(Because Starting Over Deserves Support)

- DivorceCare: www.divorcecare.org Find local support groups and workshops

- Women's Divorce Resource Center: www.wdrc.org Legal, emotional, and financial resources specifically for women

Single Parent Resources

(Because Dating With Kids Needs Extra Support)

- Parents Without Partners: www.parentswithoutpartners.org Support, resources, and community for single parents

- Single Moms Planet: www.singlemomplanet.com Empowerment network and resources for single mothers

- National Parents Organization: www.nationalparentsorganization.org Advocacy and support for single-parent families

Culture-Specific Resources

(Because Dating Experiences Vary Across Communities)

- Asian Pacific Institute on Gender-Based Violence: www.api-gbv.org (Resources for Asian and Pacific Islander communities)

- Casa de Esperanza: www.casadeesperanza.org (Resources for Latina communities)

- The National Indigenous Women's Resource Center: www.niwrc.org (Resources for Native American/Indigenous communities)

Substance Abuse & Recovery Resources

(For Dealing With Boozy Bruce And His Buddies)

Essential Resources:

- Alcoholics Anonymous www.aa.org
- Al-Anon Family Groups: 1-888-4AL-ANON www.al-anon.org
- SAMHSA's National Helpline: 1-800-662-4357 www.samhsa.gov

Additional Recovery Organizations:

- Narcotics Anonymous: www.na.org
- SMART Recovery: www.smartrecovery.org
- Celebrate Recovery: www.celebraterecovery.com

Support for Family/Partners:

- Nar-Anon Family Groups: www.nar-anon.org
- Adult Children of Alcoholics & Dysfunctional Families: www.adultchildren.org

Crisis and Treatment Resources:

- Crisis Text Line: Text HOME to 741741
- Treatment Locator (SAMHSA): www.findtreatment.gov
- National Suicide Prevention Lifeline: 988

Education and Support:

- National Institute on Drug Abuse (NIDA): www.drugabuse.gov

- Partnership to End Addiction: www.partnershiptoendaddiction.org

Specialty Resources:

- Women for Sobriety: www.womenforsobriety.org

- Refuge Recovery: www.refugerecovery.org

Narcissistic Abuse & Toxic Relationships

(Because Some Red Flags Come With A Side Of Gaslighting)

- Narcissistic Abuse Support:
  www.narcissisticabusesurvival.com

- The National Domestic Violence Hotline - Narcissistic Abuse Resources:
  www.thehotline.org/resources/narcissistic-abuse

- Out of the FOG (Fear, Obligation, Guilt):
  www.outofthefog.website

- Emotional Abuse Support Groups:
  www.supportgroups.com/emotional-abuse

- Dr. Ramani's YouTube Channel:
  www.youtube.com/c/DoctorRamani

Body Image & Self-Esteem

(Because You're Perfect Just As You Are)

- National Eating Disorders Association: 1-800-931-2237
  www.nationaleatingdisorders.org

- Body Image Resources:
  www.psychologytoday.com/us/basics/body-image

Background Check Basics

(Because Google is Your Girlfriend and Due Diligence is Your Bestie)

Before meeting that seemingly perfect match, let's channel your inner detective. Here's your investigative toolkit for some savvy sleuthing:

Start with the Basics:

- Google Search: Your first stop for basic intel
    - Search their name, phone number, and email address
    - Use quotation marks for exact matches
    - Add keywords like city, employer, or alma mater

- Google Reverse Image Search: Unmask those suspiciously perfect profile pics
    - Upload their photos to images.google.com
    - See where else they appear online
    - Verify they're not stolen from someone else

FaceCheck.ID:

- Advanced facial recognition search engine (www.facecheck.id)

    - Upload photos to search across social media, news sites, and public records

    - Provides match confidence scores to help verify authenticity

    - Can help identify if profile photos are stolen or if someone has multiple online identities

    - Useful for detecting scammers who use fake photos

Public Records Resources:

- PACER (Public Access to Court Electronic Records): www.pacer.gov Federal court cases and bankruptcy records

- National Sex Offender Registry: www.nsopw.gov

- Bureau of Prisons Inmate Locator: www.bop.gov/inmateloc

- State Prison Inmate Search Search "[Your State] Department of Corrections Inmate Search"

County and State Court Records:

- Search "[Your County] Clerk of Court Records." Look for:
    - Criminal cases
    - Civil lawsuits
    - Divorce records
    - Marriage licenses
    - Property records
    - Tax liens
    - Restraining orders
    - Small claims

- Search surrounding counties

- Check both criminal AND civil courts

- Look for:
    - Eviction records
    - Building code violations
    - Child support cases
    - Business litigation
    - Professional disciplinary actions

Professional Verification:

- State Professional License Boards
- LinkedIn (cross-reference employment claims)
- Business registrations through the Secretary of State's website

Additional Safety Checks:

- Better Business Bureau (for business owners)
- FTC Scam Alert Database
- State Bar Association (if they claim to be a lawyer)
- Medical Board (if they claim to be a doctor)
- Mortgage Electronic Registration Systems (MERS) for property ownership verification
- Local Police Department Arrest Logs: Many are published online weekly

Social Media Deep Dive:

- Check all platforms:
    - LinkedIn (work history)
    - Facebook (relationship status/history)
    - Instagram (lifestyle verification)
    - Twitter (personality indicators)
    - TikTok (recent activity)

If something feels off, trust your instincts! It's better to be safe than sorry.

Safety Tip: Create a dedicated email address for your searches to protect your privacy.

Important: A legitimate person should have a consistent, verifiable online presence. If you're finding numerous gaps or inconsistencies, that's a red flag.

Safety Apps & Digital Check-Ins

(Because Your Smartphone Should Be As Smart As You Are)

Essential Phone Security:

- Always use a strong passcode on your phone (not just fingerprint or face ID).

- Enable the "Find My Phone" feature (iPhone) or the "Find My Device" (Android).

- **Share your location** with trusted friends or family members before dates.

- Set up emergency contacts in your phone's health app for quick access.

Safety-Focused Apps:

- bSafe: Records video and audio, and sends your location to emergency contacts with an SOS button.

- Noonlight: Press and hold a button while feeling unsafe; release it without entering a PIN, and emergency services are called.

- Life360: Location sharing with trusted friends or family with check-in features.

- Kitestring: Checks on you via text at predetermined times; alerts your emergency contacts if you don't respond within a set timeframe.

- Circle of 6: Quick access to call or text pre-programmed contacts with preset messages like "Call me, I need an interruption" or "Come get me."

- WatchOverMe: Tracks you for a set period; if you don't check in, alerts are sent to emergency contacts.

Community Warning Systems:

- **Tea App:** Allows women to share information about problematic dating experiences, helping others avoid potentially dangerous matches.

- **"Are We Dating The Same Guy?"** Facebook groups: Local community groups where women can compare notes about potential matches and warn others about scammers, cheaters, or dangerous individuals.

- **Garbo:** Background check website specifically designed for dating safety, www.garbo.io

Bear in mind: While these community warning systems can provide valuable information, always verify what you learn and use your own judgment. Some reports may be subjective or contextual.

Supportive Online Communities

(Because Sometimes You Need a Digital Village)

- **The Date Safe Project** (@DateSafeProject on Twitter): Educational content about consent and healthy dating.

- **The Female Dating Strategy:** FDS (www.thefemaledatingstrategy.com:) A spinoff forum from Reddit's r/femaledatingstrategy. Community-driven advice from women for women navigating the dating scene. Exclusively for women who want to take control of their lives.

- **Baggage Reclaim** (baggagereclaim.co.uk): Blog and community focused on self-esteem and healthy relationships.

- **@jillianturecki** (Instagram): Relationship coach focusing on healthy attachment and communication.

- **@alittlenudge** (Instagram): Dating coach Erika Ettin offers practical, no-nonsense advice on crafting standout profiles, messaging strategies, and navigating the often confusing world of online dating with both humor and expert insight.

- **@violetbenson** (Instagram): "Daddy Issues" creator known for humorous takes on modern dating.

- **@thesabrinazoharshow** (Instagram): Sabrina Zohar delivers candid, relatable dating advice with a refreshing blend of humor and vulnerability, tackling everything from situationships to setting boundaries through engaging stories and actionable insights.

Dating Strategy

(Because Sometimes You Need a Battle Plan, Not Just Hope)

- **The Burned Haystack Method®** by Jennie Young: A strategic approach to dating developed by a scholar of applied rhetoric. Rather than endlessly searching for a needle in a haystack, Young's method advocates "burning the haystack" by recognizing rhetorical patterns to efficiently filter out unsuitable matches. Her approach helps women:

    - Craft profiles that attract quality matches while repelling incompatible ones.
    - Use strategic communication to quickly assess compatibility.
    - Apply rhetorical principles to dating app conversations for more meaningful connections.
    - Save time and emotional energy by eliminating poor matches early.

- Follow her research-backed methods at:

    - Facebook: "The Burned Haystack Method®" group
    - Instagram: @word_case_scanario
    - Website: www.jennieyoung.com

Digital Privacy Protection

(Because Your Digital Footprint Shouldn't Lead Straight to Your Front Door)

Before You Start Dating:

- Conduct a self-search on Google to see what information is publicly available about you.
- Review and tighten privacy settings on ALL social media accounts.
- Consider using a Google Voice number instead of your real phone number for initial contacts.
- Create a dating-specific email address to keep your primary email private.
- Remove location data from photos before sharing them (most smartphones have this option in settings).

Privacy Management Tools:

- **DeleteMe:** Removes your personal information from data broker sites.
- **Privacy Badger:** Browser extension that blocks invisible trackers.
- **Have I Been Pwned:** Checks if your email has been compromised in data breaches.

Smart Practices:

- Avoid sharing your full name until after meeting in person.
- Never share your home or work address in dating profiles.
- Be vague about specific workplaces, using general industry terms instead.

- Wait to connect on social media until you've established a level of trust.

- Consider setting up dating-specific social accounts with limited personal information.

- Regularly audit who has access to your location sharing services.

Bottom line: In the digital age, privacy is a precious commodity. Once information is online, it can be difficult to remove it completely!

Social Media Privacy Checklist

(Because Your Digital Footprint Reveals More Than You Think)

Beyond the digital privacy section already included, take these additional steps to protect yourself:

- Review and remove geotags from all photos before posting, as these can reveal your home, workplace, or regular locations.

- Audit your tagged photos across platforms, and untag yourself from photos that reveal too much.

- Check your "friends of friends" privacy settings to limit what strangers can see through mutual connections.

- Review past check-ins at locations and remove those near your home or regular hangouts.

- Consider using the platform's "close friends" features for sharing personal content rather than posting it publicly.

- Check which third-party apps have access to your social accounts and revoke unnecessary permissions.

- Set up alerts to notify you when your name appears in search results (e.g., Google Alerts or similar services).

- Consider using different profile photos across various platforms to make it harder to connect your accounts.

- Regularly search your name with various keywords to see what information is publicly available.

The Truth: A determined person can piece together surprising amounts of information from seemingly innocent social media activity. Dating app matches don't need to know where you live, work, or spend your time until you've established a level of trust.

LGBTQ+ Dating Resources

(Because Love Comes in Many Forms)

While this book reflects my personal experiences as a heterosexual woman dating men, I recognize that dating challenges and safety concerns exist across all relationship types. For readers seeking LGBTQ+-specific dating resources, here are some organizations that provide specialized support:

- SAGE National LGBTQ+ Elder Hotline: 1-877-360-LGBT (5428), www.sageusa.org (Dating advice and support for older LGBTQ+ individuals)

- National Coalition of Anti-Violence Programs: 1-212-714-1141, www.avp.org (Support for LGBTQ+ people experiencing dating violence)

- LGBT National Help Center: 1-888-843-4564, www.glbthotline.org (Peer support for dating and relationship issues)

- Her Dating App Resource Center: www.weareher.com/resources (Dating safety tips for queer women, non-binary, and trans people)

- Taimi: www.taimi.com/blog (Dating and relationship advice for LGBTQ+ community)

- @queerdatingcoach (Instagram): Dating coach specifically for LGBTQ+ individuals

- @queerloveproject (Instagram): Platform featuring relationship stories and advice

- "Queer Dating in 2023 and Beyond" Facebook groups: Community support for LGBTQ+ dating experiences

Technology & Digital Security

(Because Your Digital Life Needs Bodyguards Too)

Account Protection:

- **Two-Factor Authentication Setup:**

  ◦ Enable 2FA on all dating apps, email, and social media

  ◦ Use authenticator apps like Google Authenticator or Authy instead of SMS when possible

  ◦ Backup your 2FA codes in a secure location

Password & Account Security:

- **Password Managers:**

  ◦ **1Password:** www.1password.com (Comprehensive security features)

  ◦ **LastPass**: www.lastpass.com (Free version available)

  ◦ **Bitwarden:** www.bitwarden.com (Open-source option)

- **Unique passwords for every dating app and account**

- **Regular password audits** - check for compromised passwords

Privacy Protection:

- VPN Services (Virtual Private Networks):

  ◦ **ExpressVPN:** www.expressvpn.com (High-speed, reliable)

  ◦ **NordVPN:** www.nordvpn.com (Strong security features)

  ◦ **Surfshark:** www.surfshark.com (Budget-friendly option)

- **Use VPNs when dating on public WiFi** - coffee shops, restaurants, etc.

Evidence Documentation:

- **Screenshot Best Practices:**
    - Include timestamps and full conversation threads
    - Save to cloud storage with date/time stamps
    - Document threatening messages immediately
- **Screen Recording:** Learn how to record video calls or live interactions
- **Email Forwarding:** Forward threatening messages to a secure email account
- **Photo Metadata Preservation:** Don't edit screenshots as it can remove important metadata

Workplace & Professional Protection

(Because Your Career Shouldn't Pay for Your Dating Life)

Professional Reputation Monitoring:

- **Google Alerts:** Set up alerts for your name and variations
- **LinkedIn Privacy Settings:**
    - Limit who can see your connections
    - Turn off activity broadcasts
    - Hide your profile from search engines if needed
- Professional Email Separation: Never use work email for dating apps

Workplace Harassment Resources:

- **HR Department:** Know your company's harassment and stalking policies
- **Employee Assistance Programs (EAP):** Many employers offer free counseling
- **Documentation:** Keep records of any workplace incidents related to dating
- **Legal Consultation:** Know when dating issues become workplace legal matters

Business Owner Protection:

- **Separate Business and Personal Profiles:** Keep dating life away from business social media

- **Professional Reputation Services:** Consider services like Reputation.com for business owners

- **Review Monitoring:** Watch for vindictive reviews on business platforms

Travel & Transportation Safety

(Because Adventures Should Be Fun, Not Frightening)

Rideshare Safety Features:

- **Uber Safety Tools:**
  - Share trip details with trusted contacts
  - Use PIN verification for pickups
  - Access emergency assistance button
  - Rate your driver and report issues

- **Lyft Safety Features:**
  - Share ride details via text
  - Call emergency services through app
  - Verify license plate and driver photo

Hotel & Accommodation Safety:

- Hotel Safety Programs:
  - Request rooms not on ground floor or near stairwells
  - Use the security latch and door chain
  - Never open door without verifying identity

- **Airbnb Safety:** Read reviews carefully, verify host identity, and share details with friends

- **Check-in Protocols:** Always let someone know your exact location and expected return

Travel Dating Safety:

- **Local Emergency Numbers:** Research local emergency contacts for destination cities

- **Transportation Apps:** Download local rideshare and public transit apps

- **Embassy Registration:** Register with US Embassy if dating while traveling internationally

- **Travel Insurance:** Consider coverage that includes emergency evacuation

Recovery & Mental Wellness

(Because Healing Isn't Just a Destination, It's a Journey)

Dating Detox & Breaks:

- **Planned Dating Sabbaticals:**
  - Set specific timeframes (30, 60, 90 days)
  - Delete apps temporarily rather than just logging out
  - Focus on self-care and personal interests
- **Digital Detox Resources:**
  - **Center for Humane Technology:** www.humanetech.com
  - **Digital Wellness Institute:** www.digitalwellnessinstitute.com

Confidence Rebuilding:

- **Self-Compassion Resources:**
  - Dr. Kristin Neff's Self-Compassion Program: www.self-compassion.org
  - **The Confidence Code** by Kay and Shipman (book)
- **Body Positivity Support:**
  - **Body Positive Power** by Megan Crabbe (book)
  - @bodyposipanda (Instagram) - Body positivity and self-acceptance

Re-entering Dating After Trauma:

- **Trauma-Informed Dating Coaches:** Search for specialists in your area
- **EMDR Therapy:** Eye Movement Desensitization and Reprocessing for trauma recovery
- **Support Groups:** Look for local "Dating After Abuse" or "Survivors Dating" groups
- **Gradual Exposure:** Start with low-pressure social activities before full dating

Home & Personal Security

(Because Your Castle Needs a Moat)

Home Security Basics:

- **Address Protection:**
  - Never list your address on dating profiles
  - Use nearby cross-streets for initial meetups
  - Consider a PO Box for any mail-related activities
- **Home Security Systems:**
  - **Ring Doorbell:** Video monitoring for unexpected visitors
  - **SimpliSafe:** Easy-to-install home security
  - **ADT:** Professional monitoring services

Mail & Package Security:

- **PO Box Services:** USPS or private mailbox services
- **Mail Holds:** Temporarily stop mail delivery when traveling
- **Package Delivery:** Use Amazon lockers or workplace delivery
- **Address Changes:** Be cautious about changing address too quickly in relationships

Personal Safety Upgrades:

- **Smart Locks:** Keypad entry to avoid giving out keys
- **Security Cameras:** Monitor your property perimeter
- **Motion Sensor Lights:** Automatic lighting for driveways and walkways
- **Personal Alarm Systems:** Wearable panic buttons for immediate help

Advanced Background Check Resources

(Because Sometimes You Need to Go Full Detective Mode)

Enhanced Verification Tools:

- **FaceCheck.ID:** Advanced facial recognition search engine (www.facecheck.id)
  - Upload photos to search across social media, news sites, and public records
  - Provides match confidence scores to help verify authenticity
  - Can help identify if profile photos are stolen or if someone has multiple online identities
  - Useful for detecting scammers who use fake photos

Professional License Verification:

- **State Medical Boards:** Verify doctors and medical professionals
- **State Bar Associations:** Verify attorneys and legal professionals
- **Professional Engineering Boards:** Verify engineers
- **Real Estate License Lookup:** Verify real estate professionals
- **Teacher Certification:** Verify education professionals

Business Verification:

- **Better Business Bureau:** www.bbb.org (Business ratings and complaints)
- **State Secretary of State:** Business registration verification
- **FINRA BrokerCheck:** www.brokercheck.finra.org (Financial advisors)
- **Contractor License Boards:** Verify construction and trade professionals

Financial Scam Recovery

(Because Sometimes Love Costs More Than Just Your Heart)

Immediate Steps After Financial Loss:

- **Contact Your Bank Immediately:** Report unauthorized transactions
- **File Police Report:** Local law enforcement for documentation
- **Report to FBI:** IC3.gov for federal investigation
- **Contact Your State Attorney General:** Consumer protection division
- **Alert Credit Bureaus:** Place fraud alerts on your credit reports

Recovery Resources:

- **AARP Fraud Watch Network:** www.aarp.org/fraud (Recovery assistance)
- **National Elder Fraud Hotline:** 1-833-372-8311
- **Local Victim Services:** Search "[Your County] Victim Services" for local assistance
- **Legal Aid:** Free or low-cost legal help for fraud victims

Technology-Facilitated Abuse Resources

(Because Digital Stalking is Still Stalking)

Specialized Support:

- **Safety Net Project:** www.techsafety.org (Technology safety for abuse survivors)

- **Digital Security Helpline:** 1-234-567-8910 (Hypothetical - check current resources)

- **Cyber Civil Rights Initiative:** www.cybercivilrights.org (Non-consensual pornography)

Technical Protection:

- **Spyware Detection:** Malwarebytes, Avast Mobile Security

- **Phone Security Audits:** Check for unknown apps or location sharing

- **Social Media Privacy Audits:** Quarterly reviews of all privacy settings

- **Digital Evidence Preservation:** Professional services for legal cases

Emergency Planning & Documentation

(Because Hope for the Best, Plan for the Worst)

Personal Safety Plan:

- **Emergency Contact List:** Keep updated contact information readily available

- **Safe Words:** Establish code words with friends for different levels of help needed

- **Exit Strategies:** Plan multiple ways to leave dates or unsafe situations

- **Emergency Cash:** Keep cash hidden for emergency transportation or needs

Documentation System:

- **Dating Journal:** Record dates, locations, and red flags observed

- **Photo Documentation:** Screenshots of profiles, conversations, and concerning behavior

- **Incident Reports:** Detailed records of any threatening or concerning incidents

- **Evidence Storage:** Secure cloud storage for all documentation

Remember: Your safety is worth more than any relationship. Trust your instincts, and don't hesitate to use these resources. You deserve to feel secure and respected in all your dating experiences.

Additional Dating Safety Resources
Financial & Identity Protection

(Because Your Credit Score Shouldn't Become Collateral Damage)

Credit Monitoring & Protection:

- **Credit Karma:** Free credit monitoring and alerts - www.creditkarma.com

- **Experian:** Credit monitoring with identity theft protection - www.experian.com

- **Annual Credit Report:** Free annual reports from all three bureaus - www.annualcreditreport.com

- **How to Freeze Your Credit:** Contact all three credit bureaus (Experian, Equifax, TransUnion) to place a security freeze - this prevents new accounts from being opened without your permission

Financial Recovery Resources:

- **Small Claims Court Guide:** Search "[Your State] Small Claims Court" for local procedures to recover money lost to romance scams

- **Bank Fraud Departments:** Contact your bank immediately if you've shared financial information

- **Wire Transfer Recovery:** Contact Western Union (1-800-325-6000) or MoneyGram (1-800-926-9400) fraud departments

- **Cryptocurrency Recovery:** Report crypto scams to the FBI's IC3.gov and your crypto exchange's fraud department

Recommended Reading

(Because Google University and the school of Hard Knocks Shouldn't Be Your Only Teachers)

DIGITAL DATING & COMMUNICATION (Chapters 1-2)

- "How Not to Die Alone" by Logan Ury (Decision-making in modern dating)

- "The New Rules: The Dating Dos and Don'ts for the Digital Generation" by Ellen Fein and Sherrie Schneider (Updated dating strategies specifically designed for online dating and modern romance)

- "He's Just Not That Into You" by Greg Behrendt (Classic reality check that still applies to online dating)

- "Crucial Conversations" by Kerry Patterson, Joseph Grenny, Ron McMillan, and Al Switzler (How to handle difficult conversations and recognize poor communication patterns)

ATTACHMENT & LOVE LANGUAGES (Chapters 3-4)

- "Attached" by Amir Levine and Rachel Heller (Understanding attachment styles in relationships)

- "The 5 Love Languages" by Gary Chapman (Understanding the different ways people express and receive love, and how to communicate effectively in relationships)

- "Wired for Love" by Stan Tatkin (How our brains are wired for connection and what this means for romantic relationships)

- "Hold Me Tight" by Sue Johnson (Understanding relationship dynamics and creating secure emotional connections)

PERSONALITY EXTREMES (Chapter 5)

For Arrogance/Ego Issues:

- "The Arrogance Cycle" by Steven Fink (Understanding how arrogance develops and recognizing it in potential partners)
- "Difficult People" by Kerry Patterson, Joseph Grenny, Ron McMillan, and Al Switzler (Dealing with challenging personality types, including arrogant individuals)

For Boring/Emotionally Flat Partners:

- "Bored No More" by Patricia Love and Steven Stosny (Understanding emotional numbness and lack of engagement in relationships)
- "The Emotionally Unavailable Man" by Patti Henry (Recognizing men who can't or won't engage emotionally)

For Sarcasm/Verbal Patterns:

- "The Verbally Abusive Relationship" by Patricia Evans (Understanding subtle verbal abuse, including chronic sarcasm and put-downs)
- "Words That Hurt, Words That Heal" by Joseph Telushkin (The power of words in relationships and recognizing harmful communication patterns)

General Personality Issues:

- "Toxic Personalities at Work" by Mitchel Kusy and Elizabeth Holloway (While work-focused, excellent for understanding difficult personality patterns that carry over into dating)

FINANCIAL AWARENESS (Chapter 6)

- **"Smart Money Smart Kids" by Dave Ramsey and Rachel Cruze** (Understanding financial red flags and protecting yourself from financial manipulation)

- **"The Total Money Makeover" by Dave Ramsey** (Building financial independence to avoid dependent relationships)

- **"Women & Money" by Suze Orman** (Financial empowerment for women and protecting yourself from financial manipulation)

- **"The Behavior Gap" by Carl Richards** (Understanding the psychology behind poor financial decisions and recognizing financial red flags)

- **"Your Money or Your Life" by Vicki Robin** (Building financial independence so you're not vulnerable to financially controlling partners)

- **"The Millionaire Mind" by Thomas Stanley** (Understanding how truly wealthy people think vs. those who pretend to have money)

- **"Scam Me If You Can" by Frank Abagnale** (Recognizing financial scams and cons, perfect for spotting MLM guys and crypto bros)

- **"The Psychology of Money" by Morgan Housel** (Understanding money behaviors and red flags in how people handle finances)

- **"Financial Recovery" by Karen McCall** (Recognizing financial dysfunction and codependency around money)

- **"Mind Over Money" by Brad Klontz** (Understanding the psychology behind financial behaviors and money disorders)

FINANCIAL CONTROL & ABUSE

- **"Financial Abuse" by Shannon Thomas** (Recognizing and recovering from financial manipulation and control in relationships)

- **"In Control" by Shannon Thomas** (Understanding financial abuse as a form of domestic violence and how to protect yourself)

- **"The Money Code" by David Krueger and John David Mann** (Understanding money psychology and recognizing when someone uses money to control others)

- **"Financial Abuse: The Hidden Crime" by Lisa Aronson Fontes** (Comprehensive guide to recognizing financial abuse tactics and getting help)

- **"Why Does He Do That?" by Lundy Bancroft** (While not exclusively about money, it has excellent sections on how abusive men use financial control)

LIFESTYLE EXTREMISTS & OBSESSIVE BEHAVIORS (Chapters 7-8)

- **"Toxic Faith" by Stephen Arterburn and Jack Felton** (Recognizing when religious devotion becomes unhealthy obsession)

- **"The Subtle Power of Spiritual Abuse" by David Johnson and Jeff VanVonderen** (Understanding spiritual manipulation and control)

- **"The True Believer" by Eric Hoffer** (Understanding the psychology behind extremist thinking and fanaticism)

- **"Escaping the Rabbit Hole" by Mick West** (How to help someone caught up in conspiracy theories)

- **"High Functioning Addiction" by Sarah Allen Benton** (Recognizing addiction in people who seem to have it together)

- "Is It Love or Is It Addiction?" by Brenda Schaeffer (Understanding the difference between love and obsessive attachment)

- "The Adonis Complex" by Harrison Pope, Katharine Phillips, and Roberto Olivardia (Understanding male body image obsessions and compulsive exercise)

- "Exercise Addiction" by Heather Hausenblas and Danielle Symons Downs (Recognizing when fitness becomes an unhealthy obsession)

- "Too Much of a Good Thing" by Dan Kindlon (When positive traits become problematic obsessions)

- "Obsessive Compulsive Disorder" by Jonathan Abramowitz (Understanding obsessive thinking patterns)

UNDERSTANDING MEN & DATING PSYCHOLOGY (Chapters 9-11)

- "Act Like a Lady, Think Like a Man" by Steve Harvey (Male perspective on dating and relationships)

- "Become Your Own Matchmaker" by Patti Stanger (Professional matchmaker's guide to taking control of your dating life and finding the right match)

- "He's Scared, She's Scared" by Steven Carter and Julia Sokol (Understanding commitment phobia in both directions)

- "Men Who Can't Love" by Steven Carter and Julia Sokol (Perfect for understanding Ghosting Gary and Friends-With-Benefits Frank types)

- "Getting to Commitment" by Steven Carter and Julia Sokol (How to tell if someone is truly ready for commitment vs. just playing games)

- "Why Men Marry Some Women and Not Others" by John Molloy (Research-based insights into male commitment patterns)

- **"The Commitment-Phobic Man" by Steven Carter** (Understanding men who want love but run from it)

- **"What Men Want" by Bradley Gerstman, Christopher Pizzo, and Rich Seldes** (Three male authors explain how men really think about dating and relationships)

- **"Men Are from Mars, Women Are from Venus" by John Gray** (Classic guide to understanding different communication and thinking styles)

- **"Men Chase Women Choose: The Neuroscience of Meeting, Dating, Losing Your Mind and Finding True Love" by Dawn Maslar** (Science-based insights into male psychology and dating behavior)

EMOTIONAL IMMATURITY & PETER PAN SYNDROME (Chapter 12)

- **"Adult Children of Emotionally Immature Parents" by Lindsay C. Gibson** (Understanding emotional immaturity and how it affects relationships)

- **"Running on Empty" by Jonice Webb** (Recognizing emotional neglect and its impact on adult relationships and maturity)

- **"The Peter Pan Syndrome" by Dan Kiley** (The classic book on men who refuse to grow up emotionally)

- **"No More Mr. Nice Guy" by Robert Glover** (Understanding the psychology behind overly dependent, approval-seeking men)

- **"Stop Caretaking the Borderline or Narcissist" by Margalis Fjelstad** (How to stop mothering grown men and enabling their immaturity)

- **"The Road Less Traveled" by M. Scott Peck** (Understanding true emotional and spiritual maturity in relationships)

- **"Emotional Maturity" by Edward Podvoll** (What emotional growth looks like in healthy adults)

- **"Emotional Intelligence 2.0" by Travis Bradberry and Jean Greaves** (Understanding emotional maturity and recognizing emotional immaturity in potential partners)

BOUNDARIES & SELF-RESPECT (Chapter 13)

- **"Let Them" by Mel Robbins** (Setting boundaries and letting go)

- **"Why Men Love Bitches: From Doormat to Dreamgirl" by Sherry Argov** (Guide to setting boundaries and maintaining self-respect in relationships)

- **"Boundaries" by Dr. Henry Cloud and Dr. John Townsend** (The gold standard for understanding and establishing healthy boundaries in all relationships)

- **"Keep Calm and Cut Him Off" by Bruce Bryans** (No-nonsense guide to setting boundaries and walking away from toxic relationships)

- **"Boundaries in Dating: How Healthy Choices Grow Healthy Relationships" by Dr. Henry Cloud & Dr. John Townsend** (Establishing and maintaining healthy boundaries specifically in dating relationships)

MIDLIFE & DIVORCE RECOVERY (Chapter 14)

- **"The Male Midlife Crisis: A Survival Guide" by Jim Conway** (Classic guide to understanding what men go through during midlife transitions)

- **"Passages" by Gail Sheehy** (The landmark book on life transitions, including the predictable crises of adult life)

- **"The Wonder of Boys" by Michael Gurian** (Understanding male development and how it affects midlife behavior)

- **"Men in Midlife Crisis" by Jim Conway** (Specifically focused on the emotional and psychological changes men experience)

- "Your Husband's Midlife Crisis" by Jim and Sally Conway (A guide for wives, but excellent insights for any woman dating a man going through this phase)

- "Standing by Your Man" by Jim Conway (How to recognize if a man is working through legitimate growth vs. just acting out)

- "Falling Upward" by Richard Rohr (Healthy spiritual and emotional growth in the second half of life)

- "Crazy Time" by Abigail Trafford (Understanding the emotional stages of divorce and recognizing men who aren't ready to date)

- "Mom's House, Dad's House" by Isolina Ricci (For single mothers navigating dating while co-parenting)

DANGEROUS & HIGH-RISK BEHAVIORS (Chapter 15)

For General Red Flags & Dangerous Men:

- "How to Spot a Dangerous Man Before You Get Involved" by M.A. Sandra L. Brown (Essential guide to identifying red flags and potentially harmful personality types)

For Health Hazards:

- "Codependent No More" by Melody Beattie (The classic guide to understanding codependency and breaking free from unhealthy relationship patterns with people with an addiction)

- "Getting Them Sober" by Toby Rice Drews (Practical strategies for dealing with alcoholics and addicts, including when to stay and when to leave)

- "It's Not About You" by Debra Jay (How to help someone you love get treatment for addiction while protecting yourself)

- **"Loving Someone with an Addiction" by Cynthia Moreno Tuohy and Beverly Conyers** (Understanding addiction as a disease while maintaining healthy boundaries)

- **"Beyond Addiction" by Jeffrey Foote, Carrie Wilkens, Nicole Kosanke, and Stephanie Higgs** (Evidence-based approach to helping someone change addictive behaviors)

- **"The Language of Letting Go" by Melody Beattie** (Daily meditations for codependency recovery)

For Sexual Misconduct:

- **"The Sexual Healing Journey" by Wendy Maltz** (Understanding sexual boundary violations and healing from sexual trauma)

- **"Boundaries and Relationships" by Charles Whitfield** (Setting sexual and emotional boundaries)

For Players & Serial Cheaters:

- **"The Monogamy Myth" by Peggy Vaughan** (Understanding infidelity patterns and protecting yourself from serial cheaters)

- **"After the Affair" by Janis Spring** (Understanding the mindset of cheaters and recognizing the signs)

For Criminal Behavior:

- **"The Sociopath Next Door" by Martha Stout** (Recognizing people with no conscience who exploit others)

- **"Without Conscience" by Robert Hare** (Understanding psychopathy and criminal personalities)

- **"The Art of the Con" by R. Paul Wilson** (How to spot scammers and avoid being manipulated)

MANIPULATION & EMOTIONAL ABUSE (Chapter 16)

For General High-Conflict & Manipulative Personalities:

- **"5 Types of People Who Can Ruin Your Life" by Bill Eddy** (Focuses on identifying and managing relationships with high-conflict personalities)

- **"The Covert Passive Aggressive Narcissist" by Debbie Mirza** (Focuses on those who operate in subtle, hidden ways rather than the more obvious grandiose narcissists most people recognize)

- **"In Sheep's Clothing" by George K. Simon Jr.** (Understanding manipulative personalities and recognizing covert-aggressive behavior patterns)

- **"Psychopath Free" by Jackson MacKenzie** (Recognizing and recovering from relationships with narcissists, sociopaths, and other toxic personalities)

For Emotional Manipulation:

- **"The Narcissistic Abuse Recovery Program" by Melanie Tonia Evans** (Understanding and recovering from narcissistic manipulation)

- **"Disarming the Narcissist" by Wendy Behary** (Surviving and thriving with narcissistic personalities)

- **"Becoming the Narcissist's Nightmare" by Shahida Arabi** (How to devalue and discard the narcissist while supplying yourself - empowering strategies for survivors)

- **"Run Like Hell: A Therapist's Guide to Recognizing, Escaping, and Healing from Trauma Bonds"** (Understanding and breaking free from the psychological bonds that keep women trapped in toxic relationships)

For Manipulation Tactics:

- "Gaslighting" by Stephanie Sarkis (Recognizing and surviving psychological manipulation)

- "The Gaslight Effect" by Robin Stern (How to spot and survive the hidden manipulation others use to control your life)

For Power & Control:

- "Why Does He Do That?" by Lundy Bancroft (Inside the minds of angry and controlling men)

- "The Verbally Abusive Man" by Patricia Evans (Understanding verbal abuse and control tactics)

For Misogyny & Prejudice:

- "Men Who Hate Women and the Women Who Love Them" by Susan Forward (Understanding misogynistic behavior patterns)

- "No More Mr. Nice Guy" by Robert Glover (Understanding the psychology behind "nice guys" who aren't actually nice)

For Aggressive Behaviors:

- "The Angry Man" by Murray Cullen and Robert Freeman-Longo (Understanding male anger and when it becomes dangerous)

- "Living with the Passive-Aggressive Man" by Scott Wetzler (Recognizing and dealing with passive-aggressive behavior)

GREEN FLAGS & HEALTHY RELATIONSHIPS (Chapter 17)

- **"Getting to 'I Do'" by Pat Allen** (How to recognize a man who's truly ready for commitment)

- **"If the Buddha Dated" by Charlotte Kasl** (Finding love without losing yourself - recognizing healthy partnership)

- **"The Seven Principles for Making Marriage Work" by John Gottman** (Research-based guide to what makes relationships succeed)

- **"Getting the Love You Want" by Harville Hendrix** (Understanding what healthy, conscious relationships look like)

- **"Conscious Loving" by Gay Hendricks and Kathlyn Hendricks** (How to create a relationship that serves you both)

- **"The Soulmate Experience" by Mali Apple and Joe Dunn** (What it feels like when you find the right person)

- **"Mars and Venus on a Date" by John Gray** (Understanding healthy dating dynamics and green flags in courtship)

- **"Love Is a Choice" by Robert Hemfelt, Frank Minirth, and Paul Meier** (Recovery from codependent relationships and finding healthy love)

- **"Safe People" by Dr. Henry Cloud and Dr. John Townsend** (How to find relationships that are good for you and avoid those that aren't)

- **"The Right One" by Kevin Connor** (How to successfully date and marry the right person)

- **"Getting Real" by Susan Campbell** (The ten truth skills you need to live an authentic life and have authentic relationships)

- **"The High-Value Woman" by Melanie Schilling** (Understanding your worth and attracting quality partners)

PERSONAL SAFETY & INTUITION (Chapter 18)

- **"The Gift of Fear" by Gavin de Becker** (Personal safety and intuition)

- **"Protecting the Gift" by Gavin de Becker** (Keeping children and families safe from violence and predators)

- **"The Safety Trap" by Spencer Coursen** (How to protect yourself from security threats in everyday life)

- **"The Like Switch" by Jack Schafer** (FBI behavioral analysis techniques for reading people and situations)

- **"Dangerous Instincts" by Mary Ellen O'Toole** (Former FBI profiler's guide to protecting yourself from harmful people)

- **"Left of Bang" by Patrick Van Horne and Jason Riley** (How to recognize the warning signs that precede an act of violence)

- **"Strong on Defense" by Sanford Strong** (Survival skills and personal safety strategies for women)

CONFIDENCE & EMPOWERMENT (Moving Forward)

- **"The Confidence Code" by Kay and Shipman** (Building authentic confidence and learning to trust your instincts and abilities)

- **"It Begins With You: The 9 Hard Truths About Love That Will Change Your Life" by Jillian Turecki** (Self-reflection and personal growth guide for creating healthier relationships)

- **"Untamed" by Glennon Doyle** (Breaking free from expectations and living authentically)

- "You Are a Badass" by Jen Sincero (Self-help guide to creating a life you love)

- "The Gifts of Imperfection" by Brené Brown (Letting go of who you think you're supposed to be and embracing who you are)

- "Daring Greatly" by Brené Brown (How vulnerability transforms the way we live, love, parent, and lead)

- "Rising Strong" by Brené Brown (How to get back up after falling down)

- "Big Magic" by Elizabeth Gilbert (Creative living beyond fear)

- "The Power of Now" by Eckhart Tolle (A guide to spiritual enlightenment and present-moment awareness)

- "Feel the Fear and Do It Anyway" by Susan Jeffers (How to turn your fear and indecision into confidence and action)

- "The Four Agreements" by Don Miguel Ruiz (A practical guide to personal freedom)

- "Women Who Run With the Wolves" by Clarissa Pinkola Estés (Myths and stories of the wild woman archetype)

- "Dating with Purpose: A Single Woman's Guide to Escaping No Man's Land" by Dr. Erica Holmes (Strategic approach to intentional dating and avoiding relationship limbo)

Final Words of Wisdom

(Because Your Dating Success Story Starts With Self-Advocacy)

You're not just looking for a partner - you're protecting your heart, your safety, and your sanity. These resources aren't just a safety net; they're your personal support team cheering you on from the sidelines.

Whether you're dealing with an Alpa Al, a Boozy Bruce, or recovering from Gaslighting Gus, help is always available. Don't hesitate to reach out; your well-being is non-negotiable, your boundaries are valid, and the right relationship will enhance your life, not diminish it.

Special Note: Resources and contact information are subject to change. Always verify current contact details through official websites.

The Road Ahead

As you close the pages on this whimsical pilgrimage through the often perplexing world of online dating, it's clear that the path to finding a meaningful connection is rarely a straight line. You've laughed, cringed, and perhaps even recognized a bit of yourself or your past dates in these colorful archetypes.

From the cringeworthy antics of Dick-Pic Rick to the exhausting energy of Velcro Vic, you've surveyed the pitfalls and potholes that litter the digital dating landscape. These characters serve as humorous cautionary tales, reminding us of the importance of self-awareness, respect, and genuine communication in our quest for connection.

But as you've seen with the final gallery of "green flag" profiles, from Respectful Ryan to Brilliantly Balanced Brian, there's hope on the horizon. These positive archetypes remind us of the qualities to look for and to cultivate in ourselves as we navigate the complex world of modern relationships.

Behind every profile is a real person, with their own hopes, dreams, and yes, flaws. The goal isn't to find perfection, but to find someone whose quirks complement our own, whose values align with ours, and whose presence enhances our life.

As you continue on your your path in the world of online dating, carry these archetypes with you, not as strict categories to sort potential matches into, but as a lighthearted guide to help you recognize red flags, appreciate green ones, and perhaps most importantly, to laugh at the inevitable awkwardness that comes with putting yourself out there.

May your swipes be guided by wisdom, your matches be guided by authenticity, and your venture be filled with growth, laughter, and perhaps, if the algorithms align, a connection that makes all the frogs worth kissing.

Here's to love, laughter, and the continuous adventure of human connection in the digital age.

Happy Swiping!

Swiping Right on Gratitude

They say it takes a village to raise a child. Well, it takes a small army of supportive people and a parade of swipes and questionable dates to write a book about online dating. Time to give credit where credit is due!

First and foremost, to my family: You've been on this "journey" with me (yes, I used that term, and I'm as annoyed about it as you are). Your unconditional love, support, encouragement, patience, and advice have been as steadfast as Catfish Calvin's commitment to using stock profile pictures. Thank you for believing in me, even when I thought this book had as much chance of happening as Gym-Rat Jake skipping leg day.

To the men whose profiles I emphatically swiped left on and blocked: Your contributions to this book are immeasurable. You provided more material than a Verbose Vince on a coffee date. And to the profiles I swiped right on (what was I thinking?), thank you for the "learning experiences" that were more educational than a semester abroad.

To my amazing friends, my fellow warriors in the online dating trenches: Your stories, ranging from mildly amusing to "how are you still alive?", have been a constant source of inspiration. This book is as much yours as it is mine. May your future dates be less like chapter material and more like happily ever afters. Special thanks to Anne, Marcy, and Kristi, whose encouraging words and ongoing support in publishing "Swipe Left" are greatly appreciated.

A special shout-out to laughter, the real MVP: Without you, this book would have been a much more bitter pill to swallow. You truly are the best medicine, especially when dealing with an "All-About-Me Alden".

To the dating apps, those digital matchmakers of the 21st century:

Thank you for providing the platform that's simultaneously the cause of and solution to many of life's romantic problems. Without your complex algorithms (which I'm convinced are just bored interns playing an elaborate game of 'Hot or Not' with our profiles), we'd be forced to meet people the old-fashioned way – by actually talking to strangers in public. The horror! Your endless supply of profiles has given us more entertainment than a Netflix subscription and more surprises than a box of mystery-flavored jelly beans. From the bottom of my repeatedly broken and mended heart, thank you for being the petri dish in which this book's bacterial cultures...I mean, characters... grew.

To my readers: A heartfelt thank you to the women out there bravely navigating the freak show of online dating. This book is for you. May it bring you laughter, solidarity, and the courage to keep swiping left on the Philandering Phil's of the world until you find your person (or at least a date who doesn't think fish pics are a personality trait). In a world full of options, you chose to spend your precious time with this book instead of swiping through another hundred profiles of men holding fish. Your dedication to humor and self-preservation is commendable. May this book bring you more joy than your last match and fewer regrets than your last "u up?" response.

Remember, for every page you turn here, that's one less opportunity to accidentally super-like your ex. You're welcome.

www.ingramcontent.com/pod-product-compliance
Lightning Source LLC
Chambersburg PA
CBHW062112040426
42337CB00043B/3708